THE FIGHT FOR PRIVACY

Also by Danielle Keats Citron

Hate Crimes in Cyberspace

THE FIGHT
FOR PRIVACY

Protecting

Dignity, Identity, and Love

in the Digital Age

Danielle Keats Citron

W. W. NORTON & COMPANY
Independent Publishers Since 1923

Note to Readers: *The Fight for Privacy* is a work of nonfiction. Certain names, dialogue, and potentially identifying characteristics of individuals have been changed and some scenarios have been reconstructed or revised. References in this book to third-party organizations, tools, products, and services are for general information purposes only. Neither the publisher nor the author can guarantee that any particular practice or resource will be useful or appropriate to the reader. Web addresses included in this book reflect links existing as of the date of first publication. The publisher is not responsible for the content of any website, blog, or information page other than its own.

For information about permission to reproduce selections from this book, write to Permissions, W. W. Norton & Company, Inc., 500 Fifth Avenue, New York, NY 10110

For information about special discounts for bulk purchases, please contact W. W. Norton Special Sales at specialsales@wwnorton.com or 800-233-4830

Manufacturing by Lakeside Book Company
Book design by Beth Steidle
Production manager: Julia Druskin

ISBN: 978-0-393-88231-5

W. W. Norton & Company, Inc., 500 Fifth Avenue, New York, N.Y. 10110
www.wwnorton.com

W. W. Norton & Company Ltd., 15 Carlisle Street, London W1D 3BS

1 2 3 4 5 6 7 8 9 0

This book is dedicated to my family.

Contents

Introduction: Intimacy in the Twenty-First Century   xi

1 Spying Inc.   1

2 Privacy Invaders   24

3 Government Spies   50

4 This Is Us   64

5 Law's Inadequacy   82

6 The Right to Intimate Privacy   105

7 A Comprehensive Approach to
Intimate Privacy Violations   131

8 The Duties of Data Guardians   148

9 The New Compact for Social Norms   169

10 Hope and Change   189

Epilogue: The Fight Continues   207

Acknowledgments   213

Appendix   219

Notes   231

Recommended Reading   267

Index   273

Introduction

INTIMACY IN THE TWENTY-FIRST CENTURY

ALEX IS A NURSE IN HER LATE TWENTIES. ONE MORNING, AS always, Alex rose early, made coffee, and took a shower. She noted her blood sugar on her health band and checked her dating app. She messaged a friend to confirm dinner plans. As she made breakfast, she asked her home assistant to play her voice mails. What she heard stopped her in her tracks. A friend had left a message warning that Alex's ex had tweeted a video of her undressing in her bedroom. Alex searched her name online and found the video on several adult sites. When she checked her email, she saw messages from her mother's family in South Africa saying that her ex had sent them the video using what seemed like her email address.

Until that moment, Alex had no idea that her intimate life was under surveillance. She did not know that her ex had hidden a "nanny cam" in her bedroom. She did not want anyone watching her or posting videos of her undressing online. She was the victim of privacy violations that undermined her autonomy, her dignity, and her willingness to trust others.

In the twenty-first century, when we meet new people—many times even *before* we meet them—we Google them. Alex knew that new friends, colleagues, acquaintances, and even strangers inevitably would see her body before they met her in person. Even the people in her inner circle would see this video and have to look past it to connect with her as a whole person. And the privacy violation wouldn't just change how others saw Alex—it had already changed how she saw herself. She no longer felt safe or in control; she felt defenseless.

Alex was denied what I call intimate privacy. Intimate privacy involves the social norms (attitudes, expectations, and behaviors) that set and fortify the boundaries around our intimate lives. It concerns the extent to which others have access to, and information about, our bodies; minds (thoughts, desires, and fantasies); health; sex, sexual orientation, and gender; and close relationships. It includes our on- and offline activities, interactions, communications, and searches. It isn't just a descriptive term, but also a normative one. Intimate privacy is a precondition to a life of meaning. It captures the privacy that we want, expect, *and* deserve at different times and in different contexts. At its core, it is a moral concept.

In 1890, two American lawyers, Samuel Warren and Louis Brandeis, worried about the way emerging technologies were being used to erode the privacy of intimate life. Gossip rags were growing in popularity. Reporters used Kodak cameras to capture people in unguarded moments at home and on the street. Details of people's sex lives sold newspapers, so the press splashed intimacies "whispered in the closet" on their front pages. Warren's brother was discovering his homosexuality just as the public warned of homosexuality's deviance. Then, being gay was publicly shameful and potentially criminal. Warren enlisted his law partner Brandeis to write an article that would highlight privacy's centrality to human development. Warren and Brandeis called for a legally recognized right to privacy, by which they meant an ability to decide the extent to which one's innermost thoughts, desires, and "domestic relations" are shared with others. They underscored the spiritual and psychological harm inflicted by privacy invasions. We don't think of "The Right to Privacy" as being about intimate privacy, but that is what their writing described.[1]

Their article was a powerful opening salvo in the fight for privacy, but their goal remains elusive. More than one hundred years later, the privacy afforded intimate life has still not been given sufficient attention or protection. That must change.

Consider the privacy afforded bank account information. It protects our accounts from theft, yes, but otherwise has a limited impact on our lives. Intimate privacy, on the other hand, frees us to figure out who we are, what turns us on, and who we love. It lets us see ourselves as dignified and have others see us that way. It enables us to form and sustain close relationships. Intimate privacy is fundamental to our development in a way that a bank ledger will never be.

Privacy, as it interlocks with our intimate lives, carves out an invisible space with our bodies and thoughts so we can develop a sense of self and identity. Self-knowledge begins with our bodies—our first point of reference for our needs, desires, and aspirations.[2] Intimate privacy allows us to invite others to join us in our self-exploration in some contexts, while letting us exclude them (and anyone else) in other contexts. Close relationships require intimate privacy to thrive.[3] Love develops through a process of mutual revelation where partners share their innermost thoughts, feelings, desires, and experiences. Reciprocal sharing is the key ingredient in close relationships. We are willing to expose our true selves—to express all of who we are in mind, body, and spirit, to make ourselves vulnerable—only if we trust partners to treat our confidences with care.[4]

Instinctively, we all feel that we should have a right to intimate privacy. We should be able to live free from fear that the details of our intimate lives are being amassed and exploited. We should be able to undress in bathrooms, wear health bands, talk to digital home assistants, search adult sites, and message dates and friends without worrying about being surveilled. We should be able to share experiences, feelings, and thoughts on- and offline, with the reassurance that the firms facilitating our activities and interactions are also protecting them. We should be able to take advantage of these possibilities without sacrificing our intimate privacy.

Yet we do not live in that world. We do not have a right to intimate privacy. But we can, and we should.

As a law professor and civil rights advocate, I work to help us understand why intimate privacy matters and how its denial amounts to a massive legal, social, and moral failing. Over the past decade, I have advised tech companies about privacy and safety practices. I have talked to CEOs and safety officials interested in protecting intimate privacy. I have worked with lawmakers and law enforcement in the United States, South Korea, Australia, and the United Kingdom. I have advocated for legal and social change to prevent individuals from invading others' intimate privacy; businesses from over-collecting, using, and sharing our intimate data; and governments from manipulating intimate information to silence, blackmail, and imprison journalists and critics.

When I first started working on privacy issues in 2005, our intimate lives had just begun to be subject to digital surveillance. Facebook was in its infancy, Google would debut its first Maps product that spring, the iPhone would not launch for another two years. It was still possible to maintain some level of anonymity on- and offline. Companies soon realized that they could earn money from turning products and services into data collectors and purveyors. Firms began hoarding our personal data, and it happened so seamlessly that we hardly noticed. Although they touted their services as "free," we paid for them with our personal data and our attention, rather than with our credit or debit cards. Tech companies assured us that data collection would make our lives better—that it would be fun and rewarding, and that it would not compromise the safety of our data. "Trust us," they said, and we did.

The details of our intimate lives are a valuable commodity in the age of "informational capitalism," as privacy scholar Julie Cohen has aptly described modern data markets.[5] For advertisers, marketers, and data brokers, information generated about our bodies, health, sex, gender, and sexual orientation is a veritable gold mine. Firms use this information to personalize their services, predict our behavior, and learn our vulnerabilities. They sell our data to eager buyers. Now that storage is cheap, the default is to collect everything because even the most prosaic information—like whether we searched for hand cream or alcohol wipes—when combined with lots of other seemingly benign personal information can provide a window into our intimate lives. Computer scientists tell us that soon anyone with access to lots of unrevealing personal data will be able to infer revealing information (like our sexual orientation or health conditions) with a high degree of accuracy. Privacy invasions are central to the business model of internet platforms, devices, and services: the more information they have about us, the more they have to sell to advertisers, data brokers, and governments, who can further exploit and control us.

For website operators, intimate privacy violations like the videos of Alex mean more viewers, more ad revenue, and more data to mine. Thousands of sites peddle nonconsensual porn, hidden camera footage, and deepfake sex videos. You don't even need to visit those specialty sites: mainstream porn sites feature an array of privacy violations. At any given moment, hundreds of thousands of people are watching, sharing, and commenting on nonconsensual nudity. While viewers hail from everywhere, sites devoted to nonconsensual intimate images are often hosted in the United States, where there is scant risk of liability (thanks to a federal law that I will explore in subsequent chapters). Indeed, after authorities in Denmark shut down one notorious revenge porn site, it resurfaced hosted in Las Vegas.

Privacy invasions are a win-win proposition for sites hosted in the United States, but a grave blow for people everywhere because those sites can be accessed, viewed, and shared anywhere. What happens in the United States—what its laws sanction and enable—dictates the state of intimate privacy across the globe. The absence of intimate privacy in the United States is its absence wherever access to the internet exists. And much as we might prefer to believe that the denial of intimate privacy is happening to far-away people we don't know, it is a nearer threat than you think. Everyone is vulnerable—even you.

The more time we spend online, the greater the risk to our privacy. Australia's e-Safety Commissioner—a government agency created in 2015—reported a 249% increase in cases of nonconsensual pornography during the COVID pandemic. The helpline at the US-based Cyber Civil Rights Initiative or CCRI (of which I am the vice president) received more than 200% the number of email inquiries in 2020 as compared to 2019. According to the FBI, sextortion scams in the United States increased during the first months of the pandemic.[6] Officials in South Africa reported a similar trend.[7]

Everyone is at risk, but as with so many issues, the vulnerable suffer more intimate privacy violations and more often. Around the world, women are victims of nonconsensual pornography at higher rates than men;[8] gay and bisexual men are at greater risk than heterosexual men; and gay and bisexual women may be at the highest risk of all.[9] Racial background, ethnic background, and disability status also affect one's risk of nonconsensual pornography. Of the thousands of sites specializing in nonconsensual pornography, 98% of the photos are of women, and not because women are taking and sharing more nude selfies than men are. Law professor and CCRI president Mary Anne Franks put it well: "Men send more nude photos than women do [but] revenge porn sites don't traffic in men's pictures."

Over the course of my career, I've witnessed the entrenchment of the notion that the bodies of women and minorities are not their own, that their nude images can be traded like baseball cards, that it's no big deal—just "boys being boys." In my first brush with a case involving nonconsensual porn in 2007, local law enforcement told the Asian American woman whom I was advising that nothing could be done, that she should just turn her computer off because only kids were paying attention. These attitudes were surely an outgrowth of the fact that porn and the internet are inextricably linked: you really can't have one without the other. Sexist attitudes make it all seem as American as apple pie.

We're now facing the digital era equivalent of someone telling rape victims that their skirts were too short or that nothing bad happened to them. In this era, however, instead of one victim, there are thousands; and instead of a few bystanders, there are hundreds of thousands of people consuming images of victims' bodies. It's happening with ease because global communities of perpetrators, cheerleaders, and financial beneficiaries have embraced, spread, and evangelized frictionless, technology-enabled privacy violations and because law enforcement isn't paying enough attention. That intimate privacy violations are so popular; that there is no shortage of intimate images taken, stolen, or extorted; that site operators and posters treat it as harmless fun; and that victims are blamed; all of this has enormous expressive power. These facts tell people, especially women and marginalized communities, that they should neither expect, nor do they deserve, intimate privacy.

Social attitudes, cultural practices, and law influence how we think about privacy (and how each influences the others). They destroy our hope for and expectation of privacy and the willingness of the powerful to protect it. American policymakers view privacy through the lens of free markets, free speech, and consumer protection. Collections of personal data are understood as inherently valuable, rather than as sources of ultrahazardous risk. Privacy violations are treated as disconnected problems or normal market practices, rather than as endemic societal challenges.

Because we fail to recognize the practical and moral significance of privacy, it is easy for tech companies to design products and services without thinking about risks to vulnerable communities. US companies offering services across the globe have been caught transgressing national or regional data protection regulations, for example, by failing to obtain people's explicit permission to collect personal information. Companies pay penalties and promise to right their practices. Whoops, we won't do it again. Although data protection laws are modestly stronger in territories outside the United States (such as the European Union), their enforcement isn't what it should be.

We need a common language for how we think about the freedoms that intimate privacy enables—one that captures the crucial opportunities at stake and broadens the areas in which we expect and deserve to pursue those opportunities. We need to talk about intimate privacy in a way that acknowledges its importance to growth, dignity, and love, so that everyone has a chance to develop as an individual, partner, and citizen. We also need a term that reflects the impact that intimate privacy violations have on women and marginalized groups.

Luckily, in the United States, we have such a term: civil rights.

Civil rights are legal rights whose protection are essential for human beings to flourish, enjoy respect, and feel that they belong. They are moral rights deserving priority: they can't be traded away or denied without a good reason. Giving notice in a privacy policy or advising people to stop taking intimate images is not a meaningful response. Civil rights are fundamental entitlements owed everyone, but they also require protection against discrimination given the bigoted stereotypes and attitudes that vulnerable groups face. The civil rights approach to intimate privacy I'm offering builds on the human rights tradition—with its emphasis on dignity, self-development, and equality—but it also forges its own path.

In the United States, civil rights laws require powerful entities with control over our important rights to act as the *caretakers* of those rights. We should build on that tradition in protecting intimate privacy. This would require legislatures and courts to flesh out the duties of site operators, private companies, and governments, just as they have clarified the duties of schools, employers, and public transportation providers to provide reasonable accommodations to disabled individuals. Those duties would entail far more than existing piecemeal and procedural protections.

An American civil right to intimate privacy, if robustly protected, might have something to offer other countries as well. Whereas human rights instruments tend to focus on a state's obligations to individuals within its borders, US civil rights laws constrain public *and* private power. They recognize the structural damage to equality wrought by intimate privacy violations, and offer a pathway for comprehensive reform for individual perpetrators.

As a lawyer and law professor, I recognize that the law is only a part of the solution. Market interventions are a critical second source of pressure. Tech companies need to design their products and services with a respect for privacy, rather than scrambling to repair damage that has been inflicted, often at considerable scale. At the same time, we must be wary of technical fixes. "There is an app for that" is a response that tends to over-promise and under-deliver. Innovation often excludes women and minorities, including individuals who have been chased offline. The denial of intimate privacy is another way that society piles injustice on those most vulnerable to it while rewarding the most powerful.

This book exposes law's failure to protect intimate privacy in the United States and in other countries. But there is hope in this story. I have seen change from the ground up. Coalitions have formed that have built political will and support for reform. We can build on those successes while pressing for market solutions and global cooperation.

Join me in the fight for intimate privacy. That work is already underway. Together, we can build a world where intimate privacy is respected and protected.

THE FIGHT FOR PRIVACY

1

Spying Inc.

AMAZON HALO LOOKS LIKE A WATCH, BUT TIME ISN'T THE POINT. The wearable health device has sensors that monitor your heart rate, oxygen level, and daily steps. It analyzes your body fat from your photos, and its microphones measure the tone, energy, and positivity of your voice. It is always on, enabling real-time analysis of your body. *Wired* magazine described the Halo as the best fitness band for "feelings" because its voice-tone tracker lets you know when you sound irritable.[1]

Every day, all day long, products and services like Amazon Halo track our bodily functions, health conditions, searches, sexual activities, and correspondence, creating digital archives of our lives at unimaginable scale. We've accepted the tracking because tech companies assure us that they are making our lives better. As is often the case, that sounds wonderful in theory, but what about in practice? Companies are maximizing the amount of personal data collected so that they can make money from it—hence my shorthand for the entire enterprise, "Spying Inc." For most firms, privacy isn't a high priority because it isn't profitable. In the world of Spying Inc., intimate data is more valuable than one-time product purchases or regular subscription fees. It is so valuable that firms keep our intimate data long after we've trashed their devices or deleted their apps. Companies bury the details of their data collection efforts in privacy policies that no one has the time or inclination to decipher. Although firms and their investors understand the deal, we have no clue.

Imagine if surgeons performed operations not only to heal us but to gather information about our organs so they could sell the information to life insurance companies. What if accountants gave us tax advice not only to help us deal with authorities but to obtain our financial information to share with data brokers; or if storage companies took an inventory of our belongings not only to prevent theft but also to sell that itemized list to advertisers?

Doctors and accountants know a lot about intimate aspects of our lives, but apps tracking and recording our bodies, conversations, and love lives know far more. Yet, unlike accountants, whose professions subject them to fiduciary obligations like owing us duties of loyalty and confidentiality, and doctors, who are further subject to federal health privacy laws, these firms aren't bound by law to keep our intimate data confidential. They face few limits and even fewer responsibilities for handling our data. While doctors and accountants must keep our intimate data to themselves and certainly can't sell it—lest they face serious legal and professional consequences—apps have *no* such obligation.

Nowhere is that more true than in the United States. Law hasn't caught up to address the powerful roles that apps play in our lives. We generally treat digital services like the consumer products of the analog age—when wristwatches were just wristwatches, not instruments that monitored us and reported the intimate data back to companies. Given this country's nonregulatory approach, businesses are free to collect intimate information. Because storage costs are cheap, firms hold onto it. Companies have little to worry about if they mismanage our data. If intimate data is leaked (and it often is: there were 1,001 US data breaches in

2020), companies likely won't have to internalize costs borne by individuals. They may have to notify us about breaches and face some bad press. But, as I will explore in detail in Chapter 5, American law currently provides little protection to individuals whose data has been collected, used, shared, and otherwise handled.

While the rewards of data collection outweigh the risks for firms, the same isn't true for individuals, even when we account for all that these digital tools allow us to do. Take the Amazon Halo. You are eager to track your workouts and monitor your health, so you put it on. What you don't realize is that Amazon is not pledging to handle your intimate data to help *you*. You won't know if your data is later shared and then used in ways that negatively impact you. As long as the Halo is on your wrist, you have little control over what happens next.

Companies have convinced us to give away our intimate data without strong privacy commitments. They wield formidable powers of persuasion and seduction, so individuals end up sharing far more personal data than they realize. Companies know that people can't appreciate the potential perils because the risks from data collection often materialize in the future.

THE SEAMLESS CREATION OF OUR DATA SELVES

In an ad for its credit-monitoring service, Experian explains, "there exists another version of you made up of your financial data. Your Data Self." Although the ad doesn't let on, far more surveillance is afoot than just of your financial data. Your Data Self includes a comprehensive view of the most intimate aspects of your personal life. "Your Intimate Data Self" is more like it.

UK journalist Judith Duportail was shocked when she caught a glimpse of her Data Self. Duportail asked the dating app Tinder for a copy of her records. In compliance with the transparency mandate of the European Union's General Data Protection Regulation (GDPR, which the United Kingdom incorporated into its domestic law post-Brexit), Tinder sent her more than 800 printed pages. That included all 1,700 messages she sent to potential dates, links to her photos, photos of the men whose profiles she viewed, the number of people she matched with and their ethnicities, the times and locations of her messages, and her Facebook likes. Had she shared her HIV status on the app, that data point would have been included as well. DuPortail was aghast that Tinder knew more about her "hopes, fears, sexual preferences, and deepest secrets" than she did herself.

If Tinder wants to share UK subscribers' data, it has to ask for permission, as required by GDPR. But for US subscribers, Tinder has no need to seek their approval. Under US law, it is sufficient that the company have a privacy policy, which explains that subscribers' data might be shared with advertisers.[2] In other words, in the United States, notice and choice are presumed from the fact that companies have privacy policies. (All of the major dating apps have the same policy: no privacy for US users.)

Kashmir Hill, a renowned tech reporter for the *New York Times*, was similarly taken aback when she got hold of her 400-page dossier created by Sift, a consumer scoring company that analyzes 16,000 factors to tell clients whether you are worthy of their trust. The dossier included her Airbnb messages, delivery orders, favorite Indian dishes, and the number of times she used the Coinbase app on her iPhone. Until she started studying the growing "consumer scor[ing]" marketplace, she had never even heard of the company, though it knew a whole lot about her.[3]

We are all Duportail and Hill. Only when the hundreds of pages sit in our laps can we begin to wrap our heads around the staggering amount of information being collected (and inferred) about us. When our data is transmitted, we don't register its disclosure as we would if we conveyed it face-to-face. We swipe on dating profiles, search adult sites, and use fitness bands without realizing how much information about us is being generated and stockpiled.

Our inability to comprehend the extent of the data collection only partially explains why it happens so seamlessly. We barely notice the firms gathering our data because online interactions take so little effort: a few clicks and swipes. If we are directly asked for permission to collect our data (because a country's data protection law, like the GDPR, requires it), it's usually when we are signing onto a service, so we click yes and move on. We also click the box because we have little attention to spare. Information overload is endemic to the digital age; we constantly receive pings, texts, and emails.

Given our attention deficit, we don't notice privacy policies, but more importantly, we wouldn't have time to read them all even if we tried. A study by computer scientists Aleecia McDonald and Lorrie Cranor found that if we tried to skim every privacy policy that we encountered in a year, it would take 154 hours.[4] If a service or an app *has* a privacy policy, then that is often good enough for us. Most of us (75%) are under the mistaken impression that if a firm has a privacy policy, then it won't share our data with other companies.[5] It is a myth of epic proportion. Instead, in the United States, privacy policies are drafted to protect the company; they function as liability shields for the firm, not privacy guarantees for the user. Privacy scholar Woodrow Hartzog put it best: "privacy policies in fact usually end up being *antiprivacy* policies."[6]

Knowing all of this, firms employ every tactic available to get us to disclose as much information about our intimate lives as possible. In the astute words of privacy researcher Pinelopi Troullinou, "seductive surveillance" is the name of the game. Firms tell us that the more they know us, the more they can meet our needs, bring us joy, and simplify our lives.[7] Alexa and Siri, on our phones and from devices inside our homes, are called "smart assistants." As the founder of a wellness app promised, "Every single data point you enter and share empowers you to be in charge of your health."[8] But data collection isn't solely for our personal benefit (if only!). Rather, firms amass intimate data to analyze it, share it, and— yes—sell it.

Design is yet another tool in the data collector's arsenal. Firms develop products and services that seem more like friends than busybodies or corporate spies, so we welcome them into our lives. Smart assistants, for example, cultivate a sense of intimacy with personalized conversations and soothing voices. People activate them by saying hello—"Hey, Alexa" or "Hey, Siri" gets their attention. Amazon, a leading seller of smart home assistants, "didn't want people worrying about the new flood of data that Alexa would send its way" for devices using the voice command, so it "worked to create strong personal bonds between humans and its humanoid."[9]

Dating apps offer another example of seductive design features. To ensure that we share more and more of ourselves, firms incorporate game-like features, such as swiping and colorful graphics. We swipe (and swipe and swipe) for dopamine hits and for the highs of "social approval."[10] Tinder founder Sean Rad admitted as much when he told *Time* that subscribers don't really care if they "match because swiping is so much fun."[11] For writer Nancy Jo Sales, Rad's app was a "drug" that was "free and constantly available and always waiting for me on my phone—waiting to help me feel good."[12]

Overcollection is the business model. Computer scientists have tested smart home devices to see how often they collect people's conversations when individuals aren't deliberately engaging with the devices. A study conducted by researchers at Northeastern University found that smart speakers listening to a continuous loop of the television show *Gilmore Girls* for 21 hours had 63 false positives—that is, recordings made even though no one said a command (like "Hey, Alexa") to wake up the smart assistant.[13] Along these lines, although Apple's privacy policy says that it does not sell data collected by its smart assistant, Siri, it has shared audio recordings with contractors. According to whistleblowers, Apple's Siri has recorded people having sex.[14]

Companies are developing smart home assistants that will collect even more intimate data. For example, Amazon has a patent for smart speakers that will detect key words like "enjoyed" or "love." When the device hears those trigger words, it will "capture adjacent audio that can be analyzed on the device or remotely" to determine what exactly that person enjoys or loves. A Google patent application describes the ability to use speech patterns to identify who is in a room, the action being performed, and how quietly it is being performed.[15]

Smart devices are poised to track our every movement and activity at home. One Amazon executive promises, "There is no reason not to put [smart devices] everywhere in your house." Amazon's Echo Flex is so small that it can be plugged into your bathroom's wall outlet. The company is also pushing a new product, Alexa for Residential, for landlords to install in rental apartments. The device lets landlords "drop in" on tenants so they can discuss rent, amenities, and needed repairs. Amazon even has a smart assistant customized for hotel rooms; I was shocked to find one during my stay at a hotel in Oklahoma City. When I went to look for a landline, I found in its place a small black device and a card explaining that Alexa would connect me with anything I needed. When I went to the front desk to learn more, the manager said that I was the only guest to have ever inquired about the device in the six months that the hotel had been using them. As privacy scholar Neil Richards said to me, these devices "are literally being built into the environment, leaving us with no choice."

Even sex toys have apps that let us send texts, share photos, and livestream "what is going on in the moment." And companies are keeping those communications. Vibratissimo's database stores explicit images, chat logs, and other personal information (including sexual orientation) about subscribers to its Panty Buster toy.[16] We-Vibe records the dates and times that subscribers use their vibrators and the settings that they choose.[17]

Countless digital products and services connect to the ultimate data collectors: our smart phones. More than 2.5 billion people have smart phones capable of tracking them wherever they go (hotel rooms, doctor's offices, AA meetings); collecting whatever they search, view, or read; and monitoring whatever they type, record, and share.[18] The smart phone is a one-stop shop for our thoughts, desires, searches, photos, communications, and movements.

INTIMATE DATA AS ADVERTISING GOLD

One night, "Marc" turned on his laptop to watch porn. He enabled the private browsing mode to prevent his viewing habits from being tracked. He searched an adult site for videos, using the key words "bondage" and "fantasy play," and watched a few. The feature that he thought would protect his privacy only ensured that his browsing history wasn't stored on his computer. It didn't prevent firms from tracking and mining his activity—his IP address, his searches, page views, and the frequency of his visits.[19]

Few of us appreciate the reach of the vast ecosystem of advertising, analytics, and marketing firms that comprise the "ad-tech industrial complex." Advertising firms create profiles indicating our interests in, for instance, "pornography, gay life, hate content, sexuality, male impotence, substance use, sexually transmitted diseases, cancer, and mental health" so that we will be more inclined to click on the curated ads in our feed.[20] US law imposes no technical or legal limits on creating, using, sharing, and selling these profiles, so companies build and monetize them at a feverish pace. (In nations following the GDPR, advertising firms must ask for people's express consent to track them; giving users notice on a tucked-away part of a website and presuming their consent does not cut it, as it does in the United States.)

According to a study conducted in 2020, 93% of 22,484 porn sites allowed third parties to collect information about people's browsing habits. On average, adult sites had seven companies tracking users. Google ad trackers appeared on 74% of the sites, Oracle on 24%, and Facebook on 10%.[21] A majority of the top 100 adult sites allow third parties to place trackers that synchronize cookies across sites.[22] Privacy researcher Elena Maris put it well: "That the mechanism for adult site tracking is so similar to, say, online retail should be a huge red flag."[23]

To get a sense of the ad tracking and profiling trade, Sebastian Meineck, a journalist at *VICE*, signed up as a client of Pornhub's ad platform, TrafficJunky. Meineck placed ads based on specialized categories (like "BDSM" and "anal"), specific groups (gay, straight, trans, and "female friendly"), browsing language, and location. He was able to design an advertisement for "people watching gay porn in Bristol who are browsing in Spanish between 6 and 7 AM, and looking for content with the keywords 'threesome' and 'outdoors.'"[24] The granular detail is astounding.

You might dismiss these concerns because your loved ones aren't likely to frequent adult sites and, therefore, advertisers aren't collecting data about them. Statistics say you'd be wrong. If your family and friends have a computer or cell phone, then they have likely visited an adult site at some point or another. Every day, sometimes multiple times a day, hundreds of millions of people visit porn sites. Pornhub's monthly visits exceed those of Amazon, Netflix, and Twitter combined. In 2019, Pornhub had 42 billion visits from around the world (there were only 7.7 billion people in the world), with the United States, Japan, the United Kingdom, Canada, and France leading in daily traffic.

It's not just adult sites. Ad-tech trackers are *everywhere*. Consider ad-tech surveillance on dating sites. In 2013, security researcher Ashkan Soltani set up a fake OkCupid account and discovered 50 companies tracking his computer.[25] The ad trade has grown exponentially since then. In 2020, OkCupid had more than 300 advertising and analytics partners, while Grindr used Twitter's advertising service and its 180 ad partners (including one that was reported to have sold the data to more than 1,000 third-party providers).[26] Advertisers harvest an array of sensitive details, including information about subscribers' sexually transmitted infections.[27]

One might think that mental health apps would avoid the advertising trade because the data collected is so sensitive. But even those apps welcome advertisers, despite glaring moral, ethical, and safety concerns. US health privacy laws mostly don't apply to them—only health care providers like doctors, hospitals, and health insurance companies have legal obligations related to the handling of our personal data. (To the extent that federal law enforcers have taken a different view, as the Federal Trade Commission did in 2021, health apps just need to notify subscribers that their data will be shared. I will talk about those rules in Chapter 5.) According to a study conducted in 2019, 29 of the 36 most popular free apps for depression and quitting smoking allowed advertisers or marketing services to access some subscriber information. A couple of apps disclosed very sensitive information, including health diary entries, self-reports about substance abuse, and usernames, to other companies.[28] When then-FTC chief technologist Latanya Sweeney analyzed twelve health apps and two wearable devices in 2014, she found that subscriber information was sent to no fewer than 76 different companies. Knowing that someone has a depression or a smoking cessation app on their cell phone is "valuable health-related data."[29]

No matter what we do, we can't shield ourselves from the ad-tech industrial complex. In the United States, intimate data gets captured whenever we browse, search, or use apps. The default setting—the one that sticks—is to track data, ad infinitum. Julia Angwin, the editor in chief of the nonprofit investigative newsroom *The Markup*, spent a year trying to prevent advertisers and marketers from tracking her online, to no avail. She had no apps on her phone and carried it in a Faraday bag,* which blocked remote access to her device. She basically had to withdraw from all networked services.[30] Angwin had resources and help,

---

* Faraday bags are named after English scientist Michael Faraday, famed for his research on electromagnetism, who, in 1836, built a room coated in metal foil to block electric charges from piercing the room.

and even she concluded that ad tracking was impossible to avoid while remaining part of modern society. That is no way to have to live in the twenty-first century.

THE SECRETIVE DATA-BROKER INDUSTRY

Monsignor Jeffrey Burrill was a parish priest before becoming a top administrator of the US Conference of Catholic Bishops (UCCB). In July 2021, he resigned from that position after the Catholic news site, *The Pillar*, told UCCB that Burrill had been using the gay dating app Grindr—a serious problem for UCCB, since the Catholic Church opposes sexual activity outside heterosexual marriage. The *Pillar*'s reporter did not meet Burrill on the app, but rather "obtained information based on the data Grindr collects from its users." The data revealed that Burrill frequently used Grindr and that he visited gay bars while traveling for work. As the *Pillar* reported in its story, "the data was obtained from a data vendor," which the news site did not name. In other words, Grindr sold Burrill's "anonymized" location data and mobile advertising ID to advertising networks; the information was then sold to a data broker; the data broker sold the information to the news site, enabling the site's reporter to out the priest as gay.[31] (Somewhere along the line, Burrill's mobile advertising ID was relinked to his full name, address, and other personally identifiable information, something data brokers specialize in.[32])

"Secretive and shady" is how US Senator Ron Wyden describes the little-known yet highly lucrative data-broker industry, which collects our intimate information.[33] Secretive and shady, yes, but entirely legal in the United States. (The data broker's sale of the priest's information was entirely on the up-and-up.) In 2004, there were approximately 500 companies peddling our personal data.[34] By 2020, there were more than 4,000 data brokers, collectively with dossiers on 98% of Americans.

In the United States, data brokers face few restrictions, so they amass

and trade every detail of intimate life. Based on data that they have man-
aged to access and compile, data brokers profess to know our sexual trau-
mas, addictions, smoking habits, psychiatric problems, eating disorders,
genetic conditions, medical illnesses, sexually transmitted diseases, sex
toy use, sexual orientation, marriages, divorces, pregnancies, and dietary
habits.[35] Data brokers do this by making inferences about us.[36] They estimate our risk for certain diseases, our likely personality traits, and our
propensity for fraud, even though the information that they are analyz-
ing has been ripped from its original context and may contain inaccura-
cies.[37] They "harvest, sell, or trade mobile phone location data."[38]

Cyber law scholar Frank Pasquale and I have described the world
created by data brokers as a "scored society" where predictive algorithmic
assessments rate people along countless categories. Job candidates are
scored for their creativity and leadership; software engineers are ranked
for their contributions to open source projects; individuals are assessed
for their likelihood to vote. Individuals are turned into "ranked and
rated objects."[39]

Some data brokers specialize in aspects of intimate life. Health data
brokers sell lists of rape victims and HIV and AIDS patients. Crossix,
for example, has health data on 250 million Americans, including doctor visits, treatment histories, prescriptions, insurance claims, and medical ailments. Oracle's health profiles can tell you whether people have
searched for abortion services.[40] Where are these brokers getting data
to mine, since health records in the United States are covered by federal
and state health privacy laws? From our health-related purchases (CVS
or grocery store "discount" cards), consumer genetic testing services, our
searches, and information shared with dating and health-related apps and
services. Health analytics company GNS Healthcare calculates people's
health risks from data culled from "mobile health devices and consumer
behavior."[41] In 2018, for 153 dollars, US Date—a "dating" data broker—
supplied the dating profiles, sexual orientations, occupations, physical
traits, contact details, and photographs of one million people.[42] In 2019,

another broker sold the dating profiles of 2,000 Australian women for only 60 US dollars.[43] Data brokers obtain this information from dating apps and other sources.

Who can buy access to data-broker dossiers? Anyone—your neighbor, your ex, your former high school classmate, and, of course, reporters, as we saw in Burrill's case. For $24.86 a month (that was the price quoted to me in 2021), BeenVerified.com gives subscribers access to people's social media records, information on relationships, names of "boyfriends/girlfriends, roommates, business associates, ex-husbands/ex-wives, forgotten social media accounts, websites visited, videos, dating profiles, and other potentially embarrassing online profiles."[44]

Buyers of data-broker dossiers include private entities like alternative payment providers such as PayPal, advertising and marketing firms, colleges and universities, insurance companies, lenders, pharmaceutical companies, real estate services, and tech firms. Life insurance companies purchase access to dossiers maintained by health data brokers.[45] In most states, this is permissible. In 2019, the New York Department of Financial Services released an "industry circular letter" stating that life insurance companies may use data from "non-traditional sources" to determine premiums, if those sources are non-discriminatory. (Whatever that means is up for grabs.)

Political campaigns have long integrated data-broker dossiers into their outreach strategies. According to the *Washington Post*, the Democratic National Committee "acquires enough to understand you as a person, including unique identifiers from your phone that can be used to target ads across different apps." It spent "six figures" acquiring information from third-party vendors during the 2020 election.[46] President Donald Trump's campaigns used data brokers, including infamous Cambridge Analytica, to obtain dossiers on the American people.

Data brokers have made their mark globally. Acxiom, the world's largest data broker, says it has amassed more than 10,000 data attributes on over 2.5 billion people in more than sixty countries.[47] (For contrast, the company had 3,000 data points on practically every American in 2014).[48] Almost every adult in the United Kingdom is included in dossiers held by credit and data broker giants Experian, Equifax, and TransUnion. The data-brokerage industry generates *200 billion dollars* annually. (For comparison's sake, Google's revenue in 2020 was approximately 181 billion dollars.)

The industry's data collection has run into some snags outside the United States. In 2020, the UK's Information Commissioner's Office (ICO) found that Experian, Equifax, and TransUnion violated the UK's GDPR because they collected people's personal data without directly telling them and because they had failed to obtain people's express consent to use their data for marketing purposes. Equifax and TransUnion agreed to change their practices and to stop processing data collected unlawfully. (Experian refused to settle, so the ICO issued an enforcement notice compelling the company to make changes.) The ICO "expect[s] the [rest of the] data broking sector to make the same commitments."[49]

HYPER-SURVEILLANCE OF WOMEN AND GIRLS

Although corporate tracking of our data is mostly equal opportunity, that isn't so for our health data. Women and girls are 75% more likely to use health apps than are men and boys.[50] The femtech market includes thousands of apps tracking menstruation, fertility, pregnancies, menopause, pelvic and uterine health, nursing care, and sexual habits. Over 100 million women and girls worldwide use period-tracking apps, including one-third of the women and girls in the United States.

Femtech apps are "actively expanding the amount of data that they collect, betting that they'll eventually figure out how to make money from it." Period-tracking app Flo has *13 billion data points* for its 30 million active subscribers. Femtech users are asked to answer questions about their cramps, medications, illnesses, the consistency of their vaginal discharge, sex drive, sexual fulfillment (including whether they orgasmed or not), mood, alcohol use, miscarriages, and use or nonuse of contraception.[51] There is seemingly no end to the data collection.

Researchers studied 30 period-tracking apps that collectively had over 11.5 million Android downloads. Four apps had no privacy policies at all, while one had a link to a privacy policy that led to an error message. For the remaining 25, privacy policies were long and confusing, and downplayed privacy concerns. Not one of the 30 apps protected subscribers' reproductive data.[52] After *Consumer Reports* exposed a security flaw that enabled anyone to access Glow accounts with subscribers' email, the app became the first (and seemingly only) fertility tracking app to comply with the federal Health Information Portability and Accountability Act (HIPAA), which requires that individuals give express affirmative consent to collect and share their health data.[53]

A related issue is that femtech services have an accuracy problem, which perhaps isn't surprising given that many femtech founders are cisgender males (only 10% of venture capital funding in this area has gone to female-led startups) who lack personal experience with the services that they put on the market. According to figures compiled in 2016, 95% of 180 period-tracking apps contained misleading health information. Only 20% of the apps predicted periods accurately, and even those apps contained errors.[54] The consequences of inaccuracy can be serious: "[T]here's real cause for concern if you're using [apps] to avoid getting pregnant. If you're just one day off, it could result in an unintended pregnancy," observed Dr. Nathaniel DeNicola. Indeed. The Swedish Natural Cycles app claimed to be 99% effective at preventing pregnancy through cycle tracking, but a hospital debunked that claim with its report that out of 668 women who sought to terminate unwanted pregnancies in a four-month period in 2017, 37 had relied on the app as their only form of birth control.[55] Novelist Olivia Sudjic wrote about her experience getting an abortion after relying on the Natural Cycles app, noting, "I felt colossally naïve. I'd used the app in the way I do most of the technology in my life: not quite knowing how it works, but taking for granted that it does."[56]

Accuracy issues in femtech extend beyond cycle predictions. The Flo app offers a tool that assesses a woman's risk of polycystic ovary syndrome (PCOS), but it never conducted high-level clinical studies to evaluate the accuracy of its assessments. In September 2019 alone, the app recommended that 38% of the 636,000 women who consulted the tool speak to their physicians—and yet, according to experts, only 10% of women are likely to develop PCOS.[57] This surely generated needless worry, excessive doctor visits, and unnecessary health care costs.

Medical researchers have access to the data in anonymized form so that they can study patterns that may help detect illness and disease. Such access has the imprimatur of US law if the data is anonymized—that is, "not individually identifiable."[58] The problem with anonymization, however, is the ease of re-identification. As computer researchers have shown, anonymized data can be traced to people's identities if consolidated with data from other sources. A famous example traces back to 1997 when the Massachusetts Group Insurance Commission released anonymized data on hospital visits of state employees. Latanya Sweeney, then a computer science graduate student and now a Harvard professor, used voter registration rolls to identify the records of the then-Massachusetts governor William Weld.[59] She used identifiers like age and gender to narrow down records that could only be Weld, which revealed the details of his hospital stay, diagnosis, and prescriptions.[60] Techniques of re-identification have advanced considerably in the past 25 years, so health data stripped of identifiers can be re-identified with ease. When femtech apps say that they are only sharing de-identified data, they aren't guaranteeing anything. Promises of anonymization can easily be broken, as privacy scholar and computer scientist Paul Ohm has warned.[61]

It is estimated that the femtech industry will be worth 50 billion dollars by 2025, a fivefold increase from its value in 2020, thanks to the ad-tech market. According to Patient Privacy Rights founder Deborah

Peel, women's reproductive health data is uniquely valuable to advertisers and marketers because menstruation and pregnancy are among the few life stages when "consumers are open to brand capture." As a Bayer representative explained, femtech apps let the company "bring the right content to the right place."[62] A Flo-using teenager might get ads on tampon use, while a 30-year-old might be pitched ovulation tests.

The most popular femtech apps in the United States share subscribers' data with at least a half-dozen or more advertisers.[63] In a study of 36 period-tracking apps, researchers found that 61% transferred data to Facebook's advertising service, even when subscribers did not have Facebook accounts. The Flo app updated Facebook whenever subscribers engaged with the app. The company stopped the practice following a *Wall Street Journal* exposé and subscriber uproar.[64]

DATABASES OF INTIMATE DATA: HIGH RISK, HIGH REWARD

In the mid 1800s, water reservoirs produced steam that powered textile mills. Reservoirs operated by collecting as much water as possible and ensuring that the water stayed safely inside them. When reservoirs burst and the water rushed out, destruction followed, flooding neighborhoods and ending lives. When the water remained inside those reservoirs, society benefited. High risks for high rewards—the safety of individuals dependent on keeping water contained and secure.

Databases of intimate data are the digital reservoirs of the present day, fueling the economy, enhancing our lives in countless ways, just as water reservoirs provided energy for prior eras. But when data escapes—whether by design (for example through the ad-tech industrial complex and data broker industry) or by accident (through leaks and hacks)—it can usher in havoc.

Databases produce harms that are more varied, more diffuse, and that cannot be immediately felt, unlike a reservoir's escaping water that causes physical damage. But the metaphor is apt in the ways that matter: it reminds us that every era has employed high-risk, high-reward technologies in the business of collection and storage. Optimizing digital reservoirs of intimate data is a balancing act. We need to better calibrate how to get the most out of them while not only protecting against collecting and sharing too much, but also securing what is inside.[65]

Imagine if I asked you to throw out your cell phone or delete all your apps. If you said no to both requests, I wouldn't blame you. You might scoff at the idea of removing dating apps, because finding romance and sex can seem difficult without them. They have been de rigueur for finding companionship in the time of COVID. The same is true for countless other digital tools. We enjoy them, we can't opt out of using them, and we should not have to, so we trust firms to collect only personal data that they need to provide their services while protecting our data.

Some data collection is lifesaving. People have implanted devices that monitor their heart rhythms to detect cardiac events. They wear insulin pumps and continuous glucose monitors to track their blood sugar. Data collection could help us tackle global pandemics. Australia successfully contained COVID outbreaks for more than 18 months by engaging in swift contact tracing.[66] At the outset of the pandemic in the United States, health tech companies talked to the Trump administration about creating a "national coronavirus surveillance system." The idea was to provide hospitals with real-time information about potential cases and policymakers with information that would help them figure out where to reopen the economy. (Because the administration seemingly had no plan to protect the personal data, a colleague and I raised concerns about the proposal in an op-ed in the *Washington Post*.[67])

But even when the stakes aren't life or death, data collection may enable the provision of services that bring us joy and, yes, make our lives better. The dating apps that we use—and the data collection that enables them to operate—help us welcome partners into different aspects of our lives, deepening trust and love. Home devices have a record of all the music that we have played throughout the years—a twenty-first-century version of a mix tape based on our lives. Replaying those songs lets us relive formative moments and gives us insight into ourselves and our relationships. Wellness and fertility apps let us access support at the very moment we need it.

This was true for Sadaf Khan, a Pakistani journalist who suffered a miscarriage while she was using the pregnancy app Glow Nurture. She then switched to its companion app, Glow Eve, to track her period. Answering the app's questions about her moods helped her cope with her grief. Participating in the app's message boards connected her to other women "going through the same thing and facing similar emotional and physical fallouts." She confided more in the app than she did in her own gynecologist. As another Eve subscriber noted, it's easy to share your feelings on the app because "so many other women are talking."[68] Extended conversations on femtech apps can help women and girls feel less isolated during difficult times.[69]

We shouldn't have to do away with services and products that benefit our lives. Rather, we should address the high risks that come with the high rewards. Much data collection serves none of our short-term or long-term needs or interests. Sex toy manufacturers don't need to keep people's explicit videos, texts, and photos to provide their services. Fertility-tracking apps don't need to know about subscribers' sexual experiences (whether they were "mindblowing," "pretty good," or "eh") or the intensity of their orgasms ("YASSS," "No," or "Faked It"). They don't need to push women to turn their babies into data points before those babies can decide if they want companies tracking their every move, even before birth. And yet we answer these questions even when they are unnecessary for the service at hand. Sometimes, we must answer to keep using the service. (Firms are coercive that way.) Other times, we answer because we assume that we have to, and that no one will care about information buried in a sea of data.

We may not even recognize that answering these questions or

providing this information amounts to giving up our privacy. Doing so seems like a no-brainer because the gains are obvious while the costs aren't readily apparent. We don't immediately see or feel the costs as we use apps and other online services. We don't see or hear our data bouncing from our heads and hands into the databases of companies and then to countless other purchasing parties. We don't think about these activities as implicating our privacy because we can't wrap our heads around the avalanche of data being created about our intimate lives.

This is key to why we have such a difficult time understanding and protecting against risks associated with digital services. Indeed, the insurance industry is premised on the basic idea that it has unique expertise evaluating risks of all kinds. Assessing risk is hard for ordinary people, especially when the risks aren't physically tangible or immediately quantifiable. This is especially true for our data. When intimate information is collected, it may take a while before we realize what is going on or before it is used against us. And once our data is collected, we lose control over it. We are worse off, and it's hard to appreciate the extent of our vulnerability. The risk of harm may be hard to see, but that doesn't make it any less potent or dangerous—it is profound and real. We can't prevent downstream problems, and we won't know about them before they happen, if we ever find out. The risks are as varied as they are significant. They include our inability to take advantage of important opportunities; the entrenchment of inequality; the exposure to manipulation; loss of freedom of expression; and damage to our reputations.

Let's return to where this chapter started, with the Amazon Halo. Your Halo tracks your weight gain and your fat levels. Suppose that your data is run through an algorithm. Based on your fat fluctuations and vocal patterns, the algorithm predicts that you have an "extremely high risk" of Type 2 diabetes. This prediction leads to higher life insurance premiums. You never realized that your fitness band's intimate data would be used for anything other than helping *you* manage your health. And you certainly never imagined that your data would be amassed, mined, and shared. Spying Inc.'s tentacles reach far and wide, and may hurt your prospects for affordable life insurance.

Using algorithms to make predictions or to rank individuals isn't necessarily nefarious. It depends on how those algorithms are designed, what personal data is mined, and whether algorithmic outputs disparately impact vulnerable communities. Algorithms can, for example, entrench troubling bias against women and minorities if the algorithms themselves encode such bias (after all, they are built by human beings) or if the data being analyzed reflects invidious discrimination.[70] (The problem is often referred to as "algorithmic bias."[71]) When intimate data reflecting biased attitudes or discriminatory outcomes forms the basis for "probabilistic judgment about attributes, abilities, and aptitudes," both individuals and society lose.[72]

In 2018, Amazon developed an algorithmic hiring tool that compared previous hires with the resumes of applicants and then ranked job candidates. The system excluded resumes from candidates from all women's colleges and resumes that included the word "women's." After trying to fix it, Amazon engineers abandoned the tool because they could not be sure the algorithm would not continue to disadvantage female applicants.

A study conducted in 2019 found that Facebook's ad delivery system reinforced gender and racial stereotypes: ads for jobs in the lumber industry were disproportionately shown to white men, ads for cashier positions at supermarkets were shown to women, and ads for taxi drivers were shown to Black individuals.[73] As for Google, information scholar and CCRI board member Safiya Noble demonstrated that the search engine produced highly sexualized imagery results for searches of terms like "Black girls" and "Latina girls" as compared to searches of "white girls."[74]

Odds are great that algorithmic decision-making based on intimate data will have a disparate negative impact on women and minorities. Ovia Health, a period-tracking app, is marketing a paid version of the app to insurers and employers as a way to reduce medical costs and "shepherd new mothers' return to work."[75] Female employees at the video game company Activision Blizzard are paid a dollar a day for letting the company's human resources personnel access their Ovia Health data in de-identified form. Medical researcher Paula Castaño is skeptical about any potential benefit this would have for women because fertility apps ask them to share information that would suggest their need to miss work or to seek medical services, which would only mean one thing—more costs for firms.[76]

Our intimate data can be used to manipulate us at our most vulnerable moments by, for example, feeding us how-to self-harm videos just as our anxiety and depression symptoms are worsening. Consider the advertising service The Spinner, which promises to send targeted ads to individuals to encourage them to settle divorces or to make up with an ex. The company's most requested service is its "initiating sex campaign," which sends ads trumpeting reasons why people should have sex.

We often have no idea when intimate data has been used to our disadvantage. But when we discover that our intimate data has been collected or shared in unwanted ways, that knowledge may change how we interact with the world. We may become reluctant to express ourselves or engage with others. Although we do not want to chill our activities and self-expression, we do it to protect ourselves.

Consider the damage to individuals and to society after Grindr subscribers discovered that the app had shared their HIV status (noted as "positive," "positive on HIV treatment," "negative," or "negative on PrEP") with advertising and analytics firms.[77] A man told *Vox* that he removed his HIV status from his Grindr profile because when the "wrong people" find out, lives, careers, and family relationships are imperiled. This chilling effect disappointed physicians who had lauded Grindr for prompting people to share their HIV status and thus be more transparent and—hopefully—more likely to talk about practicing safe sex.

We saw chilling effects after women learned that their fertility-tracking apps were collecting, storing, and sharing their intimate data.

More than 100 women responding to a survey by the *Washington Post* said that they "felt trapped by an unfair choice: They cared about their privacy, but they also found the digital trackers too valuable to give up." Many wanted to get the benefit of the apps while reducing their privacy risks, so they registered under fake names, provided false information, or logged only some of their data. Others stopped using the apps entirely, for fear that their data would be misused.[78]

And on top of those difficulties, Spying Inc.'s risks also include professional, reputational, and emotional harm. Think of the people who used the adultery site Ashley Madison. The site's woeful security practices enabled hackers to steal subscribers' profiles and post them online. People committed suicide after learning that their spouses or employers found out about their use of the site. Some lost their jobs. Spying Inc.'s risks are life-altering in ways large and small, known and unknown, but all are significant.

We all have Data Selves. We often don't realize, and can't prevent, corporate surveillance of our intimate lives or the creation of our digital doppelgängers. We should be able to use networked products and services without worrying that our intimate information is being tracked in unwanted ways, or that it may be used against us or our loved ones, for, as we'll see, once this information is out in the world, it can be hard to contain it or prevent its downstream use.

2

Privacy Invaders

IN AUGUST 2020, I RECEIVED THIS EMAIL FROM SOMEONE I HAD never met:

> Hello. I am being stalked online. My computer guy says my ex has made a copy of my laptop and my cellphone. He is holding my accounts hostage. He changed the passwords to 14 different accounts. He has been posting naked photos of me from years ago and some that were taken a few months ago in my bedroom—he must have hacked my laptop. Some of the photos aren't even me but he has tagged them all with my name. I have been told that this is not illegal. My ex is wealthy and well-known. How will I ever be able to get anything back? I even shut my cell phone off and have stopped using my laptop to try to stop it. Everyone I speak to even Apple says they can't really help. I'm desperate. Can you help?

I wanted to help her. But her problem, one shared by countless others around the world, is as difficult to combat as it is terrifying.

Attacks on intimate privacy by Privacy Invaders, acting alone or in coordination, are rampant. Our intimate lives can be secretly recorded and instantly shared with anyone, anywhere. Privacy invasions are getting easier and cheaper to achieve, in ways never before achievable, reaching into areas of life never before reachable.

It's almost a cliché to acknowledge that strangers and those we know are invading our intimate privacy and yet we still treat it as urban legend, as something that happens to others in far-off places. Pop culture bears some of the responsibility for this cognitive dissonance. Television series and films feature girls sharing their nude photos with tragic results, female prosecutors stepping down from career-making cases to prevent defense counsel from publishing their stolen sex videos, and stalkers installing cameras in unwitting victims' homes. The plots are so over the top that they seem unreal, but fiction has nothing on reality.

BARRIERS REMOVED, STAKES TRANSFORMED

Intimate privacy violations are as old as time. The English language has had the term "Peeping Tom" for a thousand years: as folklore has it, Lady Godiva's sadistic husband agreed to cancel his tenants' taxes if she rode naked through town. Only Tom, the tailor, ignored her plea that people close their shutters during her ride. In the pre-modern era, intimate life could be observed only so much and only momentarily.

In the recent past, practical limits like time, money, and geography constrained what Privacy Invaders could accomplish. In the 1940s and 1950s, you needed access to mail order catalogs or spy shops that sold location trackers, miniature cameras, radio pills, and tiny tape recorders.[1] Available for purchase were bugging devices hidden in earrings, tie clasps, fake martini olives; they broadcast conversations to receivers up to a block away. In the 1960s, managers hid microphones in the walls of employee restrooms and desks; model homes and car showrooms were equipped with hidden microphones so salespeople could overhear what prospective buyers were discussing.[2] Recall Linda Tripp's secret recording of phone calls with Monica Lewinsky; the recordings ultimately resulted in President Clinton's 1998 impeachment. Because Tripp had to gain Lewinsky's trust and only their telephone conversations could be recorded, her cruel betrayal took months.

The practicalities that once protected privacy are rapidly disappearing. Hundreds of sites now sell hidden-camera clothing hooks, clock radios, phone dock chargers, air purifiers, and smoke detectors. In 2013, these devices cost about $5,000 each.[3] Today, Amazon's "hidden cameras" category includes "mini spy camera" coat hangers for $19.99 and smoke detectors tricked out with night vision, remote monitoring, and long-lasting batteries for $150. All with free delivery for Prime members. And, of course, there are our smartphones, ever ready to record.

Today's surveillance tools enable individuals to monitor intimate life from afar and in coordination with many, many others. No place, body part, or communication is safe—not the bathroom, gym, hotel room, or bedroom; not under our skirts or down our shirts; and not our calls, texts, or emails. Privacy Invaders don't even need to be near us to capture our data and record our bodies. They can download malware onto our personal devices to give themselves real-time access to our photos, texts, and calendars; they can activate the cameras and deactivate their warning lights. They count on us to bring our laptops and cell phones everywhere, including our bedrooms—and we do (just as the emailer you met at the outset of this chapter did).

Geographic barriers that once deterred Privacy Invaders have been essentially erased in the digital age. A single perpetrator can have hundreds, even thousands, of victims in different countries and across multiple continents. A man pretending to be a teenage girl tricked teenage boys into sharing nude photos and then forced the boys to send more to prevent the man from posting the photos online. Another man coerced 230 women and girls into sending him nude images and performing sex acts for him in front of a webcam—his laptop held 15,000 webcam videos, 900 audio recordings, and 13,000 screen captures.[4]

The speed and scale of distribution is striking. Privacy Invaders have thousands of sites to choose from on which to publish a person's nude photos. Those sites facilitate global connectivity so intimate information is accessible anywhere and everywhere. The only barriers are terms-of-service agreements, which may ban certain forms of content, such as spam, hate speech, and bullying. But sites tend to filter or block content only if liability is a real risk (it often isn't), while keeping up the rest, especially content that generates traffic and ad revenue, as intimate images are wont to do.

Once intimate information is posted online, it can't be escaped or erased. Unlike print newspapers, with their limited reach and eventual fate in the trash or recycling bins, search engines index content, retrieve and publish it in an instant, and keep it forever. Intimate information appears online long after strangers have spied on us and long after lovers have betrayed our trust. There is often no forgetting in the digital age.

Intimate images attract wide audiences. Sex sells. We are mesmerized by sensuality and nudity. We want to know, and we eagerly share, information about people's sexual habits and naked bodies. According to one study, 84% of men and 74% of women report that they would watch attractive people have sex or undress if they were sure they wouldn't get caught.[5] We share provocative information online—content that we might not share in person—because we feel anonymous. We struggle to connect the images and stories circulating behind screens with real-world harms that are inflicted on flesh-and-blood human beings. No wonder intimate images go viral.

It all packs a serious punch. Photographs and video and audio recordings grab our attention and stick in our memories because we trust what our eyes and ears tell us. Images make us witnesses to events, or so we think; after all, we needn't rely on what others say happened when we see or hear it for ourselves.[6] According to researchers, we are 80% more likely to remember a photograph than to remember text, and most people don't doubt an image's provenance when shown one. Renowned photographer and author Susan Sontag didn't need studies to say of her craft, "Photography furnishes evidence. Something we hear about, but doubt, seems proven when we are shown a photograph of it."[7] Or, as Oliver Wendell Holmes Sr. remarked, photographs are "mirrors with a memory."

Today, memories of our intimate lives are being created against our will by perpetrators who intrude on the seclusion that we expect, want, and deserve. That is the domain of the digital voyeur.

DIGITAL VOYEURS

Public restrooms, gym showers, and dressing rooms—here and other publicly accessible places are where miniature cameras record people urinating, undressing, or washing themselves. In South Korea, the practice is called *molka*, after a 1990s television show about hidden-camera pranks. But there's nothing funny about it.[8] The practice is so prevalent in South Korea that many women and girls either avoid going to public restrooms or bring emergency kits containing screwdrivers (to break cameras hidden inside screws), masks (to hide their faces), and silicone sealant (to fill holes that might contain cameras).[9] Kits are available on Tumblbug for less than 20,000 won (approximately $20).[10]

The story of South Korea is the story of Singapore, and the story of Singapore is the story of Israel, Australia, the United States, the United Kingdom, and elsewhere. Unfortunately, comprehensive statistics aren't available because most countries don't track crimes with minor penalties (true for most voyeurism laws) and because there aren't clearinghouses of information about the amount of spy cams around the globe.[11] But what we do know about the weaponization of cameras is startling. In a survey of 6,109 people from Australia, New Zealand, and the United Kingdom, one in three respondents said that their nude or sexually explicit images had been captured without their consent.[12] (And that is surely a low-ball estimate, given that most people don't even know that they have been taken.)

So long as perpetrators have access to places where people undress, they exploit that access. In Louisiana, a man duct-taped a miniature camera to the inside of a urinal in the men's bathroom of his workplace. The camera's memory card was later found to contain photographs and videos of several men's genitals.[13] A UC Berkeley employee used a hidden video camera to tape more than 100 people in a dorm bathroom.[14] Berkeley students also have been caught placing their cell phones in women's shower stalls.[15] In the UK, an electrician installed a camera in the women's changing room at a police station.[16] In Singapore, a man used camera sticks and hidden-camera pens to film and photograph women and girls in the dressing rooms of a clothing store chain as well as in the restroom of his church. He had 700 videos and 821 photos on his computer.[17]

Hotels and doctors' offices are prime targets. Hotel guests in Sydney, Beijing, and Miami have been filmed undressing, urinating, and having sex without their knowledge or consent.[18] Cameras hidden in wall sockets, hairdryer holders, and television boxes secretly filmed 1,600 guests in 42 motel rooms in South Korea.[19] A Johns Hopkins gynecologist used a pen-shaped camera hanging from his neck to photograph and video-record his patients' naked bodies in the examination room.[20] A Maryland rabbi used a spy-camera clock to record 150 women while they undressed for the ritual bath known as the mikvah.[21]

Privacy Invaders use cell phones and watches with hidden cameras to take photographs up women's skirts or down their blouses. Riding escalators, taking public transportation, and browsing store aisles—all pose the risk of intimate privacy violations.

In China, the latest women's fashion craze is the "safety pant," and it's not because the pants are cute. Safety pants are tight shorts designed to be worn over undergarments to protect against up-skirt photos. China's leading e-commerce platform, Taobao, sells safety pants with graphics or messages aimed at deflecting unwanted leers, including an animated horse saying, "What the f—k are you looking at?" According to an online poll, 85% of approximately 75,000 respondents living in China said that they would wear safety pants to protect themselves against predators taking up-skirt photos.[22]

Efforts to destroy zones of privacy extend beyond secret recordings, to include bombarding cell phones with sexually explicit material. Consider how subway flashing has evolved. Today, men don't have to pull down their pants to shove their genitals in a subway rider's face. (As I experienced on a Manhattan subway in 1996, flashers stand directly in front of sitting riders and pull down their pants just as the car pulls into the station, allowing them to expose themselves and get away.) Enter cyber flashers: subway riders use their iPhone's AirDrop feature to send photos of their genitals to riders near them. Cyber flashers can look for a nearby active AirDrop account with a woman's name and, voilà, they are set. While victims can reject unsolicited photos once they have seen them, they can't prevent more from being sent until they change the Air-Drop setting.[23] A female reporter received more than 100 sexually explicit images via AirDrop as she traveled on the London Underground.

Cyber flashing accomplishes what old-school flashers want but with less personal risk, because no one can see what they are doing and because victims usually shrink into themselves rather than vocalize their discomfort. Victims have to think about coerced sex from someone nearby. In Japan, the practice is so prevalent that riding the subway is synonymous with the receipt of unwanted "dick pics." It isn't just subway riders who are forced to look at someone's intimate images. According to the UK's Office for Standards in Education (Ofsted), nine out of ten girls report that unwanted explicit videos or photos are sent to their cell phones "a lot" or "sometimes." Ofsted's Chief Inspector Amanda Spielman explained that cyberflashing is so normalized that "many child[ren] and young people, particularly girls, feel they have to accept" such abuse and "don't feel it is worth reporting."[24]

Perpetrators not only invade physical and digital spaces where they are unwelcome, they also extort victims to provide intimate images, combining privacy invasions with crimes like blackmail and extortion. Sextortion, as it is frequently called, routinely involves threats to disclose victims' nude images unless they send more nude images or perform sex acts in front of webcams. The scheme begins when perpetrators obtain victims' nude images, often through hacking, trickery, or hidden cameras. It's the latter category that enabled a stranger to target Joan, a white woman from the United States, while she was traveling for work.

In September 2018, a New York hotel employee placed a hidden camera in the bathroom of the guest room where Joan stayed. Recordings showed Joan taking off her clothes and showering. Someone with the handle notabadguy2 posted the videos on several porn sites under Joan's real name with the caption, "Bathroom Voyeur Cam." The same person then started sending Joan threatening emails—the employee presumably obtained Joan's email address from the hotel's computer system. The first email included a link to the videos next to the question "this is you right?" An hour later, the second email arrived, complete with the name of her graduate school and her employer as well as a cryptic threat: "I don't want to embarrass you please reply." The next day, he wrote several more times, this time explicitly threatening that unless she sent him nude images and videos, he would continue to distribute these videos, along with her name and her employer's name. Emails said, "Promise me my own show . . . You have until midnight to send me something good or I will post videos, your name, info everywhere . . . and send to people you know." Joan did not respond, so the perpetrator emailed the videos to all of her LinkedIn contacts (she had hundreds) and posted them on dozens more porn sites. Whenever Joan got a site to take down the videos, the perpetrator would repost them and send her taunting emails: "Why'd you take down my video? It's already up on a bunch of sites. You already hit 1000 views on one."

Sextortion happens on a scale that only today's internet can provide.

We have seen sextortion rings, where perpetrators work together to extort victims and sell access to intimate images that they have obtained. From late 2018 to early 2020, 125 South Korean men tricked 26 girls (many in their early teens) and 100 women into sending them nude photos. They placed online ads for models, which led to interviews and requests for nude images. After women and girls sent the images, the men threatened to publish or email them to family members unless victims sent more revealing and sexually explicit images. Some women and girls were forced to tape themselves masturbating, penetrating themselves with office supplies, and carving the word "slave" onto their bodies. One girl had to make 40 videos. Another girl was tricked into entering a hotel room where she was recorded being sexually assaulted. The videos and photos—along with the victims' names, addresses, and schools—were posted in pay-to-view chatrooms. The chat rooms had names like "Slaves" and "Underage Girl Room." "Let's rape" was how chat room participants greeted each other. More than 25,000 people paid to access the chat rooms—the price tag for entry was $1,200 in Bitcoin per person.[25] Another sextortion ring coerced 50 women and girls to produce 3,000 sexually explicit videos and photos, which were posted on another pay-per-view chat room called "Nth Room."[26] Both operations were eventually shut down after South Korean authorities arrested the ring leaders.

Men, too, have fallen victim to sextortion schemes.[27] Michael was in his forties when he met a woman on a dating site; they began messaging and talking via Skype. On one call, the woman asked Michael to get naked and promised to do the same. As soon as they were both naked, she ended the call, sent him a video with him naked, and demanded that he pay her $400 or she would send the video to his Facebook friends. Too mortified to let his friends hear about his carelessness, he sent the money to the address in Asia as the woman had demanded.[28]

The power grabs of sextortionists have extended to other arenas. Jerry Falwell Jr. allegedly secretly taped his wife having sex with a young man, Giancarlo Granda, and threatened to release the sex tapes if Granda told reporters about the affair.[29] An associate of rap artist R. Kelly tried to force a woman to drop her civil lawsuit against Kelly by threatening to release her sexually explicit photographs.[30] The *National Enquirer* and its parent company, American Media, Inc., attempted to blackmail then-Amazon CEO Jeff Bezos by threatening to publish intimate photos of him, which he had taken himself and sent to his extramarital lover, unless he made a public statement that he had "no knowledge or basis for suggesting that AMI's coverage was politically motivated or influenced by political forces."[31]

Strangers aren't the only ones exploiting access to our intimate lives. People who we know and trust spy on our intimate activities, force us to reveal nude images, and display our naked bodies. Lovers and former lovers are frequent Privacy Invaders.

INTIMATE SURVEILLANCE, ABUSE, AND VIOLENCE

A New York financial advisor secretly recorded his sexual encounters with three women he was dating, all of whom thought that they were in an exclusive relationship with him. He stored the videos on his laptop and on password-protected YouTube and Vimeo accounts. When confronted with proof of what he had done, the man blamed his "doggie cam," claiming that he had put the camera in his bedroom to monitor his dog, not to film his sexual encounters. He said that it was just a coincidence that the videos showed him setting up the camera and angling it to focus on the bed while the women were out of the room.

The man's "doggie cam" explanation lost whatever feeble credibility it might have had after he repeatedly used his laptop to secretly film his sexual encounters with the women when he went to their apartments.

Saying he had work to do, the man would bring his laptop to their homes and leave it open on their nightstands or desks—whichever position facilitated a view of the bed. When he (presumably unintentionally) left a flash drive in the apartment of one of his unsuspecting victims, she found copies of the videos neatly organized into folders, one for each woman. One folder was labeled "Indian Research," for that woman's ethnic background. He also uploaded the videos to his private YouTube and Vimeo accounts to share them with his friends.[32]

In a profound violation of trust, domestic abusers install stalkerware on partners' cell phones.[33] To do this, they only need their victims' phone (and password) for a few minutes. Once installed, cyberstalking apps silently record and upload the phone's activities to their servers. They provide access to victims' photos, videos, texts, calls, voice mails, searches, social media activities, locations—nothing is out of reach. From anywhere, they can activate the phone's mic to listen to conversations within 15 feet of the phone. Victims are never free from unwanted monitoring. Abusers use the data they obtain to terrorize, manipulate, control, and shame their victims. When victims finally figure out what's going on, they often get rid of their phones on the advice of law enforcement, who frequently lack the technical skills to detect or remove cyberstalking apps.

Buying cyberstalking apps is as easy as searching "cell phone spy." Results return hundreds of pages. In my Google search results, a related popular search is "spy on spouse cell phone." More than 200 apps and services charge subscribers a monthly fee (as much as $100) in exchange for providing secret, real-time access to people's phones.[34] When I first began studying stalkerware in 2013, businesses marketed themselves as the spy in a cheating spouse's pocket. Ads featured photos of couples next to the message "Many spouses cheat. They all use cell phones. Their phones will tell you what they won't." Although the ads are more subtle now, affiliated blog entries are less so, with titles like "Don't Be A Sucker Track Your Girlfriend's iPhone Now: Catch Her Today."[35]

We don't have precise numbers on stalkerware victims, but domestic violence hotlines around the United States help more than 70,000 individuals every day, and as many as 70% of those callers raise concerns about stalkerware.[36] A 2014 study found that 54% of domestic abusers tracked victims' cell phones with stalkerware.[37] Security firm Kaspersky detected more than 518,223 stalkerware infections during the first eight months of 2019, a 373% increase from that period in 2018.[38] Statistics suggest that millions of people, right now, are being watched, controlled, and manipulated by partners or exes. Russia, Brazil, India, and the United States lead the world in the number of stalkerware users.[39]

Intimate partners don't stop with digital spying: they disclose victims' intimate images to others. The publication of someone's nude or sexually explicit images without permission is often called "revenge porn." That label is misleading. While some people are driven by malice, others are motivated by vanity, cruelty, or carelessness.[40] Calling it "revenge" also assumes that the victim has done something to merit revenge. In any case, focusing on the perpetrator's motive turns it into someone's personal problem, or psychopathology, and suggests that it's unusual, a symptom of extreme rage. But the perpetrator's motive isn't the point; the nonconsensual disclosure of intimate images is. Advocates for victims of intimate privacy violations call it "nonconsensual pornography" as an imperfect shorthand reference. Unfortunately, it's not rare.

Anna was living in Bulgaria when she met her husband, a native of Iceland, through an online dating site. They dated by long distance for two years. During that time, he repeatedly asked for nude photos and videos of her masturbating. She hesitated at first but eventually agreed because he assured her that the images were for his eyes only. After Anna moved to Iceland, the couple married and had a son. When their son was five years old, Anna's husband grew abusive. His angry outbursts soon led to physical attacks. When Anna said that she wanted a trial separation, her husband threatened to email the nude photos and videos to her family. Anna had not thought about those photos and videos in years—she assumed that they had been deleted. Not so.

After months of abuse, Anna asked her husband for a divorce. That was when the mass emails started. Anna's husband sent the videos and photos to her colleagues and boss at the primary school where she taught, to the parents of their son's friends, to friends from her own school days, and to the mayor of her hometown—cc'ing Anna on each of the 250+ emails. He created fake Facebook and Twitter accounts in Anna's name, friended and followed her coworkers and acquaintances, and then uploaded the photos and videos. He posted them on adult sites and sites devoted to nonconsensual pornography.

Perpetrators like Anna's husband ensure that victims can be identified. According to a 2019 study, approximately 66% of victims reported that their personal details (name, age, occupation, address, social media handle, or phone number) were posted along with their nude images. Over 30% reported that their nude images were shared on social media sites, and 20% had their nude images shared via text, email, or on sites devoted to nonconsensual intimate images.[41]

Of course, strangers are also responsible for nonconsensual pornography. A resident of South Africa left her phone in a cab in January 2019. Whoever found her phone discovered her nude photos—that person texted a relative of hers, demanding sex and cash from the woman who left the phone. When she refused, her nude photos were posted online, and they were soon trending on social media.[42]

An especially vile species of nonconsensual pornography is rape videos: there, the privacy violation compounds the damage of sexual violence. A woman from New Zealand discovered footage of her partner raping her as she lay unconscious; he had carefully set up the camera before he started.[43] A 14-year-old girl of First Nations ethnicity was sexually assaulted by two men, with a third man filming the attack; the attackers were white men. Years later, she found videos of her sexual assault on the adult site Pornhub. The titles of the videos were "teen crying and getting slapped around," "passed out teen," and "teen getting destroyed."[44] The videos had more than 400,000 views.[45]

Recordings of sexual assaults have a long and horrible history. Child sexual abuse material, also known as CSAM—itself proof of rape—has been around for as long as cameras have existed. When Nicole was four years old, her uncle videotaped his rape of her. Although Nicole's uncle was arrested and imprisoned when Nicole was nine, the photographs and videos had already been circulated on the internet. Those images are now the most widely distributed child pornography of all time.[46]

DIGITAL SEXUAL IDENTITY FRAUD

Some twenty-first-century privacy violations don't have analog-era equivalents in any conventional sense. That's especially true of what can be described as digital sexual identity fraud, technology that swaps people's faces into real porn. The manipulation of pornography got a boost with the invention of deepfake technology, which uses "deep learning" artificial intelligence to create content modeled on source data (e.g., photographs of a person's face) and inserts that content into videos. Algorithms perfect the process by detecting and fixing imperfections.[47]

In late 2017, Reddit got its first glimpse into what the person who posted under the name "Deep Fakes" had been cooking up in his spare time: a machine-learning algorithm that mashed people's faces onto porn performers' bodies. After Deep Fakes, a programmer by day and video fabricator by night, posted several of his creations, the celebrity fake porn phenomenon took off. Soon, another Reddit user created and shared an

app that lets anyone create AI-generated fake porn—no technical expertise required. In internet time (two months, give or take), the alias of the
man who started the trend was turned into a noun. Even Merriam Web-
ster has an entry for "deepfakes."[48]

By January 2018, the subreddit devoted exclusively to deepfake celebrity sex videos had more than 100,000 members. Fake hardcore porn
videos featured Scarlett Johansson, Maisie Williams, Taylor Swift, and
Aubrey Plaza. Gal Gadot appeared having sex with her stepbrother,
which of course never happened.[49] Daisy Ridley's deepfake sex video was
particularly popular. The original deepfake sex subreddits aren't available
because Reddit banned deepfakes in February 2018. But deepfake porn
quickly replicated and migrated elsewhere.

Now anyone can make realistic yet fake audio and video showing
people saying things they never said and doing things they never did.
With advances in artificial intelligence, deepfakes can be created com-
pletely de novo—no longer does one need to swap faces into preexist-
ing videos. Deepfakes are so sophisticated that even experts struggle to
distinguish the fake from the authentic. Computer scientist and CCRI
board member Hany Farid watched the rapid refinement of the technology in real time: "In January 2019, deep fakes were buggy and flick-
ery. Nine months later, I've never seen anything like how fast they're
going."[50] Deepfake sex videos can be manufactured with such sophis-
tication that victims feel exposed and viewers believe that what they're
seeing actually happened.

Noelle Martin, whose Indian-Catholic family lives in Australia, was
18 years old when she received an email from a stranger saying, "There's
deepfakes of you." The emailer sent her a link to an adult site. There, she
found an 11-second clip of a woman and a man having sex. The face of
the woman in the video was hers. But she had never made a sex tape of
any sort—let alone that one. Tags on the video included #NoelleMar-
tin, #BigTits, #Indian, and #Amateur. She searched the site and found

another video where she was performing oral sex: the deepfake was devastatingly realistic. Comments underneath the deepfake sex videos included her name, home address, and her best friend's name. Some clips featured men ejaculating onto the faked images.[51]

PATTERNS OF VICTIMIZATION

Now that we understand the different ways that Privacy Invaders violate intimate privacy, we can step back and examine the patterns that have emerged. For intimate privacy violations, women and minors are more likely to be the victims, and men are more likely to be the perpetrators. Consider statistics offered by the South Korean National Police. Of the 6,500 video voyeurism arrests in 2014, 98% of the perpetrators were male, and 84% of the victims were female.[52] Research from 2018 found that more than 40% of millennial women in the United Kingdom reported having received unsolicited photos of men's genitalia, and more than half of millennial women in the United States reported the same.[53] In 2019, the vast majority of up-skirt photo victims were women, and the perpetrators were almost always men.[54] Of the 50,000 deepfake videos posted online in 2020, about 95% inserted women's faces into porn.[55] Many of those videos feature Black women, accompanied by comments infected by misogynoir. Deepfake sex videos of Duchess of Sussex Meghan Markle demonstrate the point.

Because nonconsensual porn has attracted considerable study, we have a more nuanced picture of the phenomenon. Yet again, most studies suggest that the majority of victims are female. According to a 2017 survey conducted by Australia's eSafety Commissioner, women were twice as likely as men to be victims. Nineteen percent of LGBT individuals faced nonconsensual porn, in contrast to 11% of cisgender heterosexual individuals. Racial and ethnic minorities and disabled individuals were disproportionately impacted as well. The 2017 study found that Indigenous Australians were twice as likely to have experienced nonconsensual porn than non-Indigenous Australians, and one out of two Australians with disabilities had found themselves the target of nonconsensual porn.[56]

Children are particularly vulnerable. According to a 2016 study, 71% of sextortion victims were under the age of 18.[57] And sextortion is more serious when minors are targeted. Perpetrators are more likely to demand that children harm themselves, and threats frequently continue for more than six months. Children tend to comply with perpetrators' demands to tell no one because they believe perpetrators' threats to kill their families.[58] Online communities known as "ratters"—after the Remote Access Trojan (RAT) malware they use—hack teenage girls' and boys' laptops to watch and record them without their knowledge. (The jackpot is when victims use their laptops to take or store nude images or to look at porn themselves or when they bring their laptops into their bedrooms.) Ratters exchange photographs and recordings of their victims, whom they refer to as their "slaves." In August 2020, Interpol reported an increase in RAT attacks during the coronavirus pandemic.[59]

Heterosexual, cisgender men, too, have faced intimate privacy violations. These are typically connected to breakups or one-night stands. From 2014 to early 2018, Bryan Deneumostier ran a subscription-based website called "Straightboyz," featuring videos of men having sexual encounters without knowing that they were being recorded. Deneumostier posed as a housewife seeking anonymous sex in online ads. He instructed men answering the ad to let themselves into his house, put on blacked-out goggles, and sit down in a chair. Once the men were seated, Deneumostier livestreamed himself giving them oral sex. The Straightboyz site featured videos of 80 men, including Rich. Deneumostier posted the videos of him on Twitter and adult sites. One of the videos posted on Pornhub had been viewed more than 20,000 times.

THE PROFOUND HARM OF INTIMATE PRIVACY VIOLATIONS

Two years on from her ex's attacks against her, Anna still hadn't started dating again; the prospect of being vulnerable with another person—of taking that risk—had become unimaginable. Because friends and family often have difficulty understanding what is going on, let alone empathizing, victims feel judged and misunderstood. A study conducted by CCRI found that nonconsensual porn jeopardized the relationships that more than 30% of victims had with their families and friends.[60]

Self-esteem is shattered. Victims feel like they have lost control over their bodies, minds, and intimate affairs—that their sexual autonomy has been revoked.[61] Joan worried that her colleagues and friends would see her only as a nude body on the toilet and in the shower. Some victims experience an ongoing sense of being "virtually raped."

When Holly Jacobs, the founder of CCRI, was in graduate school, her dean advised her to change her name after her ex plastered her nude images online. Unable to bear the thought that future employers, friends, and colleagues would see the nude images when googling her name, she followed the advice.[62]

Feelings of fear and hypervigilance can be consuming. Victims are afraid to engage in the activities that led to their privacy violation—taking the bus, changing in a dressing room, sharing nude images, using their laptops. Any inkling that something is out of place opens them up to worries that Privacy Invaders are back, that the spaces that they have carved out for themselves are once again no longer their own. A New Zealand woman who was filmed in a store's dressing room subsequently became afraid to take off her clothes, even in her own home.[63] One of the women violated by the Johns Hopkins gynecologist confided, "I can't bring myself to go back. You're lying there, exposed. It's violating and it's horrible, and my trust is gone. Period."

There is no escaping the experience. Victims' lives are plagued with worry and pain. The emotional harm is severe, and it lasts for years.

According to researchers, a majority of victims suffer serious physical, emotional, and psychological trauma, resulting in chronic conditions like depression and PTSD.[64] In a survey conducted by CCRI in 2017, 93% of victims facing nonconsensual porn reported having suffered "significant emotional distress."[65] Kara Jefts, a white woman, described her experience with nonconsensual porn as an "incurable disease." Anna had frequent migraines. Joan wrestled with severe anxiety; she lost considerable weight because it seemed like a way to gain control over her body.

Tragically, minors who are victims of nonconsensual pornography are particularly vulnerable to depression and suicide.[66] Seventeen-year-old Júlia Rebeca from Piauí, Brazil hanged herself after a sex tape of her appeared online. Just before committing suicide, she wrote on social media: "I love you, I'm sorry for not being the perfect daughter but I tried, I'm sorry I'm sorry I love you so much."[67] Daisy Coleman, whose rape at 13 was filmed and the recording shared with her classmates, took her own life in 2020 at 23 years old. As her mother explained, her daughter "never recovered from what those boys did to her."[68]

Victims stop expressing themselves and withdraw from community activities.[69] After Joan deleted her social media accounts to prevent her tormentor from learning additional information about her, she felt cut off and sad because Facebook had been how she kept up with high school and college friends. Yet she felt she had no other choice. Sara, who is a member of the Church of Latter-Day Saints, started dating someone new after her divorce. On a night when her ex-husband had the kids, she invited the man over. Her ex, who had a key to her house for emergencies, had hidden a Wi-Fi-enabled video camera in her bedroom. He emailed footage of that night to Sara's parents and to members of her church. She was excommunicated, while her ex remained welcome. A church elder told her parents that she was a heretic. Afterwards, not even her parents would speak to her, much less anyone else in her community.

As victims suffer these injuries, they may internalize the invidious messages that society sends to women and minorities about their bodies and sexuality. This is part of how intimate privacy violations undermine equality and, ultimately, democracy.

ENTRENCHING INEQUALITY

Intimate privacy violations reinforce destructive bigoted and gendered stereotypes. When a white woman's nude photo appears in the search results of her name, she will be thought of as a damaged slut. If she is trans or queer, then her naked body may be viewed as disgusting, even degenerate. If she is Black, Asian, or Latina, then gender and racial stereotypes ferment further into a toxic brew, casting her as unworthy of privacy because her hypersexuality got her into the mess.

Victims internalize the demeaning messages: they feel ashamed and humiliated.[70] The woman whom the New York man secretly recorded, and whose videos he stored as "Indian Research," felt doubly shamed—as a woman and as an Indian American. The rabbi's victims felt "tainted and dirty."[71] Noelle Martin was terrified to tell her Indian-Catholic parents about the deepfake sex videos of her—"I didn't want them to suffer the shame that I felt."[72]

Many men experience a distinct kind of shame when their nude images are posted online or when they are tricked into sharing nude images only to be extorted for money: they feel embarrassed and emasculated.[73] The toxic masculinity that casts women and minorities as "less than" or as the "other" also says that men should feel ashamed for feeling like they have been sexually assaulted—in other words, as Mary Anne Franks has described, for feeling like a woman.[74]

Arizona college student Kathryn Novak had a long-distance relationship with Brandon Simpson, who was attending the University of Central Florida. Over the course of their relationship, Simpson asked

Novak to send him nude photos. Simpson posted Novak's nude images on his fraternity's private Facebook page called the "Dog Pound," where members shared explicit videos and photos of their "sexual conquests." Simpson also secretly videotaped their sexual encounters. Not only did he post the videos on Facebook, he screened them during a fraternity meeting.[75] For Simpson, the sex videos were a point of pride. Yes, they showed him naked, but they also let him show off his sexual prowess (in ways that he approved) to his frat brothers. The men could share their nudity because it gave them credibility with one another, because they controlled the situation, and because the audience was small and local.

Bigoted attitudes and stereotypes have economic consequences. Employers decline to interview or hire people because their search results featured "unsuitable photos." Victims of nonconsensual porn, who are more often women and minorities, lose their jobs and cannot obtain new ones—why would firms hire or continue to employ someone who put themselves in harm's way and who might reflect poorly on their business?

Annie Seifullah was a high school principal in New York City when her boyfriend secretly searched her old laptop and found sexually explicit photos of her from years earlier. After their relationship soured, the man uploaded the photos onto her work laptop and gave it to the school's superintendent. He also sent the photos, along with claims that she had sex on school grounds, to the *New York Post*, which published the images. Seifullah's emotional devastation coincided with the demise of her teaching career. The city initially demoted her but then suspended her for a year without pay. Although a city investigator believed that she had told the truth, New York's Department of Education dismissed her on the grounds that she had brought "widespread negative publicity, ridicule, and notoriety" to the school system and that she failed to safeguard her work computer from her abusive ex-boyfriend. Note the reasoning here: the victim of a theft is at fault for not preventing the theft. According to this argument, if a shopkeeper's safe is broken into by thieves, then the shopkeeper is to blame for not having a better safe. But we don't say that to shopkeepers, just to women like Seifullah.

Such stigma has political consequences. When victims of intimate privacy violations withdraw from online and offline activities, we are left with less diverse and less rich public conversations. For Katie Hill, a bisexual member of Congress, nonconsensual porn ended her career. In 2019, online publications published photos showing Hill naked with a woman with whom she and her husband were having an affair, along with allegations of romantic relationships with campaign and congressional staffers. The stories, written by Republican operatives working for Hill's political opponents, made hay of her "Throuple Relationship" and bisexuality.[76] As writer Quinta Jurecic noted, this was the first time that a "politically aligned publication—or, indeed, *any* publication—has released nonconsensual pornography depicting a politician of the opposing party affiliation."[77] Hill noted her disgust that opponents tried to "exploit such a private matter for political gain." A few weeks after the photos were published, Hill stepped down, saying that she worried that more photos would be used against her if she stayed in Congress.[78] Regrettably, many blamed Hill. *New York Times* opinion writer Maureen Dowd wrote that Hill made herself vulnerable by "giving people the ammunition—or the nudes—to strip you of your dreams."[79]

Of course, intimate photos don't have to be of politicians themselves; they needn't even be real. Right-wing outlet *The Daily Caller* published an article with a title suggesting that it had a nude selfie of Representative Alexandria Ocasio-Cortez, though the woman in the photo—a woman's legs sticking out of a bath with a reflection including breasts—wasn't her. After Sydney Leathers (who had gained notoriety after exchanging nude texts with former congressman and NYC mayoral candidate Anthony Weiner) said that the photo was hers, *The Daily Caller* changed the headline of its story to "Anthony Weiner Mistress Stands Up for AOC After Evil Internet Trolls Spread Fake Nude Photo."[80]

Women and minorities in public office face far more online abuse than do their white male colleagues. Amnesty International found that during the United Kingdom's 2017 election, female politicians disproportionately faced sexist online abuse on Twitter, and that Black and Asian female politicians received 35% more abusive tweets than white women.[81] A NATO study released in 2020 found that female Finnish cabinet ministers received a disproportionate number of abusive tweets containing sexually explicit and racist abuse and demeaning gendered expletives like "slut" and "whore."[82] A 2019 study found that 28% of Finnish female municipal officials targeted with misogynistic hate speech reported being less willing than they would be otherwise to make decisions that might unleash online abuse.[83] Iiris Suomela, a member of Finland's ruling coalition, has explained that her fear of misogynistic online abuse has changed the way that she addresses issues. The country's first Black woman member of Parliament Bella Forsgrén echoed her colleague in saying that she has to think twice about the discussions that she participates in and how she talks about the issues, lest she face online backlash.[84]

Intimate privacy violations adversely affect people's willingness to enter politics. Intimate privacy invasions can take future careers entirely off the table. Ben was 20 years old when he shared his nude photos with a man he met online. When Ben realized that he had been tricked into sharing his photos with a much older man, he stopped communicating with him. Seven years later, while working for a US senator, he learned that his name and the photos had been posted on a gay nonconsensual porn site and shared in a Telegram group text that had over 800 participants. Ben told me that he has always wanted to go into politics but thinks it is now impossible: "The photos will always hang over my head, ready to be leveraged against me."

As feminist writer Caroline Criado Perez has underscored, online abuse deters women from even considering political careers. A 2017 study found that 80% of Australian women surveyed reported that the media's mistreatment of female politicians made it less likely that they would go into politics.[85] The nonconsensual publication of Congresswoman

Hill's intimate images had a similar impact. According to political orga-nizer Elliot Imse, the publication of Hill's nude images exacerbated the "anxiety that LGBTQ people, young people, women and minority can-didates feel about running for office." Activist Ayah Zideyah explained that women in the United States already feel like they can't run for office because society never taught them that they could, and now it seems even more impossible given the risk of intimate privacy violations.[86] Hill wants to contribute to efforts to combat nonconsensual porn so that women and girls don't feel like they have to choose between having intimate pri-vacy and seeking public office.[87] When people don't run for office due to fears that real or fake nude images will be used against them, democracy is the loser.

White heterosexual male politicians have faced nonconsensual porn at the hands of former lovers, but they weren't blamed or shamed. In February 2020, Benjamin Griveaux was a candidate for mayor of Paris when a video of him masturbating appeared online. His flirtation with a young woman on Instagram in 2018 led to the exchange of sexually explicit videos, which the woman's boyfriend posted online. Politicians came to Griveaux's defense. The front-runner in the race emphasized that the privacy of intimate life should be respected: "Parisians deserve a dig-nified debate." Another former rival offered his support and condemned the attack as a "serious threat to our democracy."[88] Nonetheless, Griveaux dropped out of the race. In his resignation announcement, he said, "My family does not deserve this. Nobody should ever be subjected to this kind of abuse." Indeed. Nonconsensual pornography is bad for everyone, but it's worse for women and minorities.

———

WHERE IS ALL this headed? Intimate privacy violations are profitable, so engineers and tinkerers will surely continue to create new tools that facilitate them. An AI program now enables anyone to turn a photo of a clothed woman into an altered version where she is naked. I'm using the pronoun "she" deliberately, because the program only works to turn photographs of people into photos of naked women. (If you submit a photo of a man or an inanimate object, it will be transformed to include breasts and female genitalia.) The program was trained on a large database of actual women's nude photographs, so it generates fake nude photos with precision, matching skin tone and swapping in breasts and genitalia in place of clothes. The program has been commercialized—an automated chatbot now takes people's orders through an encrypted messaging app and returns photos of clothed women along with naked versions.[89] Users have to pay 50 dollars to remove the watermark covering the images. According to Amsterdam-based cybersecurity researchers at Sensity, more than 100,000 people have used the chatbot, and 63% of the bot's users said that they sent in photos of girls or women they knew in real life.[90] The chatbot, which had 95,464 active users in its first month, also assembles the AI-generated nude photos into photo galleries, which it updates daily. Although its biggest user base is in Russia, members also live in the United States and across Europe, Asia, and South America.

Soon, 3D avatars with our faces and bodies will be manipulated into any imaginable sex act, including acts that human beings aren't physically capable of.[91] Soon, sex robots will be designed to look exactly like people, from the precise shape and measurement of their body parts to the exact contour, look, and feel of their faces. Any one of us could be turned into a sex robot without our permission. Soon, there won't be a single device in our homes that isn't capable of being hacked and turned into a spy camera. Someday, hidden camera drones may be so tiny (let's say undetectable to the human eye) and so powerful (let's say capable of streaming and storing unlimited data) that we will fear continuous secret surveillance anywhere and everywhere we go. Unless something changes, these technological developments will be embraced.

We're still proceeding with the assumption that our privacy is intact, that there is some barrier concealing us from others. We're constantly being incentivized by this app or that device to share more of ourselves, and we often believe our activities and interactions are private—particularly in our consensual, closest relationships. That all-important opaque wall around our private lives appears intact—until it is punctured with incredible ease.

3

Government Spies

THE US GOVERNMENT HAS AN IGNOMINIOUS HISTORY OF WEAP-
onizing intimate information against enemies, both domestic and foreign.
That history isn't as old as you might think.

In the 1950s and 1960s, FBI Director J. Edgar Hoover directed agents
to compile dossiers on journalists, anti-war protestors, and civil rights
activists. Microphone bugs were hidden in Dr. Martin Luther King's
hotel rooms so that agents could record him from next door.[1] This led to
the discovery of Dr. King's extramarital affairs. After the press refused to
publicize the tapes, FBI agents sent copies of the tapes to Dr. King along
with a letter reading, "The American public will know you for what you
are—an evil abnormal beast."[2] Note that at Hoover's direction, the FBI
also compiled 360,000 files on government employees believed to be gay
or lesbian.[3]

Law enforcement's abuses provoked public outrage, congressional
hearings, and legislation curtailing the government's power to surveil
US citizens. Congress passed the Wiretap Act of 1968, which required
law enforcement to obtain a special warrant to listen to the private

conversations of Americans. Today, police officers can't just bug or wire-tap hotel rooms, homes, or phones of US citizens—they must get special permission from a judge. These protections do not, however, extend to foreign citizens. Although extensive rules govern foreign intelligence operations, some surveillance of non-US persons is perfectly legal. In the aftermath of 9/11, the National Security Agency amassed intimate information to "neutralize" foreign threats.[4] An NSA document revealed to journalists showed the agency's plan to discredit Muslim "radicalizers" by exploiting information obtained from tracking their porn-site activities and their sexually explicit communications with "young girls." Given the ban on pornography in Muslim countries, the exposure of these facts "would likely call into question a radicalizer's devotion to the jihadist cause." Officials leaked news that porn was found at Osama bin Laden's compound.[5]

Then came President Trump. The forty-fifth president violated the intimate privacy of US citizens (not foreigners) with Hoover's ruthlessness and cruelty. Trump and his Department of Justice (DOJ) divulged the details of text messages exchanged between two FBI officials, exceeding the bounds of federal law, propriety, and basic humanity. The result was the destruction of the intimate privacy and lives of distinguished public servants.

On December 12, 2017, the DOJ invited members of the press to view 375 text messages exchanged between Lisa Page, special counsel to the FBI's deputy director, and Peter Strzok, deputy assistant director of the FBI's Counterintelligence Division. The reporters were invited to the DOJ after normal business hours and allowed to view copies of the text messages. A DOJ official sensationalized the revelation by telling the reporters that they could not source the material to the department. Late into the night and early into the next morning, the journalists posted stories about the revelations.

Page and Strzok served on the teams that investigated Hillary Clinton's use of a private email service and Trump campaign officials' ties to

Russia.[6] During some of that time, they had an extramarital affair. They used their FBI phones to communicate with each other. In thousands of texts, they talked about work. They traded stories about their families and health. They discussed politics. In some of those texts, they "expressed anti-Trump sentiments and other comments that appeared to favor Clinton." As Page alleged in her lawsuit against the DOJ, only one-quarter of the texts could be characterized as having any connection to politics or bias against Trump.[7]

In ordinary times, Page and Strzok's texts would have remained between them. No one would have retrieved them from the FBI's electronic storage system. No one would have inquired about their political preferences. In fact, FBI policy permits employees to express their political views privately and publicly. And no one would have shared the texts with reporters. The federal Privacy Act of 1974 protects the confidentiality of agency records about US persons, including federal employees like Page and Strzok.

But these were not ordinary times. Soon came Trump's many, many tweets about the text messages and Page and Strzok's extramarital affair. Trump tweeted that "NEW FBI TEXTS ARE BOMBSHELLS!" He denounced Page and Strzok as treasonous, sick, "stupid lovers," and "bad people" (and other variations on those themes).[8] He called for Strzok's firing. Trump's tweets about Page and Strzok were retweeted and favorited *millions* of times.[9] Politicians and media personalities amplified Trump's messages. Senator Rand Paul dubbed Page the "FBI Mistress"; Ann Coulter called for Page and Strzok's imprisonment. Thousands of tweets by the president's supporters slut-shamed Page; tweets insinuated that her mother's Iranian heritage was suspicious.

The coup de grâce occurred at a Trump campaign rally in October 2019. Before thousands of people and news cameras, Trump performed dramatic readings of Page and Strzok's texts. For the crowd, he imagined conversations between Page and Strzok. " 'I love you, Peter,' 'I love you, Lisa,' " mocked the president. He pretended to orgasm, as if he were

Strzok, while saying "Lisa."[10] *Saturday Night Live* mimicked Trump's grotesque mockery of their relationship.

Little else signifies the imprimatur of the state like its president's words and actions, so the fallout from a presidential violation of intimate privacy is especially profound. The problem wasn't the FBI's possession of the texts sent and received on government-issued phones. It wasn't the agency's sharing of the texts with the DOJ in connection with the inspector general's review of FBI investigations into Clinton and Trump campaign officials. The problem was the DOJ's revelation of the texts to journalists, and the president's exploitation of those texts in tweets, interviews, and rally performances.

Over and over (and over) again, the president laid bare the intimate lives of public servants who had done everything possible to remain unnoticed so they could protect the security of the United States. During their government careers, Page and Strzok stayed out of the public eye. They did not use social media; they never gave public interviews. Before the revelation of their texts to reporters, their names and lives were of no interest to the public. According to Google Trends, interest in Page and Strzok rocketed from 0 to 100 (on a scale of 100) after news of the texts and their affair broke. Page found it excruciating to watch the president hijack her texts and romantic relationship to degrade her. As Page explained to MSNBC journalist Rachel Maddow: "I've led an entirely anonymous life and hoped to return to one. When the president did that vile sort of simulated sex act in a rally. . . . It's like being punched in the gut. My heart drops to my stomach when I realize he has tweeted about me again. . . . He's demeaning me and my career. It's sickening."[11]

No matter that the DOJ's inspector general found no evidence that the personal views of either Page or Strzok impacted FBI investigations into Clinton or Trump campaign officials, their texts and relationship remained fodder for attacks in the conservative media ecosystem for years. On March 7, 2021, Fox News personality Maria Bartiromo talked about the texts; in an October 2021 statement, Trump accused "lovers" Page and Strzok of lying about Russia. Cyber mobs have relentlessly targeted Page, Strzok, and their respective families with death and rape threats.

Before the DOJ's release of the texts to the media and the forty-fifth president's public attacks, Page and Strzok were esteemed public servants. During Page's 12-year government career, she worked on organized crime and national security matters. Strzok was considered "one of the most experienced and trusted FBI counterintelligence investigators." The violation of their intimate privacy led to the undoing of their government careers. Page resigned from her job as FBI counsel; Strzok was fired. Both have been denied the jobs that they loved. Discussions of their texts and extramarital affair dominate Google searches of their names, with no end in sight. The violation of their intimate privacy has reduced the number of people willing to interact with them, shrunk the aperture of their lives, and irreparably damaged their reputations.[12]

This recalls Independent Counsel Kenneth Starr's impact on the life of Monica Lewinsky, who was 23 years old when Starr released the official report and findings of the investigation into President Clinton. The independent counsel's office questioned Lewinsky pursuant to a properly issued subpoena—what was wrong was the report's disclosure of the details of the interviews. The 435-page Starr Report included graphic descriptions of *every single sexual encounter and communication* between Lewinsky and Clinton. The report was salacious for salacious-ness' sake, with Lewinsky suffering most of the damage. Lewinsky was blamed for their sexual relationship even though Clinton was the one with the power. After his impeachment in the House and exoneration in the Senate for lying under oath about their relationship, Clinton's popularity rose, while Lewinsky's life was shattered. As Lewinsky said in a TED Talk that she gave nearly 20 years after the report's release, the Starr Report affixed her with a scarlet "A," which has defined and tormented her. The Starr Report shattered Lewinsky's intimate privacy.[13]

The experiences of Lewinsky, Page, and Strzok demonstrate the profound damage wrought when government actors violate individuals' intimate privacy. When the state exploits your intimate communications and relationships, it legitimizes the view that intimate life can be violated with impunity. This is especially true when those government actors are high profile and their privacy violations become part of people's search results. There is no escaping the damage done, not now, not ever.

Trump (and Starr and Hoover before him) followed a playbook laid out by other countries. Authoritarian regimes are Olympic-level intimate privacy violators. As early as the 1920s, Soviet (later Russian) intelligence services lured foreign and local politicians and businesspersons to apartments where they were secretly photographed during sex, and the photos were kept for blackmail. Luxury hotels in Moscow had rooms with photographic systems hidden in ventilation holes and wall decorations.[14] Intimate *kompromat* (compromising material) was behind the political ascendancy of Vladimir Putin. In 1999, Putin used a fake sex tape to force the prosecutor general to drop corruption charges against then-president Boris Yeltsin, who ensured that upon his retirement, Putin would become prime minister.[15] That Putin might have had a "pee tape" of businessman Donald Trump is certainly within the realm of possibility.

Anyone who criticizes authoritarian regimes is vulnerable to attack. The Cambodian government used intimate information to discredit the Venerable Luon Sovath, a Buddhist monk who documented the state's eviction of 400,000 Cambodians. When even an arrest did not deter Sovath from exposing human rights abuses, the government circulated videos that appeared to show him having sexually suggestive conversations with a mother and her three daughters. Although the videos were deliberately deceptive, they had their intended effect. The Monk Council expelled Sovath from the religious order on the grounds that he had violated his vow of celibacy. He fled the country, because without the religious order's protection, he would likely be assassinated. Sovath has said that he "had no choice but to run away from [his] country and become a refugee."[16]

Journalists also have been targeted. In her writing, investigative reporter Rana Ayyub has exposed the Indian nationalist government's human rights abuses. The bridge too far for the Indian government, however, was Ayyub's criticism of Prime Minister Narendra Modi in a BBC broadcast. On April 18, 2018, a source in the Modi government emailed Ayyub with instructions to check her text messages—just as her phone began to buzz. What she saw shocked her: her face had been swapped into a porn clip. Within 48 hours, 2,000 tweets appeared on Ayyub's timeline with screenshots of the deepfake sex video. The video was shared more than 40,000 times in group text messages and on social media sites like Instagram and Facebook. She was inundated with rape threats, death threats, and texts asking her rates for sex. Her home address and cell phone number were plastered all over the internet.

Ayyub stopped writing, which was exactly what the Modi regime wanted. For months she hid at home, afraid that someone might make good on the threats. She suffered heart palpitations, anxiety, and high blood pressure. It was jarring how good the fakery was, how much it looked like her. Ayyub said that she could not shake the feeling of millions of eyes on her naked body. Of course, she knew it wasn't her body in the video, but no one else did, and a lot of people had seen it—the video had been shared with nearly half of the phones in India.

Khadija Ismayilova, an Azerbaijani journalist, was threatened with the release of sex videos unless she stopped investigating presidential corruption. Unbeknownst to Ismayilova, a video camera had been installed in her bedroom. She received an envelope from a Moscow address containing a video of her and her boyfriend having sex; there was also a warning: "Whore, refrain from what you are doing, otherwise you will be shamed." After Ismayilova refused to drop the investigation, the threat to release the video became a reality. The video was posted online; state-run media outlets ran stories suggesting that she was a foreign agent whose reports about the president should not be believed.

Obtaining intimate *kompromat* has never been easier. In 2019, Russia's intelligence and security service known as the FSB sent demands to Tinder and three other dating apps to turn over all Russian subscribers' data, including audio and video communications.[17] It ordered Tinder to store users' metadata on servers inside Russia for at least six months along with their text, audio, or video messages. Although Tinder agreed to be added to the Russian government's database of information providers, it initially refused to relay user data to the FSB.[18] There is no reporting on what happened after the company's initial refusal—though we do know that Tinder is still available in Russia. If that information was in fact disclosed to the Russian government, then it could see subscribers' activities, communications, photos, and profile information.

The US government has taken steps to prevent other countries from exploiting Spying Inc.'s reservoirs of intimate information. Chinese firm Kunlun Tech's 2018 acquisition of the gay dating app Grindr caught the attention of the Committee on Foreign Investment in the United States (CFIUS), the part of the US Department of the Treasury tasked with reviewing corporate acquisitions that may threaten national security.[19] The acquisition risked a treasure trove of intimate data being released to the Chinese government—which only needed to invoke "national security" to obtain it. Subscribers' data could be used to blackmail closeted or HIV-infected American officials or to track troops (since Grindr subscribers often post photos of themselves in military uniforms).[20] CFIUS also discovered that Kunlun Tech's leadership proposed a partnership with a team of HIV researchers at the Chinese equivalent to the US Centers for Disease Control and Prevention (CDC).[21] In 2020, the company settled with CFIUS and agreed to sell the app to a US investment group.[22]

Running in the background of all of this are routine ways that bureaucracies handle intimate information for ostensibly legitimate purposes.

BUREAUCRATIC SURVEILLANCE

Every day, the most minute details of our lives are being amassed and mined for the purpose of fighting crime and terrorism. For instance, the private communications of millions of UK residents have been collected by the country's intelligence agency pursuant to a bulk warrant issued by the home secretary. Civil liberties groups challenged the program as endangering individuals' sensitive information, including their political views and sexual orientation.[23] On May 25, 2021, the Grand Chamber of the European Court of Human Rights ruled that while bulk interception may be "essential" to combat terrorism, sufficient safeguards must be in place. According to the court, the surveillance program failed to protect "against arbitrariness and the risk of abuse."[24]

In the United States, some bureaucratic surveillance poses grave risks to minority communities without clear evidence that society is safer for it. Fusion centers exemplify the problem.

Producing actionable criminal and other intelligence is the work of the 79 fusion centers operating in the United States. Although they are not well known, fusion centers have been around since the early 2000s. They are intelligence hubs run by state police with the help of federal and local partners and private companies. According to the federal Department of Homeland Security (which helped build them), the mission of fusion centers is to identify "threats" and "hazards." Their mantra is "The more data, the better."[25]

Private companies serve as "Big Brother's Little Helpers."[26] Sometimes, that is a good thing—as when they comply with warrants, court orders, and subpoenas. At other times, there is little to no legal process governing the transfer of intimate data from companies to governments, which is legally permissible though morally troubling. Data brokers, discussed in Chapter 1, provide fusion centers with access to our digital dossiers. With analytics software supplied by companies like Palantir, fusion centers search for patterns in data-broker dossiers and public- and private-sector databases.[27] Once an address or license plate is tagged for investigation, fusion center searches will reveal an array of intimate information, including anyone who ever stayed at the address (including lovers and roommates) and anywhere the license plate was tagged by automated license plate readers that are mounted on stationery poles, road signs, and moving police cruisers (including near doctor's offices, gay bars, and twelve-step meetings).[28] Fusion centers issue reports on suspicious individuals, categorizing them as potential "terrorists, criminals, and drug dealers." Reports are shared with federal and state agencies, law enforcement, and private firms through the "information-sharing environment" portal.[29]

Although the surveillance applies to everyone included in public and private databases, it disproportionately burdens marginalized groups.[30] Fusion centers make predictions by combining intimate data with information reflecting societal biases, such as camera feeds trained on "high-risk blocks," which are often located in neighborhoods where racial, ethnic, and religious minorities live.[31] A 2021 fusion center report identified state residents as likely to have expired visas based on their immigration records, genetic links to naturalized citizens (revealed by consumer genetic testing records), and utility bills (courtesy of cable, phone, and gas companies). The report led to arrests and deportations.[32]

Because the work of fusion centers remains largely hidden from view, it is difficult to measure the negative impact on marginalized communities. But whistleblowers and journalists have uncovered troubling examples. In 2015, the Oregon TITAN Fusion Center monitored Salem residents who tweeted hashtags like #blacklivesmatter or #fuckthepolice.[33] Using a tool called "Digital Stakeout," the fusion center produced reports about individuals who expressed opposition to police violence against Black Americans. Erious Johnson Jr., a lawyer who led the civil rights unit of the state's Department of Justice, was one of the people swept up in the surveillance.[34] It wasn't until civil rights groups raised concerns about the surveillance that Oregon Attorney General Ellen Rosenblum stopped the practice.[35] And yet despite that experience, the Oregon fusion center was caught in 2019 creating intelligence reports on environmental protestors who objected to a fossil fuel infrastructure project in the state.[36]

Congress has acknowledged that fusion centers may be violating federal regulations that prohibit the collection of information about individuals based on their political, religious, or group associations.[37] In 2012, a bipartisan Senate Intelligence Committee report criticized fusion centers for their excessive and unwarranted monitoring and harassment of minority groups, as well as their failure to produce actionable intelligence. Harsh words did not, however, result in less funding.[38] In 2018, fusion centers received more than $336 million in federal, state, and local grants.[39]

Without sustained review by congressional committees, it is difficult to pin down the costs to intimate privacy and equality and to weigh them against the benefits to public safety. State and federal laws that empower the public to request information about government operations—known as "open sunshine laws"—place no duty on law enforcement to respond to such requests. This leaves questions about the extent to which intimate life is being surveilled and the impact of surveillance on women and marginalized groups. For some vulnerable people, notably pregnant women, government surveillance is more out in the open.

PREGNANCY SURVEILLANCE

Erica, a Black college student in New York City, made an appointment with the obstetrics clinic at a local public hospital at the start of her pregnancy. Her visit began with a social worker asking her increasingly pointed questions: Was Erica's pregnancy planned? Did she intend to give the infant up for adoption? Had she ever had an abortion? How many people had she had sex with? Had she ever exchanged sex for money or gifts? Had she ever experimented with drugs or been addicted to alcohol? Had she ever had a psychiatric illness? Had she ever been sexually assaulted? Did she have a history of domestic abuse? Had she ever been homeless or been expelled from school? Erica didn't think that sharing any of that history would help ensure the health of her pregnancy, but she believed, as the social worker told her, that she had to answer the questions.[40]

For poor pregnant women of color, the surveillance of intimate life is boundless and inescapable. State Medicaid rules typically require the collection of a vast amount of intimate information from pregnant women (who, like Erica, are often members of racial minorities), including their histories with abortion, sexual assault, substance use, homelessness, and school expulsion. Of course, women have some agency over the matter; no one is forcing them to seek public funds for prenatal care. But even if they don't seek public assistance for prenatal care, they will be subject to government surveillance. If women come to a public hospital for delivery without having received prenatal care, then the hospital will likely hold the infant until the state inspects the woman's home and finds her competent to raise her child.[41]

Most states, including New York where Erica lived, require the collection of excessive amounts of intimate data on poor women, much of which is not necessary for healthy pregnancies and births. A woman's history of prostitution, school expulsion, homelessness, or domestic violence sheds little light on her current physical health or the health of the fetus. It says even less about a woman's current ability to care for herself and the fetus during pregnancy and a child after birth. Nonetheless, the state requires that the details be probed, documented, and collected. Pregnant women with private health insurance are not asked these questions.

While state programs seem to gain little from that intimate data, pregnant women lose their dignity. Control, shaming, and humiliation aren't side effects of the deal; they are the deal. As legal scholar and anthropologist Khiara Bridges has argued, the state's questions tell poor women that they are the *type* of people who are addicted to drugs or expelled from school, a presumption stemming from the stigma of poverty and racial stereotypes.[42] Poor women hear loud and clear that the state doesn't think they deserve to keep deeply personal experiences—sexual assaults, domestic abuse, abortions, addictions—to themselves and to those they trust. The state's monitoring denies poor pregnant women the chance to let down their guard and to be seen (and to see themselves) as dignified.[43] Poor pregnant women get the message that they are second-class citizens.[44]

Pregnant women and girls also have been subject to government surveillance whose purpose is to impede reproductive freedom. At a hearing over whether St. Louis, Missouri's Planned Parenthood clinic would retain its license to perform abortions, the state's health department director, Dr. Randall Williams, testified that his office maintained a spreadsheet tracking the dates of patients' abortion procedures and last menstrual periods. According to Dr. Williams, the state was amassing that information to "investigate 'failed' abortions, instances in which patients needed to return a second time to complete the procedure." The state planned to use evidence of "failed abortions" to show that the clinic was "deficient."[45] Here, the state wasn't collecting intimate data to help women and girls. The goal was to strip the clinic of funding and to make it harder for poor residents of southwestern Missouri to terminate their pregnancies.

State bureaucrats aren't the only ones tracking women's pregnancies. During the Trump administration, the Office of Refugee Resettlement (ORR) collected data about girls' pregnancies and menstrual cycles, as well as their ages, abortion requests, partners' names, and sexual assault histories. In testimony before the House Judiciary Committee, the agency's former director, Scott Lloyd, noted that he received frequent updates about girls' pregnancies, including their weeks of gestation, so that he knew about any abortion requests.[46] According to emails obtained by *VICE*, the agency asked clinics handling care of pregnant minors whether progesterone could be used to reverse a "chemical abortion process."[47] We don't know the extent to which the agency refused abortion requests or ordered clinics to reverse attempted abortions. But it is clear that control over girls' bodies was extensive and, safe to say, unwanted and demeaning.

As these examples show, some bureaucratic surveillance of intimate life isn't about protecting specific individuals or public health, but rather about advancing politicians' agendas. The surveillance resembles Spying Inc., which does not prioritize people's interests but rather corporate profits. And, when it comes to fusion centers, the surveillance isn't just following the approach of Spying Inc.—companies give government access to intimate data.

———

GOVERNMENTAL POWER OVER intimate privacy is vast. Agencies can require individuals to divulge an enormous amount of personal information to obtain public services and benefits. They can pressure companies to turn over people's intimate data, or they can buy it from them. And they can rely on individuals to act as their proxies in their efforts to invade people's intimate privacy. President Trump's followers further exposed the intimate lives of Page and Strzok. Spying Inc. and Privacy Invaders thus strengthen the hand of government spies.

The question hanging in the air is why intimate privacy is so easily violated, particularly when it comes to women and minorities. What is it about social and cultural attitudes that gives permission to such abuse, that makes it seem normal? Why don't our networked tools have built-in protections for intimate privacy from the start?

4

This Is Us

SOCIAL AND CULTURAL FORCES HAVE EVERYTHING TO DO WITH the normalization of corporate, individual, and government surveillance of intimate life. Some are as old as time, some are prevalent all over the world, and some are a distinct strain of West Coast tech culture. Welcome—the view is not pretty.

At a cybersecurity conference held at Stanford University in early 2015, President Barack Obama hailed social media's promise: "I'm absolutely confident that if we keep at this, if we keep working together in a spirit of collaboration, like all those innovators before us, our work will endure, like a great cathedral, for centuries to come." Obama predicted that this work would "not just be about technology, it will be about the values that we've embedded in the architecture of this system. It will be about privacy, and it will be about community. And it will be about connection."[1]

As the years have unfolded, those values seem to have been about anything but privacy, community, and connection. Today's Silicon Valley entrepreneurs have not prioritized privacy, at least not for customers (surveillance subjects, really), who fuel their billion-dollar profits. Behind the scenes, tech CEOs vigorously protect their own privacy, doing everything from forbidding family members from using their social media services to buying property next to their homes and building hedge fortresses around them (which I saw firsthand at a dinner at Mark Zuckerberg's house). Freedom has meant total privacy for tech executives but none for the rest of us. Despite Obama's optimism, the values embedded into the architecture of Silicon Valley's products and services did not include privacy.

This wasn't inevitable. An earlier era's tech innovators saw personal computers as central to freedom and progress.[2] In 1990, Electronic Frontier Foundation (EFF) cofounder and Grateful Dead lyricist John Perry Barlow famously described the "cyberworld" as a "vast, unmapped" Wild West that needed to remain free from private and public overlords. Although the metaphor was inapt, it captured the zeitgeist of the internet's promise.[3] If Silicon Valley had an official slogan, it would have been "Information must be free." *Wired* magazine, started in 1993, spoke in starry-eyed terms about the "innate goodness and rightness of markets and decentralized computer technology."[4]

Freedom of information and freedom from government surveillance were the Valley's animating values.[5] Researchers like Tim Berners-Lee and Marc Andreessen offered tools, including the World Wide Web, for people to access, find, and share information online. Together with the business community, advocacy groups like EFF and the Computer Professionals for Social Responsibility opposed aggressive FBI oversight of their work. As tech journalist Julia Angwin brilliantly put it to me, the early tech leaders, who were mostly white men, "wanted the government's hands off their porn and weed."[6] They campaigned against the Clinton administration's 1994 proposal that would require private companies to use a new encryption technology called the Clipper chip—to which the federal government would have backdoor access.[7] In their view, the ability of the FBI or intelligence agencies to snoop on anyone's online communications was a step toward authoritarianism. It would mark the dawn of a "cyberspace police state."[8] An electronic petition opposing the Clipper chip received over 50,000 signatures.[9] The administration abandoned the idea after computer security experts made clear that backdoors made everyone less secure.

Silicon Valley went to Capitol Hill to argue that tech companies needed to regulate themselves without governmental oversight.[10] Lobbyists supported a federal bill shielding online platforms from liability for trying to remove "noxious online material" and catching too little or too much. That bill—Section 230 of the Communications Decency Act—passed in 1996.[11]

In the late 1990s, tech founders like Google's Sergey Brin and Larry Page assured state and federal law enforcers that they could be trusted with people's personal data. They promised not to be "evil," and policymakers and law enforcers took them at their word. Of course, these promises were aspirational and contingent on contemporary incentives, which later shifted to the collection of personal data so money could be made with little friction—conveniently *after* deregulation was enshrined in federal law.

Some of those companies, then startups, are now online behemoths that have embraced techno-libertarian values, but with an important twist. The freedom that advocates fought for, that *Wired* editors mythologized, that innovators demanded in the mid to late 1990s, evolved into a freedom to collect, mine, and sell personal data in the early to mid 2000s. Thanks to falling storage costs, improved processing power, expanding network bandwidth, and an exponentially growing number of people online, companies went into the data business (as we saw in Chapter 1). Privacy for consumers was not on the agenda. (A few companies like Apple have made privacy a priority because their source of income is mostly from the sale of their products, not of us.)

Today's tech companies may talk the privacy talk, but they have failed to walk the privacy walk. Their powers are nearly absolute, and perhaps we were naïve to trust that they would live by their word. Self-regulation has been a free pass to collect, store, mine, and sell personal data. And let's not forget: lawmakers' deregulatory decisions have benefited Spying Inc., Privacy Invaders, and government spies who dip into corporate databases of intimate data and exploit, damage, and ruin anyone in their way. The "Information must be free" mantra set up the conditions for the surveillance of our intimate lives.

BLIND SPOTS OF THE VALLEY BROS

What do computer code and sex have in common? Quite a lot, according to venture capitalist and Kleiner Perkins partner John Doerr. At a 2015 National Venture Capital Association meeting, Doerr told an audience that the recipe for Silicon Valley success crystalized for him when he saw programming books sitting next to copies of *The Joy of Sex* at an Amazon warehouse. According to Doerr, the "world's greatest tech entrepreneurs" were a mash-up of those books: nerdy male college dropouts in need of help with their social lives.[12]

Doerr was right: Silicon Valley is a "sea of dudes."[13] The overwhelming majority of people working in tech—as entrepreneurs, as investors, or as engineers—are white and Asian men in their twenties and thirties. In 2019, women comprised only 11% of tech executives, and women-led companies received only 2% of venture funding.[14] In the third quarter of 2020, venture funding for female founders hit its lowest quarterly total in three years.[15] The statistics are even more abysmal for women of color: just 3% of computer engineering jobs are held by Black women, while 1% are held by Latina women.[16] Women working in the tech industry also leave much faster than their male counterparts, because of a "lack of advancement, hostile macho culture, and feelings of isolation."[17]

Hiring has followed a continuous loop: young men pitch startup ideas to mostly male venture capitalists who recommend seasoned male executives to run their companies. Referrals drive employee hiring, so everyone mostly looks the same. As PayPal founder Peter Thiel admitted, startups hire the "same kind of nerds."[18] According to former venture capitalist and tech critic Roger McNamee, Silicon Valley has turned the idea of "hiring people like me" into an art form.[19]

Systemic discrimination is connected to the demographics. As historian Margaret O'Mara has shown, Silicon Valley remains steeped in troubling gender stereotypes.[20] Retrograde views are abundant, like "It's men who run businesses" and "Girls and electronics don't mix."[21] Women face sexual and racial harassment from venture capital investors, entrepreneurs, and colleagues, making work "unsafe and unpleasant."[22] Tech journalist Emily Chang has explained that if white female engineers face five to ten demeaning comments in a day, "women who are also members of a second minority—or a third minority—can double or triple that number."[23]

Biased attitudes impact the products and services tracking our lives. In 2017, Deborah Raji, a Black female engineer, was working at a startup for porn-filtering software. The company was training its algorithm on thousands of photos from adult sites, which were made up of faces mostly with darker skin, and thousands of G-rated images from stock photo services, which were made up of faces mostly with light skin. Raji's colleagues chose the photos included in these data sets, never addressing the fact that their algorithm was being trained to identify darker-skinned faces as pornographic. Critical race theorist Patricia Hill Collins coined the term "controlling images" to describe stereotypes that cast Black men as sexual predators and Black women as hypersexual.[24] The startup's algorithm was replicating controlling images.

The problem was obvious to Raji, but not to her male colleagues. Either consciously or unconsciously, Raji's male colleagues had baked controlling images into the algorithm and failed to see the problem. When mostly white and Asian male engineers choose data sets, build algorithms, write code, and review their work, they do so with *their* experiences and concerns in mind. Their blind spots may prevent them from detecting and combating algorithmic bias.

It's not just startups either; established companies have blind spots as well. AI researchers Drs. Joy Buolamwini and Timnit Gebru found that facial recognition systems created by Microsoft and IBM had higher error rates for people with dark skin. The error rates were highest for women with dark skin because the data sets used to train the systems' algorithms were populated with mostly male faces with light skin.[25]

Raji's case was a success story: when she flagged the problem, her male boss devoted time and energy to fixing the imbalance in the training data. But too many companies don't have Black female engineers, people like Raji who appreciate how prejudice manifests and works. Biases encoded into engineers' choices remain obscured from view because only company employees can access the data sets, algorithms, and programming decisions. We can't expect transparency or accountability under these conditions.

Fortunately, journalists and researchers have been able to identify some egregious examples of algorithmic bias. Reporters at *The Markup* have demonstrated that Google's Keyword Planner, which helps advertisers choose which search terms to associate with their ads, offered hundreds of keyword suggestions related to "Black girls," "Latina girls," and "Asian girls"—but the majority were pornographic. When searching for "boys" of those same ethnicities, they found similarly sexualized suggestions. By contrast, searches for "White girls" and "White boys" did not offer any keyword suggestions. (In their article, the reporters showed screenshots of the system to demonstrate the point.) As the reporters explained, "Google's systems contained a racial bias that equated people of color with objectified sexualization while exempting White people from any associations whatsoever." And they noted a concrete harm associated with those suggestions: the absence of a significant number of

non-pornographic suggestions made it more difficult for marketers trying to reach young Black, Latinx, and Asian people with products and
services relevant to their lives. After the story ran, Google denounced the
"offensive" language that surfaced in its keyword planning tool and said
that they "removed these terms from the tool and are looking into how
we stop this from happening again."[26]

Another crucial finding was that Google's advertising system allowed
advertisers to exclude nonbinary people from seeing employment or
housing ads. Companies trying to run ads on YouTube or elsewhere on
the web "could direct Google not to show ads to people of 'unknown
gender'—meaning people who have not identified themselves to Google
as 'male' or 'female.'" Again, Google responded to *The Markup*'s findings
by "pledging to crack down on the practice."[27]

We don't need the help of Black female engineers like Raji or enter-
prising news outlets like *The Markup* to unearth blatant bias. Consider
Glow's period-tracking app Eve. It refers to subscribers as "girls" and char-
acterizes sex as centered on male anatomy—a banana with a condom, a
banana without a condom, or no banana. Women who are intimate
with anyone who is not a man surely would feel alienated.[28] Perhaps we
should not be surprised given that Glow founder Max Levchin report-
edly tracked his girlfriends' bra sizes.

Exacerbating the problem of algorithmic bias is Silicon Valley's beta
test mindset, which encourages the early release of products or services.
Tech companies know that beta-stage products and services may cause
harm, especially to women, nonwhites, sexual and gender minorities,
and people with multiple marginalized identities. No matter, they cross
their fingers, release the product or service, and hope the damage will be
minor enough for a simple apology to get them out of hot water. This has
been Google's long-term modus operandi. As noted in Chapter 1, Safiya
Noble's 2012 dissertation described how searches for "Black girls" regularly featured porn sites in top results.[29] Although Google didn't issue
an official statement, it responded to Noble's discovery and fixed the

problem. The only difference now is that the company has gotten a bit better at handling public relations.

US consumers are not the only ones imperiled by American reck- lessness. US companies' pathologies are everyone's problem because their services and products are used around the globe. If you use technolo- gies built in the United States but you hail from the United Kingdom or Egypt, American biases baked into tech products and services impact your life. When gay dating apps fail to secure subscribers' accounts, the risks include discrimination in South Korea and imprisonment in Egypt. When period-tracking app Glow had security flaws that enabled strangers to access people's accounts, subscribers everywhere were placed in danger. When Silicon Valley moves fast and breaks things, it can exacerbate the exploitation of intimate life for the vulnerable around the world.

LICENSE TO VIOLATE

Although online porn has been around since even before the advent of the commercial internet in 1995, it wasn't obvious that nonconsensual intimate imagery would develop as it has. Professional pornography's pro- ducers and actors certainly aren't happy about nonconsensual porn. The porn industry is far less lucrative due to the existence of "free" adult sites, where viewers effectively "pay" sites with personal data instead of pur- chasing content from creators and producers. The advertising ecosystem means that sites profit when nonconsensual intimate images are posted.

Sites devoted to nonconsensual intimate images pair misogyny, misogynoir, gendered racism, transphobia, and homophobia, with a dol- lop of cash. When I was writing *Hate Crimes in Cyberspace*, which tackled the phenomenon of cyberstalking, my research assistants and I found 40 sites devoted to nonconsensual intimate images—and that was in 2013. By 2017, researchers found that the number had grown to 2,000. 2020's estimate exceeded *9,500* sites.[30] Sites earn money by charging subscribers monthly fees, collecting ad revenue from people's clicks, or amassing personal data, which they can sell. (Even if people are paying subscription fees, their personal data is likely being collected and shared so the sites make money both ways.)

Although sites devoted to nonconsensual intimate imagery are not keen on publishing their earnings, nor are they required to (they are not publicly traded), simple math suggests that they earn substantial revenue. Here is what we know. In 2018, the Candid Forum had more than 200,000 subscribers paying $19.99 per month to view up-skirt and down-blouse images from all over the world.[31] In 2017, another site, the Candid Board (originality isn't their strong suit), had a similar fee structure and 180,000 members.[32] In 2015, an up-skirt photo site that had 70 million daily page views was estimated to be worth 100 million dollars.[33] (As a reference point, the website for *The Atlantic* received approximately one-third as many page views in an entire month in 2021.) Most sites devoted to nonconsensual intimate images are hosted in countries where the risk of liability for privacy invasions is low.

If you look at these sites (I did so that you don't have to), you will see that site owners have done all they can to normalize the exposure of people's nude, partially nude, or sexually explicit photos. They make it acceptable—even fun—to view and comment on nonconsensual intimate images. If anyone is at fault, the sites seem to (and do) say, it is the subject of the images, whose poor choices enabled the display. A detailed view of these sites is key to understanding what we are up against.

Let's get started with a glimpse of a site's marketing. Running atop every page on the Candid Forum is a cartoon scene of two men wearing camouflage and using binoculars to watch bikini-clad women on the beach. The site's front page says that "Sexy up-skirts have never been easier to capture thanks to cell phone cameras, so we're getting more submissions than ever."

Recall the bot in Chapter 2 that undresses women's photos for a fee. The man who runs the service told the *Washington Post* that his subscribers engage in a "harmless form of sexual voyeurism" that women facilitate by posting photos of themselves "to attract attention." His service's logo is a picture of a man wearing X-ray glasses and smiling while ogling a woman.[34] Talking to the press, another purveyor of nonconsensual intimate imagery echoed this sentiment: "When you take a nude photograph of yourself and you send it to this other person, or when you allow someone to take a nude photo of you, by your very actions you have reduced your expectation of privacy." The man told the journalist that revealing his identity was off the table because he didn't want the "headache that publicity brings"—a cruel irony for women posted on his site who have no such choice.

For site operators, the more acceptable, widespread, and normal these attitudes and behaviors seem, the more users will embrace and engage with them, and the more ad revenue and subscription fees will then fill their pockets. That is why these websites display text saying that posters of nude images "appreciate COMMENTS on their work, not just clicking 'Thanks'!"

Users of these sites eagerly oblige. Popular nonconsensual intimate image sites have hundreds upon hundreds of posters and commenters who treat women's bodies as theirs to view, trade, and insult. Women are referred to as "that ass on the right," "fuckable tits," and "desperate skinny bitches." Posters invoke stereotypes in labeling photos. A downblouse thread on a hidden camera site had more than 150,000 videos with titles like "Very busty white girl spotted on Japan street with jiggling big boobs," "Black woman with dreadlocks in bikini," and "Sexy Asian Teen."

On a site devoted to nonconsensual nude images of gay and bi men and trans women with male genitalia, users of the site ask for nude photos of specific individuals, referring to them by their full names, social media handles, and locations. One typical request asks, "Anything on that guy? Been trying to see his dick for years." Users seek information about people's Grindr handle, employer name, and relationship status. Comments are demeaning: "this slave ass needs fucking," "look what a faggot whore," and "Fuck me, break me, and make me your sissy boi slave." Thousands of threads are organized by date and name of the person whose nude photo is featured or sought. A single thread can have hundreds of comments.

Gamelike behavior is the connective tissue on many of these sites. Users encourage one another as if they were true teammates. They cele-brate one another for filling in details about the people featured in photos including their real names and locations. When particularly sought-after personal information is revealed, the sharer receives the reward of more nude images as a token of gratitude. What's more, many sites turn the circulation of nude images into an actual game with cash prizes; posters of nude photos that earn the most stars can win anywhere from 75 to 650 dollars. Sometimes, sites get extra creative and host contests with themes like "Sexy Red Valentine's Outfit," "Drunk Slut at the Bar," and "Spread Eagle Looking at the Camera."

On one notorious site, users solicit nude photos of specific people via requests, such as "Huge slut back in high school, any wins on this one?" In the site's parlance, a "win" refers to a naked photo. The page displays posts by popularity; posters interested in getting a particular image to the top of the page know to write "bump" in the comments section of an image. Users offer to upload nude photos of certain women on the con-dition that others will share nude photos from their collections. Often, a woman's nude photo will be paired with her college crest and a section dedicated to her school acquaintances, alumni, or classmates.

Users collect and trade nude photos like baseball cards, earning social cachet along the way. They brag about privacy violations and revel in impressing one another with their "scores." They suggest locations where members can take photos of "great asses." During the summer of 2020, subscribers of a hidden-camera site said that Black Lives Matter protests were a goldmine for taking up-skirt and down-blouse photos. A subscriber with an entrepreneurial spirit wrote, "Let's get into how profit-able these protests are for us. For one, everyone is in a crowd and not even thinking about us recording them. I had to take advantage of a protest we had in our town, and I got 2 solid captures."[35] Journalist Amanda Hess put it well: "This is a world beyond humiliation."[36]

The excitement stems from the fact that the people in the photos do not want or expect their nude images to be shared. The images mostly feature ordinary people rather than celebrities; they tend to be less explicit than actual pornography. As writer Amanda Marcotte remarked of stolen celebrity nude selfies that went viral online, they were "downright tame" compared to real porn.[37] Although some users come to the sites to hurt ex-lovers or wives, their comments suggest that they stick around to see the nude images of other women who did not consent to their photos being shared.[38]

The more that a person thinks these actions are acceptable, the more that they think that victims are at fault, the more likely it is that the person will violate another person's intimate privacy. This is why everyday people are involved. It isn't just odd loners or impulsive adolescents. Math teachers, civil servants, and tennis coaches have been caught taking upskirt photos, recording strangers in bathrooms, and posting nonconsensual nude images.[39] Graduate students and small-town mayors have likewise been apprehended.

Alexandra Waterbury was studying at the School of American Ballet, a New York City Ballet (NYCB) affiliate, when she began dating Chase Finlay, a principal dancer. In a lawsuit filed in 2018, Waterbury alleged that during their year-long relationship, Finlay secretly recorded and photographed her during sex, and shared the explicit files with two other male dancers and a ballet donor. When Waterbury borrowed Finlay's laptop to check her email, her eyes automatically locked onto the messages that popped onto the screen. Finlay and his friends were swapping nude images—both of her and of her female classmates. Waterbury was devastated but not shocked, given NYCB's "fraternity-like atmosphere" and the sense that male dancers feel entitled to the bodies of female students.

Studies from across the globe help us understand perpetrators' thinking. Responding to a 2017 nationwide survey, 159 of 3,044 adults admitted to having shared another person's nude images without consent. (104 were men, while 55 were women.) Of those, 79% of the 159 individuals explained that they wanted to share the images "with friends"; 25% found it fun to share the images; 11% said that it made them feel good; and 6% said that they did it for "upvotes, likes, and retweets." Only 17% of those 159 people reported that they did it for revenge against the person in the image, and most of those individuals said that they would not have shared the images had they known that they could have faced punishment, including potentially having to register as a sex offender.[40]

The office of the Australian government's e-Safety Commissioner surveyed 16 people (mostly young men) who had been caught taking, sharing, or posting nude images without subjects' consent. Asked why they took or shared other individuals' nude images, the study participants offered expected rationalizations: "everyone does it," the victim chose to share images with them, and it was fun. The desire to earn praise and an elevated social status served as another key motivator. Many of the perpetrators remained nonchalant about their actions when answering questions, which psychologists and defense attorneys suggested was due to the ubiquity of pornography. Respondents had little to no awareness that intimate privacy violations carry legal implications in Australia. One of the psychologists interviewed for the study noted that because most young people face no legal consequences for nonconsensually capturing or sharing nude images, they have no incentive to stop. On the contrary, the applause from peers encourages it.[41] Nonconsensual intimate imagery sites further help build the structures that permit the violation of intimate privacy.

LICENSE TO IGNORE

Law enforcement has a long history of dismissing harms disproportionately suffered by women, especially women from marginalized communities, and gender and sexual minorities. This has long been true of sexual assault and domestic violence, and it is true of intimate privacy violations. Intimate privacy violations are a global phenomenon, as is their trivialization by police officers.

In South Korea, the police ran advertisements suggesting that hidden cameras in public restrooms were the handiwork of immature boys and that cheerful teasing would get them to change their ways. The ads literally turned their suggested response into a game: they encouraged bystanders to "find life-size cutouts of people resembling 'man boys,' take photos of them, and upload them to Instagram."[42]

Even when privacy invasions are not so explicitly reduced to a game, police officers routinely trivialize what happened as "no big deal." Officers in Illinois told Kara Jefts, whom you met in Chapter 2 and whose ex shared her nude images online without her consent, to ignore her ex's posts because "images could not hurt her." Victims have been told that they should be flattered that someone had posted their nude image online. A police officer in New York told Jen that she should feel good about appearing on "cum tribute" sites that showed videos of men masturbating to her nude photo, which was posted without her permission. According to Jen, the officer continued: "It's like posters are saying that you are as hot as Pamela Anderson Lee, so take it for the compliment that it is."

Many police officers approach the line of victim blaming, while others cross into that zone explicitly and unapologetically. Victims are told that they should never have trusted the perpetrator or taken nude photos of themselves because "all nudes leak." In 2018, thousands of women in South Korea signed a petition saying that when they reported hidden cameras in public restrooms, police officers blamed them because they "did not dress modestly."[43] Of course, a hidden camera in a bathroom stall has nothing to do with the identities of the people being recorded or with how they dress—everyone shows their genitals and buttocks when going to the bathroom. The absurdity of the response, however, does not alter its power.

It gets worse. When Marley told local law enforcement in Florida that her husband had been texting nude images of her to other men, officers asked Marley if she sent the photos to the men herself. To the officers, the most obvious explanation was that Marley was lying. Then, even though the officers told her that they could not help, they insisted that Marley email them the nude images. Marley reluctantly sent the nude images to the officers after they implied that her hesitation eroded the credibility of her complaint. Marley feared that the officers kept her nude images, or worse, shared them with others.

These themes recurred in nearly all of my interviews with victims, including those from the United States. For instance, officers told Alex (whom you met in the introduction and whose ex secretly taped her undressing in her bedroom and posted the videos online) that her ex just wanted her attention and that she should not give it to him by involving the police. FBI agents were hostile to Joan (Chapter 2's target of sextortion and nonconsensual pornography, thanks to a hidden camera in a New York hotel room), even suggesting that she took the video of herself in the shower and shared it online. I had to get personally involved to convince the agents to look into her case, but their investigation ended because they said that they could not identify the perpetrator, even though it was almost certainly a hotel employee. Joan and I both interpreted that to mean that the agents did not consider her case important enough to pursue. Victims from Iceland, the United Kingdom, and India told me that police officers dismissed their reports or suggested that they had done something wrong. Law enforcement in New Delhi told Ayyub (the journalist you met in Chapter 3) that "boys would be boys" and that nothing could be done, since the deepfake sex video had already been shared millions of times.

These experiences with law enforcement can leave an indelible, painful mark. Early on in my career as a law professor, a student knocked on my office door. She explained that her ex-boyfriend was using her nude photos to post fake ads that claimed she was a prostitute. Terrified, the student contacted her local police precinct in Baltimore, Maryland, who asked her to come in to report the incident. She was initially relieved to see that two female officers would be interviewing her, but then they asked why her ex had the nude photos in the first place. Upon hearing her explanation that she let her ex take the photos because he promised to keep them confidential, the officers asked why she had been so gullible; they said that she should just take it as a lesson learned and ignore the posts. When the student added that men were frequently calling her in response to the fake ads, the officers told her that she was lucky that her ex had only included her cell phone number; she should be grateful that he hadn't listed her home address.

The student sobbed as she told me about her experience with the officers. She wanted to know if the officers were right. Was it her fault? Was there nothing that could be done? I had worked on the law criminalizing nonconsensual porn in the state (Maryland), so I knew that the perpetrator's actions arguably constituted a crime. But even though I explained the law and offered to return to the precinct with her, she said that she would never, ever go back there. A few weeks later, still wrestling with the posts and the calls that they provoked, she returned to my office; she said that she could not stop feeling embarrassed and foolish that she had thought that the police would care about her and her privacy. It was difficult to hear that reporting the abuse had made her feel more alone, more afraid, and more embarrassed than she'd felt when she first walked into the precinct.

And most depressing, law enforcement officers have been perpetrators, too. The first two individuals who ever contacted me about nonconsensual pornography were both targeted by ex-boyfriends who were police officers. One was a businesswoman living in Hawaii whose ex forced her to pose for nude photos—he threatened to hit her otherwise. After she broke up with him, he posted her nude images on a nonconsensual intimate imagery site next to racial slurs about her Asian heritage. She went to the police, but the officers were her ex's friends; they denied that they could do anything to help her, yet still they requested that she send them links to the photos. The officers took zero action after she filed her complaint.

We have also seen law enforcement officers collude in intimate privacy violations. University of Utah senior Lauren McCluskey faced sextortion at the hands of her ex, who said that he would publish her nude photos unless she sent $1,000 to a Venmo account. She paid the money and contacted campus police. The officers asked McCluskey to email them copies of the nude photos, but then refused to help her because, they said, she had "just been hacked." Weeks later, after McCluskey's ex murdered her, campus police discovered that officer Miguel Deras not only had repeatedly accessed McCluskey's nude photos but had shown them to many male colleagues, too; Deras even shared McCluskey's nude photos with another officer at the scene of her death.[44] By the time campus police issued its report on his treatment of McCluskey's nude images, Deras was a member of the Logan Police Department, which terminated his employment.[45]

INTERNALIZING DESTRUCTIVE ATTITUDES

Licenses to violate and ignore say to victims that any space can be invaded—no matter how personal that space might be. The very fact that nonconsensual intimate imagery sites are so popular, that there is no shortage of images taken in violation of intimate privacy, that site operators and law enforcement trivialize it, tells not only victims, but also all women, especially women of color, and LGBTQ individuals that they have no entitlement to intimate privacy.

Victims internalize the view that they are to blame.[46] A nationwide 2017 study of Australian adults found that when victims of nonconsensual intimate imagery went to law enforcement, many felt that the officers did not believe them.[47] Lack of proper law enforcement training seems to be its own issue. The UK's Law Commission Report on Intimate Image Abuse found that police routinely fail to understand the relevant laws and that they do not know how to investigate the offenses. As a result, "victims reported feeling dismissed and blamed for their abuse."[48]

That message is as effective as it is corrosive. Lane, a Londoner whose bus seatmate took photos up their skirt, talked to me about why they never went to law enforcement. As a nonbinary queer person, they felt like they had no privacy rights that the police would recognize. Lane internalized the message that they could neither hope for nor expect privacy in their body, so they had become resigned to live without it.

Lane's worldview isn't unusual. The 2017 study referenced above found that 75% of victims took no steps to contact law enforcement after their intimate images were taken or shared without their permission; 29% of victims felt that reporting what happened "would not change anything," while 22% simply had no idea what to do; another 18% felt too ashamed to file a report.[49]

So many victims who contacted me said that they believed that filing a report would, at best, accomplish nothing and, at worst, exacerbate the situation. I don't blame them; I've seen how law enforcement officers react. Victims recognize the wrongfulness and harm of their perpetrators' actions and are infuriated by it all, but the systems that should protect them fall short.

———

SOCIAL ATTITUDES AND cultural forces have brought us to this predicament, and they likely will not change on their own. We can and should look to law—it says so much about who we are, what sorts of values we hold dear, whose interests will be protected, and what we aspire to be as a community. But law is not up to the task, as the next chapter explores.

5

Law's Inadequacy

KELLY CONVIRS-FOWLER IS A REAL ESTATE AGENT WHO SERVES IN the Virginia House of Delegates. Because women in her state, as in other states, had been bombarded with unwanted nude images on their mobile devices, she sponsored a law in February 2021 to criminalize cyber flashing, the trend typified by sending nude images via text or AirDrop to Apple phones, which I explored in Chapter 2. The bill would have punished people who send unsolicited photos of their genitals to another person without the recipient's consent with up to a year in jail, a fine of up to $2,500, or both. Flashing was already illegal in Virginia, so Delegate Convirs-Fowler tried to update the law to cover cyber flashing.

The bill had unanimous support in the House, but the Senate voted it down after the Senate Judiciary Committee allowed a mere nine minutes for discussion. As Delegate Convirs-Fowler saw it, her colleagues shut their ears to the problem rather than take it seriously.[1] There may have been practical reasons why the bill failed. Committee members raised concerns that the bill was overly broad in violation of the First Amendment. State Senator Scott Surovell called to ask me how the bill might be revised to ensure that it comported with free speech commitments. Perhaps not enough time was spent generating support for the bill in the Senate before bringing it to the committee. It also isn't hard to see how troubling social attitudes might have made things more difficult. All eight state senators who opposed the bill were male; two female senators supported it, and one female senator abstained.[2]

The bill might have faltered for a more fundamental reason, one that has plagued other reform efforts. The law lacks a clear conception of what intimate privacy is, why its violation is wrong, and how it inflicts serious harm. Legal tools—criminal law, tort law, and consumer protection law—tackle privacy problems, but few (if any) adequately capture the full stakes for intimate privacy. Too often, the autonomy, dignity, intimacy, and equality implications of handling intimate data are ignored. This leaves us with an impoverished view of the problem, resulting in inadequate and weak protections.

Our conceptual problems are paired with practical ones. Current state and federal laws are hopelessly out of date. Because networked technologies and the threats that they pose evolve rapidly and lawmakers move slowly, there are considerable gaps in legal protections. By the time that law catches up to one type of intimate privacy violation, other types of intimate privacy violations have emerged that the law does not touch. Also, policymakers view privacy violations in silos, so they pursue reforms in a piecemeal manner. One day, proposals focus on cyber flashing; the next, they center on nonconsensual pornography; the next, the confidentiality of people's COVID statuses, and so on. To the extent that the law is updated (which is never guaranteed), the reforms are often overly narrow.

The conceptual, cultural, and practical problems compound. Because reform proposals are not addressed as aspects of a single phenomenon— intimate privacy violations—lawmakers don't see the full breadth of the harm. When reforms do make their way into law, they don't fully capture the wrong and thus are ineffective and weak. Without the proper conceptual apparatus, lawmakers have an easier time walking away from reform efforts. Too many times, federal and state lawmakers have told me, "I just could not get buy in," or "We tried; maybe next term." We are left with piecemeal and outdated laws.

Getting the conceptual approach right is essential. Law is our teacher and guide. It changes the social meaning of activities by signaling that they are wrong, that they inflict grave harms, and that they are morally unacceptable. It helps us understand that those behaviors are off limits, that a just society does not countenance them. As we internalize law's lessons, social attitudes and cultural practices change, for the good of individuals and society.

SECTION 230'S LEGAL SHIELD

One piece of US federal legislation has cut off important legal pathways, preventing victims from seeking relief from sites enabling privacy violations. That legislation has made it impossible to see how federal and state laws and common law claims would respond at all.

A brick-and-mortar business that makes it easy for third parties to stalk and invade the privacy of victims faces tort liability for enabling the abuse. A hard-copy magazine that published user-submitted non-consensual porn encounters a blizzard of privacy lawsuits. But when those activities happen online, companies are shielded from liability. We have Section 230 of the Communications Decency Act (CDA) to thank for that.

To supporters, Section 230 is an article of faith, nothing less than the law that "created the internet."[3] But the story is more complicated than that. Section 230, broadly interpreted by the courts, gives social media platforms a free pass to host posts by civil rights protestors, like members of the #MeToo movement, *and* child predators, like the people who gather on hacking sites to share footage from children's computers.

It lets sites solicit restaurant reviews, as Yelp does, *and* hidden camera footage, as the Candid Forum does. It enables companies to design their platforms to enhance the visibility of religious texts, as the site Beliefnet. com does, *and* deepfake sex videos, as the site MrDeepFakes does. Section 230 is why the internet is filled with #blacklivesmatter tweets *and* hidden camera feeds; encyclopedia entries *and* nonconsensual porn; restaurant reviews *and* rape videos.

To understand how we got here, we need to look at the law's history. In 1995, federal lawmakers faced a challenge. They wanted the internet to be open and free, but they also realized that openness risked the posting of illegal and "offensive" material. They understood that federal agencies could not deal with all "noxious material" on their own and that they needed tech companies to help moderate—remove, block, or filter—content.

However, a New York trial court signaled that *any* effort to filter or remove online content was risky and probably foolish. It did this in a case involving self-proclaimed "Wolf of Wall Street" Jordan Belfort. On a message board hosted by internet service provider Prodigy, someone accused Belfort's firm of fraud. Belfort and his firm sued Prodigy, the deep pocket, for hosting the allegedly defamatory posts, rather than the poster, who likely had no funds. Prodigy argued that it wasn't a publisher (like a newspaper) with strict responsibility for content hosted on its message boards. The court disagreed. Because Prodigy had used software to filter out profanity (it wanted to be a "family-oriented" platform), it had taken on the role of a publisher. The court held that Prodigy's efforts to moderate content had *increased* its liability for defamatory posts.[4]

The Prodigy decision alarmed then-congressmen Chris Cox and Ron Wyden. It caught their attention even though it would not bind any other court (unlike rulings by state or federal appellate courts). Cox and Wyden worried that tech companies would learn about the case—the first in the country to address the liability of an online service provider for its subscribers' speech—and heed its message. The decision suggested that if tech companies proactively removed or blocked "noxious material," they would be strictly liable for defamatory posts that they failed to remove or block; there would be no such risk if they sat on their hands and waited for people to complain. Why would companies bother to proactively moderate user-generated content if it would heighten their legal exposure?

To nullify the New York trial court's ruling, Cox and Wyden drafted Section 230(c) of the CDA. They wanted to incentivize private efforts aimed at combatting "offensive" material. That legal incentive materialized as a shield from liability for, as the title of Section 230(c) says, "protection for Good Samaritan private blocking and screening of offensive material."

Section 230(c), adopted in 1996, has two key provisions. Section 230(c)(1) addresses the under-removal of content. It says that "no provider or user of an interactive computer service shall be treated as a publisher or speaker of any information provided by another information content provider." Section 230(c)(2), conversely, concerns the over-removal of content. It declares that providers will not be held liable for "any action voluntarily taken in good faith to restrict access to or availability of material that the provider or user considers to be obscene, lewd, lascivious, filthy, excessively violent, harassing, or otherwise objectionable, whether or not such material is constitutionally protected."[5] The legal shield has a few exemptions, including violations of federal criminal law, intellectual property claims, the Electronic Communications Privacy Act (which regulates certain forms of government surveillance), and, as of 2018, the knowing facilitation of sex trafficking.[6]

In 1996, we could hardly have imagined the role that the internet would play in modern life. Cox and Wyden were certainly prescient. In their view, if this "amazing new thing" was "going to blossom," companies should not be "punished for trying to keep things clean." Cox, who retired in 2005, told National Public Radio in 2018, the "original purpose of [Section 230] was to help clean up the Internet, not to facilitate people doing bad things on the Internet." Wyden, now a senator, agreed, noting that the key to Section 230 was "making sure that companies in return for that protection—that they wouldn't be sued indiscriminately—were being responsible in terms of policing their platforms."[7]

The judiciary's interpretation of Section 230, however, has not squared with this vision. Rather than treating Section 230 as a legal shield for Good Samaritans endeavoring to moderate content, state and lower federal courts have stretched the provision far beyond what its words, context, and purpose support. (As of April 2022, the US Supreme Court had not taken a case that would check this interpretation, though litigants have tried; CCRI has filed amicus briefs in support of those efforts.)

Bad Samaritans have been immunized from liability. Sites that deliberately republish illegal content have enjoyed immunity from liability; this was true for The Dirty, whose site operator curated and posted "scoops" about people (including nude images) sent directly to him by commenters. Sites that solicit users to engage in tortious or otherwise illegal activity have enjoyed immunity from liability; this was true for the nonconsensual intimate imagery site Texxxan.[8] Likewise, sites that enhance the visibility of illegal activity while ensuring that perpetrators could not be identified and caught have been shielded from liability; this was true for Backpage's promotion of sex trafficking ads (before Congress amended Section 230 in 2018 to exempt sites that knowingly facilitate sex trafficking).

Courts have attributed this broad-sweeping approach to the fact that "First Amendment values" drove Section 230's adoption.[9] But Congress's stated goals also included "the development of technologies which maximize user control over what information is received" and the "vigorous enforcement of Federal criminal laws to deter and punish trafficking in obscenity, stalking, and harassment by means of the computer." As Mary Anne Franks has wisely noted, "in other words, the law [was] intended to promote and protect the values of privacy, security and liberty alongside the values of open discourse."[10]

Consider Matthew Herrick's terrible predicament. He sought gay dating app Grindr's help after his ex-boyfriend began using the dating app to impersonate him. Fake profiles featured Herrick's nude photos and invited men to his apartment to play out "rape fantasies." As Herrick explained in countless emails to Grindr, his life was in danger. Every day, as many as 23 men came to his apartment expecting sex, having been told to view his resistance as part of the "fantasy." Over the course of ten months, 1,400 men confronted him at all hours of the day and night. Grindr was his last hope; his police precinct had done nothing. Grindr's security team should have been a key mechanism for minimizing the damage and the danger, but the company ignored Herrick's messages. All Herrick received was an automatically generated email: "Thank you for your report."[11]

A trial and an appellate court dismissed Herrick's case, citing Section 230 immunity, and the Supreme Court refused to hear an appeal of the ruling. Even though Grindr was in the best position to minimize the harm by fixing its software so that the app could block IP addresses (a common practice for dating apps) like the one for Herrick's ex, even though it knew with arithmetic certainty that people were using the app to invade others' intimate privacy, even though the company profited from the data that the fake profiles generated, the company had no duty to do anything. It did not have to internalize the costs that it had externalized. Too bad, so sad for Herrick, said the courts. Carrie Goldberg, Herrick's attorney, told me that she has "lost hope in there being a judicial fix to Section 230." She noted with regret, "It used to be that for the cost of an index number [to file a lawsuit], the poorest person in the world could hold the most powerful corporation accountable for the harms they caused. Those days are gone."[12]

The bottom line and the common thread weaving through these examples is that judicial opinions have sapped Section 230's Good Samaritan concept of its meaning. Sites have no liability-based incentive to take down illicit material, especially if that material gets them extra clicks, while victims have no legal leverage to insist otherwise. Digital platforms wield enormous power yet bear no responsibility.[13]

Section 230 is why nonconsensual intimate imagery sites are hosted—and thriving—in the United States. When nonconsensual intimate imagery appears on sites hosted in the United States, little can be done if the images feature people from other countries. Attorneys in Italy or South Korea have no leverage to pressure sites to take down their clients' images; courts in their countries can't order the sites to do anything because they lack jurisdiction over them. Hoping for the voluntary cooperation of Big Tech, law enforcement officers in other countries have asked me to connect them with US tech companies, but those efforts have met little success.

The lack of geographic borders online gives Section 230 an outsized impact. When non-US sites remove nonconsensual intimate images, perpetrators do the next best thing—they post the images on US sites. The images will likely remain up, no matter how much victims complain. In short, perpetrators can always torment victims on sites hosted in the United States, and victims' home countries can't do anything about it.

Paired with this practical reality is Section 230's extension to other countries via trade agreements. The United States has exported Section 230 to Canada and Mexico through the United States-Mexico-Canada Trade Agreement, which went into effect on July 1, 2020. It pledges signatories to refrain from measures that treat interactive computer services as liable for content created by others.[14] The tech industry lobbying group, the Internet Association, pressed hard for this development, illustrating just how crucial companies like Google and Facebook think the immunity is to their continued profitability. A federal law has further extended the immunity's reach by making foreign libel judgments unenforceable in the United States unless the judgment would comport with the First Amendment *and* Section 230.[15]

It doesn't have to be this way. In the EU, sites can face liability for third-party content if they receive notice and fail to expeditiously remove that content.[16] In Germany, under the Network Enforcement Act of 2018, social media companies with more than two million subscribers must remove "clearly illegal" content within 24 hours of receiving a complaint.[17] In the United Kingdom, sites are shielded from defamation liability only if they follow a notice-and-takedown procedure set forth in the Defamation Regulations of 2013.[18]

Sites and platforms hosted in the United States say to victims, "Leave me alone; go sue your attackers." But suing attackers is a tall task. Victims face considerable practical and legal roadblocks when they try to hold Privacy Invaders accountable.

PRACTICAL HURDLES

"What do you want?" It's one of the first questions that attorney Elisa D'Amico asks her pro bono clients. In 2014, D'Amico and David Bateman, partners at the law firm K&L Gates, cofounded the Cyber Civil Rights Legal Project (CCRLP) to provide free legal help to victims of nonconsensual pornography. Invariably, clients answered that they wanted the abuse to stop and for their intimate images to evaporate from existence. They hoped that law could minimize the damage to their safety, health, careers, and relationships. They asked if they could obtain compensation for, and some acknowledgment of, their suffering.[19]

Getting victims what they want is exceptionally difficult. The legal cards are stacked against them. Even if sites have policies against nonconsensual intimate images, they often ignore reports of violations—and Section 230 means they can.[20]

Some of D'Amico's clients own the copyrights of their nude photographs because they took them. Section 230 has no bearing on federal intellectual property claims, so these clients could sue sites for copyright infringement. Some Bad Samaritan sites, however, ignore takedown requests from individuals, opting instead to leave up images until courts order their removal. Remember, these sites are financially incentivized to keep up the images due to advertising revenue or subscription fees. As a notable exception, Google and Bing allow victims to request that non-consensual pornography be de-indexed from searches of their names. (I will return to this development in Chapter 10.)

Curbing ongoing abuse is challenging. While some perpetrators might be persuaded to back off if they were to face criminal charges, only the most extreme cases—often those involving children—are likely to attract law enforcement's attention. If perpetrators have taken pains to protect their anonymity, it can be hard to identify the responsible parties.

Jurisdiction is yet another hurdle in US courts. Criminal charges or civil claims can't be brought against perpetrators over whom the courts have no legal power. If a perpetrator lives outside the United States and beyond the reach of US legal process, then there is little that civil or criminal law can do. Within the United States, local law enforcers often play jurisdictional hot potato, pointing to other municipalities or states (such as the ones where the perpetrators live) as the right authority. But this is really an excuse to skirt responsibility for cases. When victims contact those other authorities, they get sent back to the same place as before, or to another entity entirely; everyone points the finger at someone else, and nothing is done. Officers could help victims navigate the system by calling another jurisdiction on their behalf, yet they rarely do.

Victims can bring civil lawsuits against US-based perpetrators in the states where they live. Although jurisdiction isn't a barrier, those lawsuits are still expensive. The demand for pro bono assistance is enormous. CCRLP averages five requests per day and can only handle an average of 100 cases at a time; it took on more than 1,000 cases between 2014 and 2019. Unfortunately, there aren't a lot of lawyers doing this sort of work. As privacy scholar Ari Waldman has documented, cases involving intimate privacy violations require tech savvy, special expertise in gathering evidence, and a deep commitment to victims.[21] Attorneys

seeking profitable cases under a contingency structure won't pursue intimate privacy cases if perpetrators don't have funds to recover, which is
often the case.

Another problem is that courts may require that plaintiffs bring
lawsuits under their real names—a rule that risks unleashing even more
unwanted publicity and exposure on plaintiffs who are simply trying to
assert their right to privacy. Once word gets out about a lawsuit, especially
a suit about privacy invasions, the very fact of the litigation may be used
as ammunition. Actress and singer Barbra Streisand discovered this after
she sued a photographer for taking aerial photos of her home. In what has
since been dubbed the "Streisand Effect," online posters tormented the
actress about the lawsuit, suggesting that she was trying to "censor" the
photographer. The message was: if you dare to sue for privacy invasions,
you will face more.[22]

Unfortunately, courts fail to appreciate the extent to which lawsuits
can exacerbate the harm of intimate privacy violations. Their rationale
is—unbelievably—"Well, your nude images are already online, so it's not
like things can get worse." But things can, and they do. A plaintiff sued
her former lover and a photographer (whom she had worked with) after
they posted her nude images online without her consent. The photos,
which showed the plaintiff's face and distinctive tattoo, appeared next
to her contact information. As a result, strangers called and emailed her.
Before initiating the lawsuit, the plaintiff filed the photos that she took
of herself (and shared with her ex) with the US Copyright Office, as federal law requires.

The plaintiff asked the federal trial court for permission to proceed under a pseudonym. The court denied her request, finding that
her privacy did not outweigh the public's interest in the transparency
of court proceedings. Part of the court's reasoning rested on the right
of defendants to know their accusers' identities. That rationale made
little sense because the perpetrators surely knew plaintiff's identity.[23]
(After all, they allegedly had personal and professional relationships

with her.) The court further explained that the plaintiff's privacy interest did not outweigh the judicial system's interest in transparency because her identity was already "known or discoverable" and because she had registered some of the photos with the Copyright Office. But here again the court ignored the facts on the ground: first, it wasn't that her identity wasn't known, but rather that the lawsuit would draw more attention to the posts; second, registering the photos was crucial for the plaintiff to protect her property interest in the photos she took of herself because only by showing proof that she owned the copyrights in them could she serve copyright takedown requests. This case illustrates how courts fail to recognize the heightened privacy risks inherent in bringing privacy claims.

As far as I can tell, the plaintiff dropped the lawsuit after the court refused to grant her request. This is as unsurprising as it is depressing. The first victim of nonconsensual pornography who ever contacted me sued the perpetrator, who was her ex-boyfriend. She asked the court for permission to sue under a pseudonym. When the court refused, she dropped the lawsuit.

Some victims don't sue their attackers for psychological reasons. After talking about the possibility of civil lawsuits with pro bono counsel, some clients decide against it because they don't want to further expose their lives to their attackers. During a guest lecture in my privacy law class in 2018, D'Amico and Bateman explained that some of their clients feared the exposure that discovery entails. They did not want to sit across from perpetrators during a deposition. Looming over the decision is the fear that lawsuits may provoke physical violence. This is especially true when perpetrators are former intimate partners. Too many women are killed by former partners, and victims don't want to be another statistic.

These practical hurdles make it difficult for civil lawsuits or criminal prosecutions to get off the ground when civil claims and criminal laws are available. The substantive reach of the law is another problem.

INADEQUATE LEGAL TOOLS

Although US criminal law addresses examples of video voyeurism (often as misdemeanors with light penalties), this isn't the case for deepfake sex videos, up-skirt photos, and cyber flashing. When the law fails to tackle intimate privacy violations, we lose the chance for law to make clear that the activity is wrong and harmful. Unfortunately, a piecemeal approach is a global trend. As the UK's Law Reform Commission on Intimate Image Abuse has found, the criminal law in the United Kingdom does not cover deepfake sex videos, photos taken down someone's blouse, threats to post someone's nude images, or sextortion.

To the extent that US lawmakers have updated the law, they have not done it well. Reform around nonconsensual pornography demonstrates the point. In many states, the unauthorized disclosure of intimate images is a misdemeanor, which police are not inclined to pursue given the significant resources required for investigations. Most laws don't include civil penalties, which might incentivize the state to get involved if they were significant enough to warrant spending resources to investigate. They don't have enhanced penalties for bias-motivated abuse often present in intimate privacy invasions—people taking up-skirt photos or hiding cameras in bathrooms know little about victims except their gender.

The laws are also overly narrow. Most require proof that defendants "intended to harm or harass" victims, a motive requirement that ultimately dissuades prosecutors from bringing cases because intent is difficult to prove. Some laws only ban intimate images posted on the internet, thereby excluding nude images sent to colleagues, friends, and family via email or text. In 2013, I worked closely with Jon Cardin, representative in the Maryland House of Delegates, and the Maryland ACLU on drafting the state's law; despite our best efforts, the bill that emerged from committee only applied to images posted on the internet.

Cramped notions of privacy are part of the problem as well. Criminal and tort law rely on "underinclusive bright line rules to determine the difference between public and private."[24] Certain spaces—bedrooms, hotel rooms, and bathrooms—are afforded privacy protection, but once people leave those spaces, the protection ends. Even though people expect and deserve privacy for the parts of their bodies that they cover, they often do not enjoy privacy protection when on the street or in other public places. The blunt view that we don't have privacy in public prevents us from tackling the intrusive surveillance of our bodies that today's digital technologies—like miniscule hidden cameras—can accomplish. A Georgia court struck down the conviction of a man who had taken up-skirt videos of women at a local grocery store because the video voyeurism law only covered "private places."[25]

Other aspects of the law do not accord with how we experience intimate privacy violations. When the ballet student Alexandra Waterbury's nude images were shared with a ballet donor and two principal dancers, her sense of self-worth and confidence were shattered. No matter, she would not have been able to bring a privacy tort claim against her ex-boyfriend for sharing those images with three other people because he did not disseminate them to the public at large. To bring a civil claim for public disclosure of private fact, nude photos must be disclosed to a wide audience. The presumption is that there is little damage when a small group of people view nude images. But disclosure to such groups—employers, family members, and colleagues—is often the most damaging. (She might have sued her ex-boyfriend for intentional infliction of emotional distress, but that can be a tough claim to prove.)

For adult victims of sextortion, different federal and state criminal charges have been used to prosecute perpetrators, but those charges produce disparate sentences with "no clear association between prison time meted out and the egregiousness of the crime committed."[26] Anton Martynenko received a 38-year sentence for tricking 155 boys into sending him nude photos and extorting even more.[27] Michael Ford was sentenced to over 4.5 years in prison after sextorting 75 adult women.[28] The sentence disparity stems from the dramatically different ways that federal and state law treat minors and adult victims. Under federal law, the sextortion of an adult is usually prosecuted as computer hacking, extortion, or stalking; such laws carry light sentences compared with child pornography laws that apply when sextortion involves minors. This disparate legal treatment reflects societal attitudes about the blameworthiness of adult victims, especially when those victims are female, nonwhite, and LGBTQ.

Around the globe, intimate privacy violators seldom face consequences beyond modest fines, analogous to the way parking tickets are addressed in the United States. Min-seo, who lives in South Korea, noticed a hole in her work restroom's toilet seat cover. Inside, she discovered a tiny camera whose memory card had hundreds of video clips and photographs of women urinating. She went to the police after her supervisor admitted that he had installed the camera—the supervisor blamed his behavior on the fact that he was sexually estranged from his wife. After initially brushing off the incident as no big deal, the police eventually questioned the perpetrator before letting him walk away with a nominal fine. The perpetrator kept his job. Min-seo resigned.[29]

We saw the same in the case brought against the New York financial advisor discussed in Chapter 2. He secretly recorded his sexual encounters with three women he was dating. Despite the overwhelming evidence against the man, the women feared that he would face little punishment because the Manhattan district attorney's office expressed little interest in the case. To the prosecutor, the privacy violations were of little consequence because the man only posted the videos on private accounts for his friends to see. The women had to explain repeatedly their humiliation at being sexually objectified and how damaging the man's abuse of trust was to their sense of safety and security. Two years after being charged with 31 felonies (a felony for each separate recording), he struck a deal to plead guilty to a *single* misdemeanor. He was sentenced to ten days of community service and no prison time. As one victim's attorney summed it up, "Ten days of community service is both a gift to the defendant and another slap in the face of the victim."[30]

AMERICAN PERMISSION TO CONSUME AND SELL

Robert Bergeron was one of Grindr's several million subscribers. Having assumed that Grindr was taking care of his intimate data because, after all, it caters to people who have long been victims of hate crimes and discrimination, he was shocked to learn that his chat messages, HIV status, height, weight, precise queer subculture that he identified with, location data, and device ID were being shared with third parties.[31]

Although Grindr's data practices were detrimental to intimate privacy, equality, and public health, they did not violate US law. A grab bag of siloed federal privacy statutes covers specific activities like credit reporting, banking, health care, children's information, and unwanted telephone calls, but those laws don't apply to Grindr's sharing of intimate data or many of the data practices discussed in Chapter 1.

The Health Insurance Portability and Accountability Act (HIPAA)—familiar to (yet often misunderstood by) anyone who has been to a hospital or a doctor's office since 1996—does not protect health information collected by dating apps like Grindr. HIPAA sets rules for the collection of personal data only in the course of providing health care and only to so-called "covered entities." In its essence, HIPAA is a health care portability law with a side of privacy protection, not a health privacy law.[32] HIPAA's privacy regulations (known as the HIPAA Privacy Rule) afford no protection for Bergeron and other subscribers who shared their HIV status because Grindr isn't in the health care business and is not a covered entity.

In the United States, the corporate sector's handling of personal data is treated as a consumer protection matter, largely policed by state attorneys general and the FTC. Under the consumer-protection approach, data collection is a perfectly legal and acceptable business practice. Federal and state laws set some ground rules—rooted in process-oriented "fair information practices"—for the handling of personal data. For instance, companies must notify consumers about their data practices in publicly available privacy policies, follow certain security protocols, and refrain from violating laws against "unfair and deceptive commercial acts and practices," also referred to as UDAP laws.[33]

As of February 2022, only California, Colorado, and Virginia allow residents to ask companies of a certain size to delete or stop selling their data. The sign-up page for Zen, a meditation app, says it uses subscribers' identifying information to track them and to link to their purchases, search history, and usage data. If you click on the link to the app's privacy policy, you will discover that you can request a copy of your personal data and unsubscribe to advertising. Most people, however, do not read the privacy policies of sites and apps that they interact with (nor do they have time to do so), let alone invoke their rights to see their data or to stop it from being shared with advertisers.

For the most part, so long as companies have privacy policies and don't lie about their practices, they can collect, use, and sell intimate data. This permissive approach has prevailed, even though state attorneys general and the FTC can bring cases that set norms around "unfair and deceptive" behavior. No surprise—available resources are a big part of the problem. Because state attorneys and the FTC have limited funds, they can intervene in very few cases.

Grindr has faced no legal consequences for peddling Bergeron's and other subscribers' intimate data in the United States. Grindr's privacy policy says that the app is sharing intimate data with third parties, so its actions weren't viewed as deceptive. Privacy advocacy groups filed complaints with the FTC and the state attorneys general, arguing that Grindr's actions constituted unfair business practices in violation of UDAP laws because subscribers had no way to stop the app from sharing their intimate data.[34] But law enforcers have done nothing. Their inaction sends the message that Grindr's data practices are acceptable.

The story has played out differently for Grindr in countries with laws more protective of data privacy. When a company collects and processes data from people living in another country, then the laws of that country apply. The European Union, members of the European Economic Area (Norway, Iceland, and Liechtenstein), and the United Kingdom (through its domestic law) are governed by the General Data Protection Regulation.[35] The GDPR conceptualizes data protection as a fundamental right, although it provides less robust protection than one might think. It leans heavily on fair information practices like notice, consent, use limitations, and deletion rights, but with far more bite than US-style procedural protections of notice in privacy policies and the presumption of choice. That bite made a difference in the Grindr case. Under the GDPR, unlike US law, consent is not inferred from the presence of a privacy policy. Individuals must be explicitly asked to consent to the collection of sensitive data, including data about their sexual orientation, which Grindr failed to do for subscribers protected by the GDPR.

In early 2021, the Norwegian Data Protection Authority (DPA) brought a case against Grindr for failing to obtain subscribers' explicit, affirmative consent before sharing their intimate data with third parties. As the DPA explained, thousands of Norwegian subscribers viewed the app as a "safe space" and expected, but did not get, discretion. The Norwegian DPA initially sought a €10 million fine, which amounted to "approximately 10% of the company's turnover." The DPA took the position that a "fine of high magnitude" was necessary to address Grindr's "grave violations of the GDPR" and to prevent other companies from relying on "take-it-or-leave-it 'consents.'"[36] In December 2021, the Norwegian DPA announced that the fine ultimately levied against Grindr was €6.5 million.[37]

The FTC and state attorneys general have yet to address or acknowledge the costs to self-expression, dignity, close relationships, and equality imposed by the over-collection and pervasive sharing of intimate data. Law enforcers have tacitly endorsed the ad-tech ecosystem's shell game even though consumers can neither control nor understand what is happening to their intimate information or where it goes.

The FTC and state attorneys general have not been totally hands-off.

They have stepped in to make clear that certain data practices—the most egregious ones—are unacceptable. For instance, the FTC investigated the fertility app Flo after journalists revealed that the company had been lying to subscribers about its data sharing practices. Flo said that it wasn't selling people's intimate information when it really was.[38] Recent guidance from the FTC suggests that health apps are covered by the federal Health Breach Notification Rule, which means that they have to directly notify subscribers that their health information has been shared with third parties, just as individuals must be contacted and told that their identifiable health information has been involved in a data breach.[39] (This would be a modest improvement over the general notice-and-choice presumption that individuals know their information is being collected and shared based on the fact that companies have detailed their practices in their privacy policies.) The Vermont attorney general's office and the FTC sued the owners of Ashley Madison, a site designed for people seeking extramarital affairs, after hackers stole *36 million* subscribers' profiles and posted them online. The complaint alleged that the site had engaged in deceptive practices in failing to delete customer profiles after charging customers for the "Full Delete" option, and to adopt reasonable security practices that would protect the "sensitive data" entrusted to them. Consumers suffered damage to their reputations, relationships, and personal lives and faced an increased "risk of identity theft."[40] The FTC and the Vermont AG, on behalf of 13 states and the District of Columbia, settled the case for 1.6 million dollars and the promise to implement a comprehensive data security program, with third-party assessments.[41]

In another case, the first brought against a stalkerware provider, the FTC sued Retina-X for enabling spying on unsuspecting consumers' cell phones (recall that stalkerware lets subscribers observe everything that phone owners do with their phones) that endangered their physical safety. Although the settlement ensured that the company would ask future purchasers to agree to use the product only for lawful purposes—an absurd ask for a tool marketed to infiltrate unsuspecting devices—it permitted

Retina-X to remain in business, demonstrating the limits of governance-by-settlement-agreement.[42] After Lina Khan took over as FTC chair in 2021, the commission took bolder action in its second case against a stalkerware provider (SpyFone) by banning it from the surveillance business altogether and ordering it to delete all of the stolen data.[43] And yet, as privacy scholar Julie Cohen astutely noted, this approach—stepping in to address exceptionally bad actors—"tends to validate the mainstream of current conduct rather than meaningfully [shift] its center of gravity."[44]

What about lawsuits? After all, the United States is often associated with tales of trial attorneys winning massive judgments against companies. That image is more a product of John Grisham novels than of our actual judicial system. Often forced out of court and into arbitration—a far more hospitable place for companies to defend their actions—individuals like Bergeron face an uphill climb if they want to hold accountable the companies that have collected, used, and shared their intimate data in unwanted ways. In 2021, a federal trial court dismissed Bergeron's class action suit against Grindr, pointing to the arbitration clause in its terms-of-service agreement.

Plaintiffs whose cases are permitted to proceed in court are still often unsuccessful because civil claims are not well suited to tackle twenty-first-century privacy problems. The most logical starting point is the field of privacy torts, which grew out of Warren and Brandeis's famous article "The Right to Privacy" (discussed in the introduction and explored in detail in Chapter 6) but narrowed under legal scholar William Prosser's influence. Today, US courts only recognize as wrongful four types of privacy-invasive activities—wide publication of hyper-personal private facts, advertisements that use someone's likeness or identity without consent, interference with the enjoyment of private spaces, and depicting someone in a false light. Privacy violations related to the handling of personal data don't fit this mold, so privacy torts offer scant hope for many of today's plaintiffs.

Under the public disclosure of private fact tort, a defendant may be liable for giving publicity to someone's private, "non-newsworthy" information if its publication would highly offend a reasonable person. But Grindr sold Bergeron's intimate data to advertisers rather than publishing them to the public, as the disclosure tort requires. The tort known as "intrusion on seclusion" involves the invasion of someone's solitude in a manner that would be highly offensive to the reasonable person. Giving advertisers access to Bergeron's data would not be understood as an invasion of his solitude—that tort works well for hidden cameras in bedrooms, but not data handling practices. The "appropriation" tort involves the use of someone's identity to sell products and services, but Grindr did not leverage Bergeron's name or likeness in its online advertisements— even though it certainly monetized his intimate data. Courts have refused to recognize companies' use of personal information to create advertising profiles as appropriation because plaintiffs were not deprived of any value inherent in their names or identities.[45] The "false light" tort applies where the publication of private facts creates a misleading narrative about the person, akin to defamation, that would be highly offensive to the reasonable person, but here Grindr did not falsely depict Bergeron or publish his advertising profiles to the public at large. In short, none of the privacy torts apply.

Plaintiffs have cast a wide net for recourse and tried nearly every type of civil claim, but to no avail.[46] They have brought claims for negligence, breach of contract, unfair and deceptive actions, and breach of warranty against companies that have broken their privacy promises or failed to secure personal data. You name the claim, plaintiffs have tried and struck out. Overly narrow harm requirements are the source of the problem. Courts dismiss claims because plaintiffs have not suffered tangible injuries like economic or physical damage. Federal courts use the same rationale to deny the same plaintiffs standing.[47]

Privacy harms are often intangible—emotional distress, anxiety, thwarted expectations and other denials of autonomy, loss of trust, the chilling of expression, damaged reputations, and discrimination. These injuries are real. When Grindr shared Bergeron's intimate data with advertisers, the company increased Bergeron's risk of discrimination and undermined his autonomy. But Bergeron can't hold Grindr accountable for those injuries.

Besides overly narrow harm requirements, information asymmetries pose another obstacle. People cannot seek redress for harms they don't know about. That companies are collecting and selling their intimate data won't be visible or obvious unless whistleblowers come forward or independent researchers devote time investigating privacy violations. Bergeron, for example, only filed his lawsuit against Grindr after the *Wall Street Journal* shined a light on the company's practices. When employers use third-party hiring services to score job candidates, as discussed in Chapter 1, candidates remain oblivious that their intimate data selves played a role in their being rejected.

Plaintiffs aren't the only ones facing information asymmetries. As career staff from several state attorney general offices have told me, it is difficult to investigate companies whose algorithms mine intimate data in ways that end up having a disparate impact on protected groups. Staff need a reason to suspect that companies are engaged in "unfair or deceptive practices" before beginning investigations, but they have no visibility into entities using algorithmic systems to make decisions about consumers. Engineers building those systems may not know how intimate data interacts with algorithms and to what extent intimate data shapes outcomes. Let's imagine that a state attorney general's office has identified a company on which to serve a subpoena (called a "civil investigative demand"); the company may resist the subpoena on the grounds of trade secrets. Then FTC commissioner and now head of the Consumer Financial Protection Bureau Rohit Chopra has explained that regulators can't assess algorithmic systems if companies have trade secret protections to fall back on.

Because courts dismiss privacy lawsuits for the absence of cognizable harm, privacy violations continue. State attorneys general and the FTC bring too few cases to make a difference, and nearly all end in settlements. The law, together with practical considerations, affords no viable avenue for individuals to obtain justice when their intimate data is handled in ways that they do not want or expect.

———

LAW FAILS TO understand and thus provide sufficient protection to intimate privacy. It protects sites not only that have yet to earn a liability shield by behaving like Good Samaritans, but that have done quite the opposite, making a mockery of the concept by encouraging and cashing in on intimate privacy violations. Two sides, same coin.

We have our work cut out for us. As a starting point, we must understand intimate privacy as a fundamental right deserving of protection. In the next chapter, I explore the importance of recognizing intimate privacy as a civil right and as a human right.

6

The Right to Intimate Privacy

IN A 2019 PRESS RELEASE, NEW YORK ATTORNEY GENERAL LETITIA
James highlighted the significance of her office's settlement agreement
with the dating app Jack'd for LGBTQ people. For an entire year, the
company had ignored reports that subscribers' private photos were not
stored securely. AG James condemned the company for ignoring the
problem knowing that 80% of its subscribers were gay, bi, and trans
people of color who might face hate crimes and bullying from photo
leaks. The app had wrongly prioritized its profits over subscribers' privacy and safety.[1]

AG James could have centered her remarks on the company's "unfair
and deceptive" practices—after all, that was why her office had jurisdiction over the app's security failure. Instead, she emphasized privacy's
inextricable link to equality. Subscribers would only feel free to engage in
sexual expression if the app could be trusted to keep their photos secure
from those who might discriminate against them due to their sexual orientation, race, or gender nonconformity.

As AG James made clear, privacy invasions aren't solely consumer

protection matters. Spying Inc.'s activities don't just involve broken promises or unfair commercial practices, though Jack'd had violated its pledge
to "maintain reasonable security practices" and ignored reports that its
databases were insecure. Violations of intimate privacy, at the hands of
Privacy Invaders, aren't harmless antics or the residue of bad breakups;
they aren't ordinary bureaucratic overreach or power grabs at the hands
of governments. Corporate, individual, and government privacy invaders
would like us to view them that way—all the easier to maintain the status
quo. Invasions of intimate privacy are not only sources of profit, retalia-
tion, or law and order. They are far more than that.

To combat invasions of intimate privacy, we first need to recognize
intimate privacy as a moral and legal right. Everyone deserves intimate
privacy to create a life of meaning, respect, and love and to feel that they
belong as citizens. We can and should recognize intimate privacy as a
civil right. In doing so, we show our appreciation of its significance for
individuals, groups, and society. In the United States, the recognition of
a civil right has legal significance and moral resonance. Our civil rights
tradition secures strong protections for crucial rights. Lawmakers can
insist upon robust duties to protect intimate privacy and to remedy its
violation. The recognition of a civil right to intimate privacy is urgent for
women and minorities who suffer discrimination due to attitudes stig-
matizing their bodies and intimate lives. Although modern civil rights
laws are principally antidiscrimination laws, that should not be their sum
total. A civil right to intimate privacy can and should combat invidious
discrimination *and* secure basic entitlements for all.

INTIMATE PRIVACY, A CIVIL RIGHT

Every year since 2016, Georgetown University Law Center has held a conference entitled "The Color of Surveillance," which explores the disparate impact of government surveillance on Black, poor, and immigrant

communities. At the first conference and in her ground-breaking work, African Studies scholar Simone Browne discussed how eighteenth-century laws required Black, mixed-race, and Indigenous enslaved people to carry candle lanterns while walking in public after sunset without the company of a white person, deputizing private people to stop anyone who failed to comply. The logic of those laws continues in the stop-and-frisk policing of Black and Brown people and the use of floodlights by police in Black neighborhoods.[2] In 2020, conference organizer (and FTC commissioner, as of May 2022) Alvaro Bedoya argued that privacy is a civil liberty *and* a civil right: marginalized communities deserve freedom from government surveillance (the civil liberty) and privacy protections against discrimination (the civil right).[3]

Underlying Bedoya's argument—and that of AG James in the Jack'd case—are the antidiscrimination principles governing modern civil rights laws. Under state and federal law, powerful entities, both public and private, are prohibited from depriving people of important opportunities because of their race, age, national origin, religion, gender, disability, and sexual orientation. People have a right to work, attend school, obtain loans, use public transportation, vote, and secure housing free from invidious discrimination.

Bedoya and AG James are right—gender, sexual, and racial equality and intimate privacy are a package deal. Women, LGBTQ individuals, nonwhites, and disabled people shoulder a disproportionate share of privacy invasions, which makes them vulnerable to destructive discrimination. Recall from Chapter 1 that Amazon's AI hiring system excluded female candidates, dropping those who had degrees from women's colleges, because they did not resemble people working at the company. Annie Seifullah, whom you met in Chapter 2, lost her job as a school principal after her ex broke into her laptop, stole her nude photos, and shared them with her boss and the media. Her employer, the New York Department of Education, blamed *her* for her ex's privacy invasion and fired her on that basis. Journalist Rana Ayyub, whom you met in Chapter 3, has not been able to publish her work in her country's news outlets since the government circulated the deepfake sex video of her.

Following the development of modern civil rights laws, a civil right to intimate privacy would combat privacy invasions amounting to invidious discrimination. It would limit or ban data practices that imperil the opportunities of women and marginalized communities because of their membership in protected groups. That is the approach of the federal Genetic Information Non-Discrimination Act (GINA), which prohibits companies from using genetic information in employment decisions. GINA was inspired by the historical threat of discrimination against Black people due to their disproportionate development of sickle cell anemia.

But a civil right to intimate privacy should not only be a right to combat invidious discrimination: it should also be a right to baseline protections for intimate privacy for everyone. In making this argument, I draw on legal philosopher Robin West's conception of civil rights. As West explains, civil rights should be understood—and protected—as "human or natural rights" that enable "our most fundamental human capabilities." They are rights *to* something—entitlements that let us "thrive and be social," feel like we belong, and engage as citizens. Civil rights deserve recognition and protection because they "secure the preconditions for a good life."[4] In the United States, civil rights protections have been operationalized through the interpretation of constitutional rights, the passage of state and federal laws, and the enforcement of existing laws that foreground those rights.

Understanding civil rights as human rights with basic entitlements has a rich history. In 1792, political theorists Thomas Paine and Mary Wollstonecraft argued for a civil right to public education because it facilitates human development and participation in civil society.[5] Legal historians George Rutherglen and Edward White have explored how the federal Civil Rights Act of 1866 protected common law rights—the ability to buy property and to enter into contracts—because they were fundamental to participation in civil society, requiring protection from discrimination.[6] Legal historian and dean of the University of Virginia School of Law Risa Goluboff has highlighted how, in the 1940s, lawyers at the Department of Justice's Civil Rights Section focused on eliminating barriers to pursuing one's chosen occupation because employment was an inalienable and natural right.[7]

The notion of civil rights as securing human rights receded in mid-twentieth-century America. As historian and African American Studies scholar Carol Anderson has explained, President Truman and Eleanor Roosevelt rejected civil rights activists' calls for the recognition of human rights because of the term's association with communism. In turn, the NAACP abandoned the call for protections of inalienable rights like education and employment and instead focused on securing protections against discrimination in important contexts. Civil rights should, as the NAACP argued in its early history, both secure our entitlement to fundamental rights—including intimate privacy—and combat the discriminatory denial of those rights.[8]

Of course, not every interest implicates a civil right. Lots of people like to buy alcohol on Sundays, but they wouldn't have a civil right to purchase it for Super Bowl parties. (Don't get me wrong, I like whiskey, but I would still have a fulfilling life if I could buy it only six days a week.) We enjoy access to parks, but we wouldn't have a civil right to enter them at night. Civil rights are rights considered fundamental because they enable us to flourish as whole individuals and active members of society.

Although intimate privacy has not been recognized as a civil right (understood as both a basic entitlement and an antidiscrimination mandate), it should be. Doing so would clarify the moral significance of intimate privacy. It would give us the vocabulary to understand its centrality to the development of an authentic and dignified identity. It would signal that intimate privacy is a precondition to love, friendship, and civic engagement. It would convey the necessity of intimate privacy for individual *and* community development. It would communicate to Spying Inc.

that intimate privacy deserves strong protections rather than empty gestures; to Privacy Invaders that intimate privacy violations aren't harmless antics; to governments that demeaning data collection corrodes democracy; and to each and every one of us that our intimate privacy matters.

The recognition of intimate privacy as a civil right would also draw proper attention to its structural role in combating discrimination against protected groups and protecting equality. It would highlight the troubling social attitudes that turn women's and minorities' naked bodies and intimate information into stigmatized bodies and sources of blackmail, humiliation, and destruction. It would acknowledge the unique harms suffered by women and minorities, often intersectionally, and the corrosive impact that discriminatory attitudes have on psyches, careers, educations, and more.

Appreciating that sexual activity, nudity, and other intimate information (real or fake) can be viewed as discrediting, humiliating, and shameful, and result in discrimination, does not mean that they *are* discrediting, humiliating, and shameful. Our naked bodies, sexual practices, and innermost desires are not dirty. They are not despicable. They are not blameworthy. If and when destructive attitudes recede (one can dream!), a civil right to intimate privacy will still matter for reasons that I am now going to explore.

The scaffolding for my argument for a civil right to intimate privacy traces back to 1890, when two Boston lawyers called for a "right to privacy" essential for human agency and dignity.

THE "MOST FAMOUS" LAW REVIEW ARTICLE

In the 1880s, the penny press splashed stories about the private lives of the rich and famous on their front pages. Reporters had no shame when it came to catching scoops; they climbed through windows and stared through keyholes. Photographers stood on city streets, taking snapshots of every person who seemed remotely famous with newly invented Kodak snap cameras. Much like today's "Stars—They're Just Like Us" columns, these photos were popular because they were "candid and revealing."⁹ The lives of politicians, stage actresses, singers, socialites, and even some ordinary people were simply fodder for the press.

Just as gossip rags were becoming popular, Samuel Warren started a law firm in Boston with his law school classmate, Louis Brandeis. Although Warren wasn't much of a draw for reporters, his new wife Mabel Bayard—the vivacious daughter of a US senator—was. The *New York Times* covered their 1883 wedding, noting that the reception and "two banquets" were attended by foreign dignitaries.¹⁰

Press attention wasn't ideal for Warren: his younger brother Ned was embracing his homosexuality just as society had begun to criminalize and pathologize it. Warren and his family knew about Ned's sexual orientation, having spent time with his partner and roommates at Oxford. In 1889, the public was preoccupied with a series of "sensational trials" about "upper-class men paying for sex with telegraph delivery boys." The coverage of homosexuality as "sexual deviance" made clear that if the press wrote about Ned's sexual orientation, he might be prosecuted and the family subject to social ruin.¹¹ Gay men were especially vulnerable to persecution if there was a "paper trail" of their romantic and sexual interests; Ned had an extensive body of unpublished poems and letters that put him at risk.¹²

Warren did what any creative lawyer would do to protect his brother's privacy—he enlisted his law partner to cowrite an article defending what they called the "right to be let alone."¹³ The article decried journalists' "sordid spying" on the "domestic circle" and broadcasting of the "details of sexual relations." Individuals and society suffer, Warren and Brandeis argued, when "intimacies whispered in the closet" are "proclaimed from the house tops." Exposing the "fact" of a "domestic occurrence" without consent risked "spiritual" and emotional harm even greater than "material" and physical harm. In their view, individuals needed to control what others knew about their domestic lives and their "thoughts, sentiments, and emotions." They called for tort law to recognize a "right to privacy" in the "sacred precincts of private and domestic life."

To make their point, Warren and Brandeis asked readers to imagine a man who was writing a letter to his son to explain that he would not be dining at home with his wife. They argued that the man had the right to decide if anyone could see the letter. It did not matter that no one would care about his plans. The nonconsensual revelation of the letter would be an affront to the man's agency, dignity, and "inviolate personality." Law should protect "all persons, whatsoever their position or station, from having matters which they may properly prefer to keep private made public against their will."[14]

The article struck a powerful chord, even though it mostly focused on the technical details of intellectual property, defamation, and contract law as precursors to a tort right to privacy. Legal scholar Roscoe Pound wrote in 1916 that Warren and Brandeis had done "nothing less than adding a chapter to our law."[15] As Neil Richards has observed, the article is "the foundation of American privacy law."[16]

Courts heeded the call for a common law right to privacy. In 1905, the Supreme Court of Georgia found that tort law secures a person's right to "live a life of privacy as to certain matters, and of publicity as to others."[17] The majority of the early privacy plaintiffs were women whose images had been used in advertisements and films without their permission or whose nude bodies were viewed without their consent. Historian Jessica Lake unearthed the stories behind those cases and found that those female plaintiffs used privacy tort law to object to unwanted "optical violation of their exposed bodies" and to being reduced to "objects of consumption" or "shameful hookers or divorcees." Although court decisions tended to attribute privacy redress to the preservation of female "modesty" and "reserve," the plaintiffs did not frame the cases that way. Litigation documents show that the plaintiffs sought to "claim ownership over their life experiences and to protest against the appropriation and exploitation of those experiences."[18]

The privacy torts could have evolved in a way that provided robust protection for the right to intimate privacy that Warren and Brandeis described, but as we saw in Chapter 5, they have morphed into four narrow tort claims. Nonetheless, the "most famous law review" article serves as an important building block for a civil right to intimate privacy. Warren and Brandeis began a conversation about intimate privacy's role in securing human agency and dignity that has continued through the ages, one that we can develop and expand.

SECURING AUTONOMY, IDENTITY, AND RESPECT

As Warren and Brandeis suggested, self-development and sexual autonomy are impossible without the ability to decide who has access to our bodies, intimate activities, and intimate data. We figure out who we are and what we want through our bodies: they are our "basic reference" for self-development.[19] We derive a sense of self-worth by being in "possession and control" of our bodies.[20] We also develop our sense of selves in physical spaces such as the home where we develop habits and arrange things that have meaning to us. As feminist philosopher Iris Marion Young has underscored, privacy afforded our physical bodies in important spaces like the home enables us to feel a sense of ease critical to identity development.[21]

When we can retreat to on- and offline spaces alone or with trusted others, when we can show parts of our bodies to who we want, when we can think, search, and communicate without worrying about being observed, judged, and ridiculed, we can let our guards down. When we can determine who gets close to us, physically and emotionally, we can develop a sense of individuality. With intimate privacy, we can explore unpopular ideas, play with our identities, and figure out our *future selves*—the ever-evolving notion of the selves we want to be. As philosopher Hannah Arendt has explained, when we have the psychic and physical space that we need to develop ourselves, we emerge as more critical and independent thinkers who can contribute to public discourse, which is central to a well-functioning democracy.[22]

Intimate privacy lets us see ourselves as having agency over our intimate lives and present ourselves to others as dignified. It enables us to show ourselves as whole, fully integrated people who command respect. It permits us to express our moral worth in letting us choose how others see our bodies and innermost selves.[23] Legal scholar Robert Post talks about respect for the privacy of our bedrooms as "civility rules" that "accord respect . . . integral to both individual and social personality."[24]

Being able to reveal our naked bodies, gender, or sexual orientation at the pace and in the way of our choosing is crucial to identity formation. With intimate privacy, Marc, whom you met in Chapter 1, could have viewed adult videos without concern that Spying Inc. might be sharing his viewing habits with advertisers; Alex, whom you met in the introduction, could have undressed without worrying that Privacy Invaders like her ex might have hidden a secret camera in her bedroom; Rana Ayyub could have posted her photo on social media without worrying that the government might insert her face into porn without her permission.

When we are denied the ability to decide who knows about our intimate information at pivotal moments, it can shatter our sense of self. We can become alienated from ourselves. Privacy scholar Anna Lauren Hoffmann explains that for transgender people, when their former names and gender are revealed without permission, it can "trigger feelings of dysphoria and humiliation."[25] Unwanted exposure of our naked bodies makes us acutely aware that others see us *as objects* that can be violated, rather than as human beings deserving respect. Philosopher Jean-Paul Sartre talked about that phenomenon as "pure shame"—not shame in others knowing something undesirable about us, but rather shame in knowing that we are being seen as objects, or as less than human. As Sartre explained, when we clothe ourselves, we are claiming our right to be seen without being seen as an object.[26]

When intimate information is "removed from its original context and revealed to strangers, we are vulnerable" to being defined by, and reduced to, that information.[27] The unwanted exposure of people's nude bodies and sexual activities can give them a "diminished status," which is often internalized as a "lack of full self-esteem."[28] As legal philosopher Martha Nussbaum explains, "sexuality is an area of life in which disgust often plays a role." Sex signifies our animal nature because it "involves the exchange of bodily fluids." In nearly all societies, "people identify a group of sexual actors as disgusting or pathological, contrasting them with 'normal' or 'pure' sexual actors (prominently including the people themselves and their own group)." That group often includes those who don't fall in line with heteronormativity, such as women who have had more than one sexual partner, LGBTQ individuals, or individuals in multiple sexual relationships.[29] When the details of our sexual activities are exposed, we may be reduced to them; women and marginalized individuals are especially likely to be seen as unseemly, promiscuous, and disgusting.

Throughout my interviews, people targeted with nonconsensual pornography felt disrespected and defenseless because they were denied the ability to decide how others saw their physical selves. Recall that Joan, discussed in Chapter 2, felt a deep sense of shame and vulnerability after the hotel employee emailed videos of her showering to her contacts and posted them online. She reasserted her autonomy over her body by changing her appearance. She got a tattoo with her grandmother's name; the tattoo was her armor. Leah Juliett, whose nude photos were posted online by a high school classmate and who identifies as nonbinary, explained to me that they changed their hair color and got tattoos to vanquish the body that had been "stolen" from them. "I rebuilt my body in my own way."

None of this is to suggest that our bodies, sex, gender, and sexual orientation are the essence of our identities. The recognition of intimate privacy as a civil right does not mean that our bodies, sex, gender, or sexual orientation exclusively define who we are, just as our reading habits and online searches do not define who we are. Instead, intimate privacy recognizes the significance of autonomy over our intimate lives that lets us form, develop, and reshape our identities.

Of course, what constitutes our choice depends on the context and setting. Consent must be informed, voluntary, and clearly manifested. Consent is nuanced; it doesn't operate like an on-off switch. Context can help us sort out the parameters of a person's consent. My view, and one that I will explore in more detail in Chapter 8, is that consent must be limited to the precise contexts and settings in which it is given, absent clear instructions otherwise. Just because someone takes off their clothes in a friend's bedroom does not mean that they have consented to being videotaped doing so, unless the friend informed them and got their permission. The reasonable expectation is that there is no video camera in the bedroom.

We should not presume consent to the handling of our intimate data. The ease with which intimate data can be taken out of its original context and viewed, used, copied, and shared demands a parsimonious and exacting approach. We have discussed the shock and anger of subscribers of dating apps and fertility tracking services when they learned that their intimate data was shared with advertisers, even though companies included warnings in their privacy policies. There will be hard cases, but the context, settings, and expectations can help us assess whether our consent has been manufactured, as is often true for Spying Inc., or instead reflects an informed, voluntary, and clearly manifested decision.

ENABLING INTIMACY

In 1947, philosopher Martin Buber described the essential roles of love and friendship in giving meaning to his existence: "Only he who himself turns to the other human being and opens himself to him receives the world in him. Only the being whose otherness, accepted by my being, lives and faces me in the whole compression of existence, brings the radiance of eternity to me."[30]

Our close relationships are central to human flourishing, and they require intimate privacy to thrive.[31] Privacy "forms the necessary context for the intimate relations of love and friendship, which give our lives much of whatever affirmative value they have."[32] Social psychologists explain that close relationships develop through a process in which partners come to know the "innermost, subjective aspects of another, and are known in a like manner."[33] As sociologist Erving Goffman explains, we feel guilty when we don't tell our intimate partners about our "invisible failings"—"it casts a shadow over the relationship if we don't tell them."[34] We are honest about our desires, secrets, and painful past experiences if our partners are honest about theirs. Reciprocal vulnerability generates confidence that our partners will not hurt us intentionally. We share our deepest secrets with our partners because we believe that they will treat our information as we hope and expect rather than as we fear.[35] We don't hide or self-censor personal facts and feelings because we trust that our partners will guard our confidences. Falling in love depends upon our partners treating our personal information with care.[36]

Intimate privacy lets partners engage in that process of mutual revelation—it lets them know one another and be known to one another. It gives them the space to be their honest and raw selves, so that they can become and see themselves as an "us." It enables partners to be spontaneous and vulnerable with one another, physically and emotionally.[37] For example, revealing one's history with sexual assault is difficult, and conceivable only if a partner can be trusted to be discreet. In these and so many other ways, intimate privacy is an essential ingredient for intimacy and love.[38]

That isn't to say that seclusion and confidentiality inevitably operate in intimacy-enabling, respect-securing, and autonomy-facilitating ways. We have seen the powerful invoke their own "privacy" to conceal their violations of other people's intimate privacy. Indeed, this has been a hallmark of the sexual harassment and assault cases uncovered in the entertainment industry since 2017. TV host Matt Lauer had a button installed on his desk so he could lock his office door when female staffers entered, allowing him to initiate inappropriate contact while knowing that nobody would see. Film director Harvey Weinstein had employees guard his hotel rooms and office from entry except for the actresses whom he groped and raped.[39] Victims were pressured into signing confidentiality agreements that shielded attackers from public reckoning.[40] Harassers and assaulters like Lauer and Weinstein eviscerate women's intimate privacy while protecting their own personal privacy, forcing women to reveal their bodies in settings that keep the abuse and privacy violations secret.

We have a regrettable legacy of invoking privacy to conceal privacy-destroying activities. In the past, the privileged summoned the privacy that they wanted. White men used that privacy to undress and rape enslaved Black women. Upper- and middle-class white women enjoyed little intimate privacy in the "family home."[41] As political philosopher John Stuart Mill wrote in 1869, husbands colonized their wives' "sentiments" and bodies.[42] The home was treated as a "secluded domain" where husbands could batter their wives without intervention. Late eighteenth- and early nineteenth-century courts invoked the concept of the "private sphere" to justify shielding spousal abuse from accountability. As far as society was concerned, battered women had no privacy to claim. Their husbands monitored and controlled their activities, beating them if they stepped out of line. Only the privacy of husbands mattered, justified by the now-rejected view of "spousal discipline."[43] Domestic violence was left unaddressed until the battered women's movement gave it a name and helped ensure its criminalization in the 1970s.

Some scholars point to this history to argue that we should get rid of privacy. Feminist legal scholar Catharine MacKinnon has described privacy as bad for equality because it secures the "right of men 'to be let alone' to oppress women one at a time."[44] But male invocation of privacy in service of female subordination does not itself *allow* for the denial of women's intimate privacy; it merely *highlights* it. The history of male abuse of women's intimate privacy does not diminish the significance of intimate privacy to enable autonomy, dignity, and companionship. If anything, it provides urgent reason for its protection for everyone. That is precisely what feminist privacy scholar Anita Allen powerfully argued in her foundational book *Uneasy Access*: the fact that women once had no intimate privacy does not undermine their entitlement to it.[45]

RIGHTS IN VIEW AND IN BALANCE

The recognition of a civil right to intimate privacy would change the social meaning of the surveillance conducted by Spying Inc., Privacy Invaders, and government spies. It would say that the stakes—human flourishing, democratic engagement, and equality—are too high for lawmakers to wait for the "next session" to adopt robust protections for individuals; for the FTC and state attorneys general to do nothing in the face of the over-collection of intimate data; for judges to treat invasions of intimate privacy like parking violations and to let the privacy torts fade into irrelevance at just the time that we need them to grow and fully capture the wrongs and harms of intimate privacy violations; and for policymakers to ignore demeaning government surveillance that has little legitimate purpose.

A civil right to intimate privacy would signal to the public that the erosion of intimate privacy and the threat of invidious discrimination are neither inevitable nor acceptable. It would say that invasions of intimate privacy are not simply the price that we pay for well-tailored ads, bad breakups, or subsidized health care. It would expose the violation of intimate privacy for women and minorities as a structural problem. It would make clear that intimate privacy can't be easily bartered away for the sake of efficiency or profits. In some contexts, it would signal that it can't be bargained away at all.

Elevating intimate privacy to the status of a civil right would change social attitudes and practices in several ways. The public would see invasions of intimate privacy as violations of human agency, dignity, intimacy, and equality. Victims would be more likely to come forward, since reporting online abuse would not seem fruitless; they might even join efforts underway to demand legislative reform. Their loved ones would be more likely to convey support rather than embarrassment and rejection. Some potential perpetrators would see privacy violations as wrongful and damaging to identity, respect, and intimacy. Many who previously tolerated or made discriminatory decisions based on intimate information would no longer view the nude bodies and intimate activities of women and minorities as disgusting and discrediting. Companies would devote time and money to eradicating or preventing bias from being baked into algorithms and automated systems rather than waiting for enforcement activity or legislative mandates. A civil rights mandate would change our "cultural software"—our "collectively created tools that constitute us as persons that we use to interact with others and express our values."[46] Intimate privacy and its protection would become the moral law within us.

Acknowledging intimate privacy as a civil right provides a moral mandate for robust legal reform. As a civil right, intimate privacy would warrant vigorous and comprehensive protection, rather than US law's current light touch. A civil rights approach would treat data collectors as data guardians with strong affirmative obligations to individuals, as I will discuss in Chapter 8. And it would work to remove the barriers that prevent women and minorities from enjoying crucial life opportunities on equal terms.

A core feature of civil rights laws is injunctive relief—ordering parties to do something rather than just compensating those injured for their suffering. A civil rights approach to intimate privacy would enable courts to order parties to stop handling intimate information as well as to take down nonconsensual intimate images. (I will take up the specific contours of those duties and remedies in my plan for reform in Chapters 7 and 8.)

Once enacted and adopted, those legal reforms would educate the public. Laws protecting a civil right to intimate privacy would teach us about the centrality of intimate privacy to a life of meaning and a healthy democracy. They would inform the actions of individuals, so that intimate privacy would be honored rather than violated. They would shape the design of products and services, so that far less intimate information would be collected and exploited. They would change the surveillance practices and policies of government agencies and officials, so that intimate privacy would be protected and prioritized rather than destroyed and ignored. The lessons of those laws would shape our behavior, securing opportunities for intimate privacy that we want, expect, and deserve.

In our current regulatory environment, Spying Inc. invades intimate privacy without having to justify its data handling practices. The public need only be given a heads-up about *what* Spying Inc. is doing, in vaguely written privacy policies, but not *why*. US tech companies don't have to justify their surveillance to anyone—not to lawmakers, courts, or agencies—unless they face investigations for acting deceptively or unfairly. Privacy Invaders and their enablers—sites specializing in nonconsensual intimate imagery—don't have to, nor do they, ask individuals for permission to record, manufacture, or share their nude images. Government spies operate under the same assumption.[47] Government engages in a "gargantuan data grab," as criminal procedure and constitutional law scholar Barry Friedman puts it, without asking anyone for permission.[48]

If we recognize and protect intimate privacy as a civil right, that unjustified presumption of permission would disappear. As legal philosopher Frederick Schauer has explained, when we say that something is a right, it means that the right can't be denied without a good reason.[49] Spying Inc. and government spies would need a good reason to

handle intimate data. Law could limit or ban outright certain practices if no good reason justifies them. What counts as a good reason
to abridge a civil right to intimate privacy would be difficult to satisfy.
Boosted corporate profits and reduced administrability costs would
not cut it.

No doubt, US companies monetizing intimate data won't be thrilled.
Corporate lobbyists will object. They will insist that collecting intimate
data serves efficiency because it pairs people with useful products and
services and enables innovation and discovery. Their arguments will be
premised on a whole lot of *possibilities*, but not *certainties*. Companies
insist that the world will be far better off so long as they can collect, use,
and share intimate data, but as far as I can tell, they haven't provided much
proof of concept. Or in economic terms, they will have difficulty showing that the marginal benefits of data collection outweigh the marginal
costs to intimate privacy. Lobbyists will simply assert that individuals are
better off (as if such assertions prove themselves), but aside from fattened
corporate profits, they likely will not offer much support for their claims.
A civil right to intimate privacy is indispensable to self-development, dignity, and close relationships as well as equality—we cannot sacrifice it
without a darn good reason.

Appreciating the significance of a civil right to intimate privacy is
a crucial first step. The next is to think about what it would mean for
policymakers wrestling with competing rights. A civil right to intimate
privacy would not automatically trump all other crucial rights and liberties, including competing intimate privacy rights and free speech rights.
When individual rights conflict, "it is the job of the government to discriminate. If the government makes the right choice and protects the
more important at the cost of the less, then it has not weakened or cheap-
ened the notion of a right."[50] Institutions weighing competing rights have
to approach the task with care.

Privacy rights can clash with free speech rights, but not every privacy right impinges upon free speech in the same way, and not every free

speech right is the same. Free speech protects our ability to freely express ourselves, to listen to and share information so that we can figure out the kind of world we want to live in, to develop civic courage, and to let truths compete in the "marketplace of ideas." When Privacy Invaders hijack your computer camera and blackmail you into sharing nude images, when government spies demand to know your history of abortions, prostitution, and domestic abuse before they will provide prenatal care, as in Erica's case discussed in Chapter 3, when Spying Inc. collects, exploits, and shares information about your favorite porn videos, HIV status, or mental health struggles without your consent, they are not informing public discourse, readying people for political participation, or offering truths for debate. To the contrary, they are undermining free speech principles by making it less likely that you will feel comfortable seeking help, browsing adult sites, finding partners on dating apps, and engaging in sexual expression on your devices and at home. In these contexts, a civil right to intimate privacy would be good for intimate privacy *and* free speech.

We need careful assessments of the speech and privacy rights at stake to figure out whose rights should prevail. From the start, the conversation about a "right to privacy" has wrestled with competing rights to free speech. In their article, Warren and Brandeis argued that people about "whose affairs the community has no legitimate concern" should not be "dragged into an undesirable and undesired publicity," especially in cases involving "flagrant breaches of decency." By contrast, they argued, the media should be free to publish stories about "matters of public and general interest."

What counts as expression essential for self-governance, civic courage, and personal development can be a complex inquiry. But sometimes it isn't that complex. Following the posting and circulation of a video showing the rape of a fourteen-year-old girl (discussed in Chapter 2), Pornhub addressed titles similar to the rape video, stating: "We allow all forms of sexual expression that follow our Terms of Use, and while some people may find these fantasies inappropriate, they do appeal to many people around the world and are protected by various freedom of speech laws."[51] As a matter of free speech values, rape videos add nothing to public discourse—they not only normalize sexual violence and perpetuate fantasies based on the absence of consent but, most obviously, they are evidence of a crime.

When digital communications are involved, plaintiffs and defendants alike may have privacy *and* free speech rights at issue. If Joan, whom you met in Chapter 2, had sued the perpetrator who posted and emailed the video of her showering and urinating (she didn't), her privacy and speech interests would have clashed with that person's speech, whose emails and posts would be viewed as their expression because they authored them, *and* their privacy because Joan would need to get a court order to unmask the identity of the author of the emails and posts. As for the perpetrator's free speech rights, the videos that they posted and sent didn't educate anyone about matters of legitimate concern to the public like art, culture, or politics; they were not facts or ideas to be debated in the service of truth; the subject of the videos—Joan—isn't a public official or figure, so the public doesn't have any legitimate interest in her private life. As for Joan, the posts and emails involved her coerced expression; their publication also chilled her from expressing herself. Recall that Joan shut down her social media profiles, not because she wanted to, but because she did not want to give her tormentor a way to contact and humiliate her again. Joan's privacy in her hotel room warranted greater protection than the perpetrator's interest in hiding their identity from accountability. In similar cases where private individuals' intimate images were posted without permission, courts have prioritized their privacy and expression over perpetrators' privacy and speech interests.

Courts and policymakers are equipped to balance a civil right to intimate privacy and free speech rights. The human rights approach outside the United States does it all the time.

INTIMATE PRIVACY AS A HUMAN RIGHT

"A porn scandal . . . and sexual antics between priests and their students has thrown the diocese in disarray." That was the title of an Austrian news magazine's article about the Catholic Church officially condemning homosexuality yet unofficially tolerating it in its ranks. Included in the article was a photograph of the principal of a Catholic seminary with his hand on another man's crotch during a party at his home. According to the article, the principal had sexual relationships with seminarians.

The principal sued the magazine for violating his privacy rights, as guaranteed by the European Convention on Human Rights, which was drafted by the Council of Europe in Strasbourg and signed by the 47 member states of the Council in 1950. Austrian courts found that the magazine had the right to publish a story about the Church's hypocrisy and the principal's relationships, but not to publish the photograph, which wasn't necessary to inform the public and just satisfied "an appetite for scandal." The newspaper appealed the Austrian court's finding to the European Court of Human Rights (ECHR) as a violation of its free speech rights under the Convention.

The ECHR upheld the injunction as striking an appropriate balance between the newspaper's right to free speech and the principal's right to privacy. The court explained that the magazine could inform the public about the Church's hypocrisy without showing the photo of the principal's consensual homosexual relationship. The court emphasized that "a person's image constitutes one of the chief attributes of his or her personality, as it reveals the person's unique characteristics," and the right to control the use of one's image is "one of the essential components of personal development," especially when it concerns one's consensual relationships.[52] For the ECHR, the privacy of photographs of one's image, especially when those photographs concern close relationships, mattered more than the media's right to publish.

All over the world, privacy and free speech are considered fundamental human rights. The "right to privacy" or private life and the right to freedom of expression are enshrined in the Universal Declaration of Human Rights. Under the Convention (the human rights document litigated in the Austrian case), Article 8 secures the right to respect for everyone's "private and family life . . . home and . . . correspondence" and Article 10 guarantees the freedom "to receive and impart information and ideas without interference by public authority."[53] Policymakers including courts like the ECHR balance competing rights, which is referred to as the "concept of proportionality." As then-UN Special Rapporteur on the Promotion and Protection of the Right to Freedom of Opinion and Expression David Kaye explained to my free speech class in the spring of 2020, "When you say human rights, what you mean is to start talking about the values rooted in the proportionality inquiry."

Although the human rights approach and my proposed civil rights framework for the United States might come down differently in particular cases, they have shared commitments that could enhance diplomatic trust and encourage trade. The first is the common recognition and protection of intimate privacy as a fundamental right. Human rights courts like the ECHR recognize the importance of privacy regarding information about the "core of a person's life," including health, sex, and personal relationships, which aligns with my conception of intimate privacy.[54] The second is the shared recognition of intimate privacy's importance for equality. The UN Special Rapporteur on Violence against Women considers nonconsensual porn to constitute gender discrimination;[55] the UN Special Rapporteur on the Right to Privacy has called for an examination of the "embedded gender and other biases in algorithms."[56] These are just the sort of antidiscrimination commitments underlying my call for a civil right to intimate privacy.

To be sure, a civil right to intimate privacy wouldn't replicate a human rights approach in all ways. An importance difference is the First Amendment, which would limit the reach of a civil rights agenda, especially concerning the publication of private facts. In a US court, the Catholic principal likely would have lost his suit on the grounds that the public has a legitimate interest in seeing photographic proof of the Church's hypocrisy, a matter of legitimate concern for the public, and because no nudity was involved. Let's return to Representative Hill's case. Recall from Chapter 2 that news sites published partially nude photographs of Hill and her female lover. The California trial court prioritized the publisher's free speech over Hill's privacy, reasoning that the public had a right to see the photos because they were proof of her affair with a campaign staffer. The First Amendment is uniquely protective of free speech rights. The human rights proportionality approach tolerates more restrictions on free speech to protect privacy, as we saw in the Austrian case brought by the principal.

Another difference is the way that human rights law views the state's obligations to individuals. A human rights approach only applies to state actors whereas a civil rights agenda pertains to both government and private actors. Then too, under a human rights approach, states must both refrain from data processing or surveillance practices violating individuals' privacy rights *and* protect individuals' privacy rights by prosecuting Privacy Invaders. While a civil right to information privacy would provide the moral mandate for strong privacy protections, it would not impose duties upon the state to prosecute Privacy Invaders. Law enforcement in the United States has broad discretion to investigate and bring cases, and it is hard to imagine lawmakers taking away that discretion and requiring prosecution in intimate privacy cases, given the broader societal struggle with over-incarceration, especially of Black men.[57]

Azerbaijani journalist Khadija Ismayilova, discussed in Chapter 3, sought the help of a local prosecutor after a video of her having sex with her boyfriend was posted online. Recall that Ismayilova had received a letter warning that, unless she ceased investigating the Azerbaijani president, the video—taken with a hidden camera—would be released. The prosecutor did nothing beyond issuing a status report that disclosed personal information about Ismayilova, her boyfriend, family, and colleagues, including their names and occupations. In the weeks following the posting of the video, newspapers with ties to the government published articles accusing Ismayilova of anti-government bias and immoral sexual behavior. Although more sex videos (both real and manufactured) were posted online, the police took no steps to try to identify the posters.

A year later, Ismayilova sued the prosecutor for failing to pursue her case in violation of Articles 8 (privacy) and 10 (free expression) of the Convention. The ECHR found that the covert filming of Ismayilova's sexual activities and posting of the sex videos amounted to a "grave intrusion into her private life and an affront to her human dignity," and the blackmail letter constituted an attempt to chill her free expression. Although the evidence was insufficient to show that the Azerbaijani government was responsible for the nonconsensual recording and posting of her sexual activities as well as the blackmail attempt, the court found that the government had violated its obligation to conduct a criminal investigation of the matter. Ismayilova was awarded 15,000 euros in damages.[5]

————

US LAWMAKERS AND law enforcers have signaled that they are thinking about intimate privacy as a civil right, though principally through the lens of antidiscrimination, which is consistent with the focus of modern civil rights laws. In the wake of the COVID-19 pandemic, senators Richard Blumenthal and Mark Warner proposed a bill that would prohibit discrimination based on "emergency health data," including infection with the COVID-19 virus. The bill, framed as a "right to privacy" in emergency health data, prohibits providers of public accommodations and voting facilities from discriminating against someone based on their emergency health data; it requires them to adopt reasonable safeguards to prevent such discrimination. Though the bill was not adopted into law, its premise reflects a promising shift among federal lawmakers toward a vision of privacy as a matter of civil rights.

True to its long-standing commitment to consumer privacy, the California attorney general's office sued the fertility app Glow for failing to adequately secure subscribers' intimate information, including medications, fertility test results, sexual experiences, miscarriages, abortions, and stillbirths. For three years, the app automatically granted anyone's requests to access subscribers' accounts without ever asking them for permission, giving stalkers and strangers access to women's data. As part of its settlement with then-attorney general of California Xavier Becerra, Glow agreed to undertake an annual privacy risk assessment, which would consider the "online risks that women face, or could face, including gender-based risks, as a result of privacy and security lapses."[59] AG Becerra went a step further than New York's AG James by incorporating an assessment of gendered risks into the compliance part of the settlement agreement. Although California's settlement agreement only applied to Glow, it signaled to other fertility apps with subscribers living in California (undoubtedly most such apps) the importance of considering concerns about gender discrimination. The California AG's office turned antidiscrimination commitments into action in the Glow case, an important start.

The FTC has expressed its concern about racial and other bias replicated and spread through algorithmic decision making. In a blog post, the FTC noted that companies need to consider how uses of artificial intelligence can "inadvertently introduc[e] bias." Invoking its authority to combat unfair and deceptive practices and to enforce the Fair Credit Reporting Act and Equal Credit Opportunity Act, it urged companies to ensure that the data sets on which they train AI models aren't missing data from legally protected groups, to test algorithmic systems for biased outputs, and to ensure that their practices are not doing more harm than good.[60] In February 2021, Acting FTC chairwoman Rebecca Kelly Slaughter gave a speech in which she signaled her interest in investigating the disparate impact that privacy violations by health apps have on vulnerable communities.[61] Privacy practitioners carefully read FTC blog posts and commissioner speeches as if they are agency white papers. Those forms of soft policymaking have an impact on the advice that attorneys give to their clients, and what kinds of protections their clients implement in their products.[62]

None of these steps have the force of a comprehensive law protecting a civil right to intimate privacy, but they show that a civil rights framework aligns with policymaker thinking. If we adopted such an approach, it would bring the United States closer to the human rights approach of so many countries around the globe. Indeed, if done right, a civil rights approach could offer even stronger protections than current data protection regulations.

Ordinary Americans are coming to see privacy in this way too. A 2020 study sponsored by the consulting firm KPMG found that 97% of survey respondents said that data privacy was important to them and 87% of survey respondents characterized data privacy as a human right. A majority of survey respondents said that they did not trust companies to ethically collect, use, or sell their personal data, and wanted law to protect it.[63]

Intimate privacy deserves to be recognized as a civil right. We all need intimate privacy to flourish, grow, and love; the most vulnerable among us are now particularly disadvantaged without it. A civil right to intimate privacy is within reach. We need reform in two areas—law and norms. While each avenue has the capacity to protect intimate privacy and equality, together law and norms provide the necessary reinforcements for a lasting compact to protect intimate privacy. In the next two chapters, I lay out the legal agenda, which borrows from the US civil rights legal tradition, and then I turn to the social agenda.

7

A Comprehensive Approach
to Intimate Privacy Violations

IN THE 1960S AND 1970S, THE WOMEN'S RIGHTS MOVEMENT first had to name and describe the harms of domestic violence before reform efforts could begin. Until that time, police officers in the United States dismissed domestic violence reports as "lovers' quarrels"; victims "chose" to stay with their abusers, so there was no need to help them. The women's movement changed how we saw and understood spousal battering—as a profoundly harmful social problem. Thanks to that work, law changed, and its treatment of battered partners is better today than it was 50 years ago.[1]

Advocates and scholars faced a similar task nearly 50 years later. In 2013, when Mary Anne Franks wrote the first model nonconsensual porn statute, and in 2014, when we wrote the first law review article on the topic, a crucial part of our task was educative.[2] At the time, the nonconsensual posting of intimate images was being sensationalized as "revenge porn." We had to convince lawmakers, journalists, and the public to stop blaming victims for trusting ex-lovers with nude photos and dismissing the abuse as the revenge of jilted lovers. We took the term "revenge porn" and refashioned it as "nonconsensual pornography" to emphasize the denial of someone's sexual autonomy and the ability to display their bodies on their own terms. Back then, describing the abuse as an invasion of intimate privacy likely would not have caught lawmakers' attention in the way that framing the issue as nonconsensual porn did.

But now we are at a pivotal moment. It is time for the law to make clear that nonconsensual pornography is only one manifestation of what it means to violate a person's intimate privacy. We need legislators and courts to treat the constellation of intimate privacy violations as a single problem. In my writing and conversations with policymakers, I have been shifting the conversation to its proper place—a civil right to intimate privacy. That concept captures the breadth of the wrongs and the stakes.

I hope that one day soon, victims can safely trust that the law is on their side, that justice can be theirs, and that our legal system will protect them rather than tolerate the abuse. Civil suits can help victims obtain justice. They can recognize the wrongs and suffering that victims have endured.[3] We need the legal system to acknowledge victims' loss and pain.

The people you've been meeting in this book need the justice system to *see* them. They need to know that the wrongs that they faced and the harms that they endured matter—that *they* matter—in the eyes of the law and society. Recall that the lawyer Elisa D'Amico, whom you met in Chapter 5, has represented victims in civil actions on a pro bono basis. In one case, the defendant posted his ex-girlfriend's photos on adult sites and social media and sent her nude photos to her law school classmates. In granting a default judgment after the defendant stopped showing up, the court issued a $6.4 million damages award for, as the judge put it, conduct that "ranks among the most vile and outrageous . . . imaginable."[4] In a different nonconsensual porn case, the jury awarded the plaintiff $8.9 million; the jurors hadn't been provided with a suggested sum—they came up with that number.

In both cases, D'Amico's clients knew that the defendants could not afford to pay those sums, so practically speaking, they were judgment proof. And yet, as D'Amico explained to me, those verdicts were important to her clients. The judicial rulings and awards said to her clients that what happened to them was wrong. They allowed her clients to see themselves as fighters with rights, rather than as naïve individuals worthy of shame, blame, or pity. No longer did her clients feel alone and helpless. They felt validated. The court's explanations and the multimillion-dollar verdicts signaled the judicial system's recognition that the defendants' violations were wrong, that they inflicted corrosive injuries, and that society assigned substantial value to intimate privacy. The verdicts were a testament to the ongoing nature of each victim's ordeal. Those verdicts were worth a whole lot more than money.

We need the judicial system to work for victims, letting them sue pseudonymously and helping them obtain counsel on a pro bono basis. But we also need the judicial system to secure more than money (though money matters for what it says even if victims can't recover all of it). Victims need relief that will mitigate the damage—and civil rights laws provide guidance on that score.

REMOVING BARRIERS

Law needs to remove the barriers that have made it difficult for victims to seek justice in the courts. Reforming the rules around pseudonymous lawsuits is crucial. D'Amico's clients were permitted to sue as Jane Does in their cases, but, as we know from Chapter 5, that permission is not always granted.

Legislatures should require courts to allow (or to accord a heavy presumption in favor of allowing) plaintiffs to sue under pseudonyms in cases involving intimate privacy violations. The defendants will inevitably know who's suing them. The rest of the world does not need to read victims' names in the caption of their cases and the court docket.

The public does not need to know a plaintiff's real name to witness the work of the judicial system. This approach would better facilitate justice, and it would do so without the risk of exacerbating the harms of privacy violations.

Permission to sue under a pseudonym would not alleviate the angst that victims experience when they face the individuals who violated their intimate privacy. It won't make them feel comfortable sitting across from their attackers in a deposition or at trial. But it would signal that the judge understands the harm wrought by publicity and is trying to counteract it. It would say that the court system is on their side, that it can vindicate the civil right to intimate privacy without exacerbating its violation.

Another puzzle piece involves getting more attorneys to take on intimate privacy cases on a pro bono basis. Right now, victims lack access to good legal representation because attorneys are reluctant to take on cases if they are unlikely to get paid (recall that there are no deep pockets to sue, thanks to Section 230, and most Privacy Invaders aren't wealthy). And yet most attorneys do some form of pro bono work. Although no state requires pro bono work as a condition of a law license, some states require attorneys to report the number of pro bono hours they perform. In Florida, where D'Amico practices, lawyers must report their pro bono hours to the state bar with their membership dues. (The American Bar Association encourages at least 50 hours of pro bono work a year.)

While pro bono cases traditionally involve representing people of limited means or nonprofits serving the poor, bar associations should also urge attorneys to take cases involving the civil right to intimate privacy. K&L Gates—which spearheaded the Cyber Civil Rights Legal Project— and Foley Hoag are among the few practices that devote pro bono time to victims of intimate privacy violations. Carrie Goldberg, a noted lawyer running what is perhaps the only law firm in the United States dedicated to intimate privacy, can take on only a few cases pro bono because she must prioritize cases that will enable her and her associates to earn a living. If more attorneys take on these cases, they can mentor others to do the same, creating a virtuous cycle of lawyers ready to put the tort system to work on behalf of victims who currently feel that nothing and no one will help them.

Whenever I give talks about my work on intimate privacy, students come to me afterwards to ask how they can get involved. They want to help victims, but financial constraints and their firms' policies on pro bono cases limit their ability to volunteer their time. If state bar associations encouraged pro bono hours devoted to intimate privacy cases and if law school clinics were created to address online abuse (right now, I can count on one hand the number of law schools doing that work), then we could harness that enthusiasm to help the civil justice system work for victims.

GETTING VICTIMS WHAT THEY WANT

Law should help victims get what they often most urgently want—the removal of their intimate images (whether real or manufactured). Plaintiffs should be able to obtain what is called "injunctive relief"—where courts order parties to *do* something. Injunctive relief in the form of a court order *directing the removal, blocking, or de-linking of intimate images* would not undo the damage already done, but would thwart further harm.

Court orders to remove, block, or de-link nonconsensual intimate images—what we can call intimate privacy injunctions—would have practical and expressive value. They would halt violations from continuing without end. They would relegate intimate privacy violations to the past, rather than letting them live online in perpetuity. They would thwart future harm, though they could not undo past harms. Intimate privacy injunctions would allow victims to reclaim their bodies and to be seen as their whole selves. They would ensure that online platforms treat victims with the respect that they deserve, rather than as purveyors of their exploitation. They would change the social meaning of sites devoted to nonconsensual intimate images. Privacy injunctions would establish that those sites are not lawless zones where intimate privacy can be violated.[5]

What plaintiffs urgently want—injunctive relief—is the cornerstone of civil rights remedies.[6] We can look to the different ways that courts have ordered defendants to fix violations of the Americans with Disabilities Act. Courts have ordered stores to rearrange furniture, so wheelchair users have equal access to their services.[7] They have required businesses to fix their websites, so people with visual disabilities can use them on equal terms.[8]

Lawmakers would need to, first, recognize that courts have the power to order injunctive relief for intimate privacy violations, and second, amend Section 230, so that content platforms and search engines can be sued for such relief. We need legislation that recognizes the judiciary's power to order the removal of nonconsensual intimate images (real or fake). Courts are often reluctant to grant injunctive relief without clear legislative permission.[9] Given the way that the First Amendment works, as I will discuss below, such legislation should exempt intimate images related to matters of public concern, which would accommodate free speech concerns.

Lawmakers don't have to reinvent the wheel. Some interesting ideas have been percolating. For instance, the Uniform Law Commission proposed the Uniform Civil Remedies for Unauthorized Disclosure of Intimate Images Act, or UDII Act. Under that proposal, victims can seek injunctive relief and reasonable attorneys' fees and costs for the nonconsensual posting of intimate images except when images concern a matter of public interest.[10] In 2021, Arkansas, Iowa, South Dakota, Nebraska, and Colorado adopted the UDII Act into law.[11] We would need to extend the provisions of the UDII Act to all violations of intimate privacy, including manufactured intimate images like deepfake sex videos.

New York Civil Rights Law provides another helpful template. Under Section 51 of that law (which is a statutory codification of the misappropriation tort discussed in Chapter 5), "any person whose name, portrait, picture, or voice is used . . . for advertising purposes or for the purposes of trade without [their] written consent" may sue to "restrain the use" of their "name, portrait, picture, or voice." Under my reform agenda, the law would have to cover all intimate privacy violations, not just instances where an intimate image is used for commercial purposes.[12] A compelling feature of Section 51 is that it applies to instances when individuals have not provided their *written consent* for the use of their intimate images. Lawmakers should incorporate that feature into the law. Written consent is practically feasible and crucially important. Sites could offer drop-down screens that would allow posters to upload the written permission that they received to post the subject's intimate image. Written consent—if obtained under noncoercive circumstances—would signal that the subject of the image considered and agreed to have their image disclosed. It is qualitatively different from presumed consent, the coin of the realm in the consumer protection approach to privacy, explored in Chapter 5, which says little to nothing about what the plaintiff in fact knows and agrees to.

Courts have granted injunctive relief in cases brought under Section 51 involving fake nude portraits of celebrities. Famed boxer Muhammad Ali sued *Playgirl* magazine for publishing a portrait of a nude Black man sitting in the corner of a boxing ring with the tag line "The Greatest," Ali's catch phrase. A trial court ordered the magazine to stop selling copies of the magazine with Ali's fake nude portrait. The court explained that Ali had a right to be let alone to protect his "sentiments, thoughts, and feelings" from "unwanted commercial exploitation."[13]

To ensure the effectiveness of an order for injunctive relief, Congress would need to amend Section 230. I lay out my broader reform proposal for Section 230 in the next chapter, but for now, let me describe a modest fix that would accompany that proposal. As it stands, the statute's legal shield effectively negates any remedies, even ones that are easy and inexpensive to administer and that significantly improve victims' situations.

Setting the wrong example for other courts, the California Supreme Court ruled that Section 230 effectively excused an online platform from complying with a court order to remove content found to have been posted illegally by one of its users.[14]

Congress should amend Section 230 to make clear that platforms and search engines can be sued for injunctive relief in the form of deleting, blocking, or de-linking intimate images that have been published without written consent. The amendment should allow plaintiffs to recover attorney's fees, which would increase the likelihood that lawyers will take their cases. When online platforms and search engines can be sued for injunctive relief and attorney's fees, lawyers gain access to deep pockets from which to recover those fees.

Legal recognition of injunctive relief would bring US law into alignment with the GDPR's Article 17, which enables individuals to request that "irrelevant" personal information be deleted or removed, and Article 9, which "prohibits the processing of personal data revealing" information about a person's sex life or sexual orientation without explicit consent. European Commissioner for Justice, Fundamental Rights, and Citizenship Viviane Reding said of this right: "If an individual no longer wants his personal data to be processed or stored by a data controller, and if there is no legitimate reason for keeping it, the data should be removed from their system."[15]

Before the GDPR went into force in 2018, the Court of Justice of the European Union (CJEU) had already recognized a "right to be forgotten." In 2010, Mario Costeja González complained to the Spanish data protection authority after a local newspaper and Google refused to remove a ten-year-old story about his personal bankruptcy, which had been resolved. The Spanish DPA rejected the complaint about the newspaper as inconsistent with free expression, but treated Google differently. The office ordered Google to remove links to the story in searches of the man's name.

The CJEU endorsed that position, finding that search results have a unique and significant impact on the "fundamental right to privacy." It ruled that search engines can be ordered to remove links to articles from search results if those articles contain information that is outdated, and the public does not have an interest in learning about the information. Search engines considering requests should strike a fair balance between an individual's right to privacy, including the sensitivity of the information, and the public's interest in that information.[16] In a subsequent decision, the CJEU found that search engines do not have to apply the right to be forgotten globally.[17] Google has developed geo-blocking technology that prevents links to articles from being included in searches conducted in the European Union.[18] (Presumably, that technology could be applied to other regions and nations.) My proposal would only apply to privacy violations involving intimate images. By contrast, the European approach applies more broadly to *any* outdated and "irrelevant" personal information like Gonzalez's 10-year-old bankruptcy.

Of course, a court order for one site to remove a plaintiff's intimate image would not automatically apply to a different site. If intimate images are removed from one site and perpetrators put them up on others, victims can show those sites the court order as proof of the legitimacy of their claims. Sites might honor those requests given the likelihood that plaintiffs might sue them for injunctive relief and attorney's fees. If those sites refused, victims would need to file a new lawsuit for injunctive relief. So, this approach is not perfect, but after talking to victims, it is a valuable response. Victims want to have a sense that the law will help them mitigate their damage, and this approach will do that. We can't let the perfect be the enemy of the good.

Victims also deserve a chance to obtain monetary relief that meaningfully captures the harms that they have suffered. We can reform the privacy torts to do that. The original vision of the privacy tort, set forth by Warren and Brandeis, provides inspiration for courts and lawmakers. Warren and Brandeis called for a right to determine whether and how we reveal our intimate lives to others. We should shift away from the four privacy torts to a broader focus on the "right to privacy."

Vindicating the "right to privacy" would allow courts to flexibly apply the privacy torts to disclosures of intimate data to small groups of people and intrusions on people's privacy in public. Privacy harms can be equally, if not more, profound when intimate images are exposed to smaller groups of people who matter to us—our colleagues, our family members—as when they divulge our intimate selves to the broader public. And they can be equally, if not more, profound when our right to intimate privacy is invaded in public, as is true for up-skirt or down-shirt photos. Just because we are out in public does not mean that we have exposed every part of ourselves to public inspection.

We also need to provide meaningful redress for the privacy harms suffered. Recall Annie Seifullah, the high school principal you met in Chapter 2 who lost her job after her boyfriend stole her sexually explicit photos from her laptop and shared them with her employer and the press. The New York Department of Education fired her, blaming her for failing to prevent the release of the images. Seifullah should have been able to recover for the discrimination harms that she suffered due to her ex's privacy violations. The privacy torts should provide recourse for the harm to equality. Intimate privacy violations entrench patterns of subordination that disadvantage women and minorities. Stigma, especially regarding nudity and sexual activities impacts the job market for women, nonwhites, and LGBTQ individuals. Victims need the privacy torts to redress those harms.

Now to explore reforms to the criminal law.

RETHINKING CRIMINAL JUSTICE

Discussions of the criminal law must begin by acknowledging the pathologies that beset the operation of the criminal justice system. In theory, criminal law deters wrongdoing and signals that society thinks the defendants' actions are wrong (those are important ways to view criminal law's role). But in practice, its burdens disproportionately fall on the shoulders of nonwhites—especially Black individuals—due to discriminatory attitudes and practices. As civil rights scholar Michelle Alexander has shown in her groundbreaking work, mass incarceration of Black men is "this century's Jim Crow."[19] My proposals should not protect intimate privacy at the overall expense of equality, at least not if I have anything to say about it. For that reason, I write cautiously about criminal law reforms, lest their enforcement—if such enforcement materializes—disproportionately fall on the shoulders of Black individuals and people of color due to invidious attitudes.

Another difficulty, one that might seem contradictory at first, lies at the intersection of race and gender. Criminal law is woefully under-enforced when the illegality involves *gendered harms* like privacy violations and sexual assault where the victims are mostly female and LGBTQ individuals. Here, again, troubling attitudes are to blame. Also, as my work and experience suggests, defendants who have been prosecuted have tended to be nonwhite men or women, which likely has far more to do with invidious attitudes than who is responsible for violations of intimate privacy. (We don't have empirical studies on this point—and we need them.)

In an ideal world, the criminal law would help deter intimate privacy violations and educate the public about the wrongfulness of this behavior. It would make clear to potential perpetrators that intimate privacy violations are so serious that they warrant criminal punishment and the potential deprivation of their liberty. The criminal law, if enforced, would tell victims that they were wronged in a way that society thinks warrants criminal punishment. It would send the message that society is harmed when anyone's intimate privacy is violated. I want us to live in that world.[20]

To help us get there, we need to educate law enforcement officers about the seriousness of intimate privacy violations, so that victims are not dismissed and their suffering is not trivialized. We need to teach them about existing laws and available technologies to investigate intimate privacy violations, so that they can follow up on victims' complaints. We need to teach them about implicit bias, which leads to prosecutions of defendants who are disproportionately Black or nonwhite. We should not replicate the pathologies that make the criminal justice system unjust as we pursue a more just world where intimate privacy is protected.

If we worked to address those pathologies, how might we fix the criminal law? The criminal law has moved in fits and starts to address intimate privacy violations. In seven years, we have gone from three state laws criminalizing nonconsensual porn to 48 states, plus the District of Columbia and Guam, and a bipartisan federal bill. As of 2022, California, Hawaii, New York, and Virginia criminalized the disclosure of digitally manipulated intimate images and videos.

The first task is for the criminal law to treat the constellation of intimate privacy violations as a *single problem*. The piecemeal approach is conceptually flawed—it fails to recognize and tackle the full breadth of the wrongs and injuries at hand. The second task is clarifying the scope of criminal law's application to intimate privacy violations. The criminal law should focus on intimate privacy violations involving the nonconsensual photographing, filming, recording, digital fabrication, exploitation, extortion, sending, or disclosure of intimate images. Why just images? Because of the lasting destruction wrought by intimate images. Images make it nearly impossible to forget violations of intimate privacy. The very notion that they might exist, that they might be seen, shared, or displayed, haunts victims. Intimate images ruin people's life opportunities. They tell other people that they are next. The grave damage to victims, groups, and society warrants criminal sanctions.

The law should include enhanced penalties for bias-motivated privacy violations. This would draw attention to the structural impact of the abuse and signal that the eradication of stigma, shame, and discrimination is a central legislative goal.[21] Along these lines, the DOJ urges federal prosecutors to seek hate crime penalty enhancements for defendants who electronically harass victims because of their race, gender, sexual orientation, or religion.[22] We see moves in that direction in the United Kingdom. The Law Commission, an independent body that advises the government about the laws in England and Wales, is considering whether sex or gender should be considered protected characteristics under hate crime laws.[23]

To ensure that criminal laws provide clear notice about what is unlawful and do not chill innocent behavior, they should apply only if a defendant knew or was reckless as to the fact that the subject of the intimate images did not consent to the privacy violation at issue; and only if intimate images do not relate to issues of legitimate public concern, such as when they show public officials engaged in criminal activity. When Anthony Weiner was running in the New York City mayoral race, he allegedly sent a photo of his crotch to an underage girl and encouraged her to do the same, which would amount to the solicitation of child pornography. Those photos, if posted online, might be of interest to the public, though we don't need to see his genitals (they should be blurred) for the public to appreciate the nature of his misconduct.[24]

Criminal penalties should be calibrated to reflect the conduct's wrongfulness. Intimate privacy violations should be treated as felonies. This would be a significant change in the law. Most states treat intimate privacy violations as misdemeanors, which means that the laws are hardly enforced. The possibility of significant prison time would be a more effective deterrent, and it would have a powerful expressive impact. It would also give law enforcers a reason to spend resources on investigations.

Without question, some circumstances deserve higher penalties than others. Recall that the hotel employee who secretly taped Joan as she showered, which constituted video voyeurism, tried to extort more nude images from her, which constituted attempted sextortion, and then he retaliated by posting the videos online when she refused to give in to his sextortion, which constituted nonconsensual pornography. The employee violated Joan's intimate privacy in three different ways, and he posted the video of her showering on countless sites—whenever one was taken down, he would repost the video on the same site or other sites. If he were prosecuted (recall that FBI agents dropped their investigation after saying that they could not identify the perpetrator) and convicted, his sentence should then reflect the compounded and aggravated nature of his violations.

FIRST AMENDMENT OBJECTIONS

These proposals will face objections on First Amendment grounds, but none of the objections are likely to succeed. Some argue that because data privacy laws regulate "speech," they are inconsistent with First Amendment doctrine. Free speech scholar Leslie Kendrick has described these "everything is speech" arguments as "First Amendment expansionism"— the tendency to treat speech as normatively significant no matter the speech in question. Free speech is a "term of art that does not refer to all speech activities, but rather designates some area of activity that society takes, for some reason, to have special importance."[25]

Rules governing the filming, recording, or otherwise collecting of intimate images or information raise few, if any, First Amendment concerns because they separate the public sphere from the private. Trespass laws, intrusion on seclusion, and video voyeurism laws have withstood constitutional challenges. Computer hackers cannot avoid criminal penalties by insisting that they were only trying to obtain information that the public would benefit from knowing about. Even the media enjoys no privilege against the application of trespass laws in their efforts to collect newsworthy information.

What about the argument that the disclosure of intimate images involves the discloser's speech so it can't be the basis of civil remedies or criminal penalties? When the government regulates speech based on the

content of that speech, it usually must satisfy what is called "strict scrutiny review." Strict scrutiny is a difficult standard to meet because government should not be in the business of picking winning and losing ideas.
Laws can satisfy that tough standard if they serve a compelling interest
that cannot be promoted through less restrictive means.

Criminal laws banning nonconsensual pornography, crafted with
the help of Franks and the support of CCRI, have faced constitutional challenge and survived the crucible of strict scrutiny review.
The Vermont Supreme Court upheld the state's nonconsensual pornography statute. The court emphasized that "[f]rom a constitutional
perspective, it is hard to see a distinction between laws prohibiting
nonconsensual disclosure of personal information comprising images
of nudity and sexual conduct and those prohibiting the disclosure of
other categories of nonpublic personal information" like health data.[26]
The supreme courts of Illinois, Minnesota, and Indiana upheld their
states' nonconsensual pornography statutes on the grounds that the
statutes were justified by the compelling governmental interest in preventing the "permanent and severe" harms posed by nonconsensual
intimate images and that the statutes were narrowly tailored to serve
that interest.[27]

The First Amendment would preclude prosecutions if the public
would have a legitimate interest in seeing nonconsensual intimate images.
To be clear, though, the fact that the public is interested in someone's
intimate images does not turn those images into matters of legitimate
public interest. That is true both for private individuals whose intimate
lives are not under public inspection and celebrities whose intimate lives
are public obsessions.

Consider a case involving a sex video made by a celebrity couple, Bret
Michaels and Pamela Anderson Lee. A federal district court ordered an
online adult subscription service to stop distributing the sex video, which
the couple had never consented to being made public. The court ruled
that the public had no legitimate interest in graphic depictions of the

"most intimate aspects of" a celebrity couple's relationship. "Sexual relations are among the most private of private affairs"; a video of two people
having sex "represents the deepest possible intrusion into such affairs,"
noted the court in 1998.[28]

On the other hand, voters have a right to learn about intimate information that sheds light on the credibility, trustworthiness, and fitness
of political candidates or officeholders. We can look to former congresswoman Katie Hill's claims against the *Daily Mail* for publishing nude
images of her with her female lover, a former campaign staffer, and an
image of her with a bong in her hand. The *Daily Mail*, a major media gossip outlet, asked a California court to dismiss the lawsuit against it, arguing that its publication of the photos involved a matter of public interest
that superseded Hill's privacy interest. The court dismissed Hill's suit
because, it reasoned, the photos shed light on Hill's fitness for office given
her possible recreational drug use and affair with a campaign staffer. The
court rejected Hill's argument that publishing the photos was a gratu-
itous invasion of her privacy with little upside for public discourse.[29] I
am with Hill—the public did not need to *see* her nude photos to have a
conversation about her private activities, and the *Daily Mail* should not
have published them; but that is not the way that the court assessed the
competing rights at hand.

What about the First Amendment implications for the regulation
of fake intimate images? First Amendment doctrine classifies harm-
causing lies as unprotected speech. Federal and state laws punish certain impersonations of government officials consistent with the First
Amendment. Those types of lies, free speech scholar Helen Norton has
observed, concern the "source of the speech." Lies of this kind—about
who is speaking—can be proscribed because they threaten significant
harm to listeners who rely on them as a proxy for reliability and credibility. These laws are largely uncontroversial as a First Amendment
matter because they "address real (if often intangible) harm to the public as well as to the individual target."[30] The regulation of deepfake sex

videos concerns whether someone was in fact engaged in pornography, an objectively verifiable determination.

Intimate privacy protections and free speech are not at odds, but instead reinforce each other. The reform proposals laid out here would make it more likely for people to express themselves, fall in love, reveal themselves to others as they truly are, and experiment in vast and sundry ways. Without strong protection for intimate privacy, private expression will be chilled. Victims will not be inclined to engage in sexual expression. In *Bartnicki v. Vopper*, the Supreme Court noted that the "fear of public disclosure of private conversations might well have a chilling effect on private speech."[31] The reforms suggested in this chapter would combat that possibility.

8

The Duties of Data Guardians

LAWS AIMED AT INDIVIDUALS ARE NECESSARY BUT NOT SUFFI-
cient to protect the civil right to intimate privacy. The second part of a
legal compact to protect intimate privacy involves the duties of private
companies and government entities.

Every year, the International Conference of Data Protection and
Privacy Commissioners brings together 100 data protection authorities
(DPAs) from more than 70 countries. At the fortieth conference held in
Brussels in 2018, Apple CEO Tim Cook gave a keynote speech, a first
for a corporate executive at the conference. According to Cook, his company shared the DPAs' view of privacy as a "fundamental human right."
Honoring that right meant that companies had to "design and develop"
technologies "to serve humankind, and not the other way around," and
to treat personal data "like the precious cargo that it is." That might mean
not collecting personal data, he explained. Cook condemned businesses
"weaponizing against us . . . our likes and dislikes, our friends and families, our relationships and conversations."[1]

Cook's message was that companies should act as the guardians of our personal data.[2] The DPAs in the audience likely agreed with the sentiment, given their nations' privacy commitments under various human rights treaties. But Cook wasn't just preaching to the choir. He was sending a message to US companies whose products and services optimize data collection and exploitation: intimate privacy is a fundamental right deserving robust and complete protection.

Historically, US civil rights laws have focused on the responsibilities of entities in charge of physical spaces—schools, workplaces, hotels, public transportation, voting booths—where people were guaranteed an equal chance to learn, work, travel, and cast their ballots.[3] Now, to guarantee the civil right to intimate privacy, civil rights laws must lay out the duties of entities in control of virtual platforms and personal data.[4]

Congress should start by reforming Section 230 and its overbroad judicial interpretation that frees content platforms from legal responsibility. On Capitol Hill, the commitment to blanket immunity is no longer airtight. Politicians across the ideological spectrum have called for reform. Some believe, as senators Brian Schatz and Mark Warner do, that content platforms leave up too much destructive speech, while others like senators Josh Hawley and Ted Cruz criticize content platforms for taking down too much conservative-leaning speech. (If you had told me in 2009, or even in 2017, that congressional committees would someday take my reform proposals seriously, I would not have believed you—my suggestions were rejected as heretical to a "free" internet.) Let me explain the approach that I have been pitching to federal legislators.

Rather than getting rid of Section 230, we should focus on fixing its under-filtering provision, Section 230(c)(1). That provision shields platforms from liability if they publish or otherwise host user-generated content, no matter how destructive, with no conditions on that immunity. Recall, as discussed in Chapter 5, that the over-filtering provision, Section 230(c)(2), conditions its legal shield for removing or filtering user-generated content on "good faith" efforts. That provision should stay as it is—it effectively restates "the right of non-government actors to restrict, ignore, or refuse to associate with other people's speech."[5]

Section 230(c)(1) should be amended to reserve the immunity for platforms acting like responsible guardians of our intimate privacy. In 2017, national security expert and Lawfare founder Benjamin Wittes and I teamed up to write statutory language that federal lawmakers could use to reform that provision. As we proposed, Section 230 should condition the under-filtering legal shield on a showing that a content platform had taken "*reasonable steps to address unlawful uses of its service that clearly create serious harm to others.*" The concept of illegality or unlawfulness refers to activities that would violate existing laws.

To secure the immunity, a platform would have to convince a judge at the outset of a case (in what is called a "motion to dismiss") that it had taken reasonable steps to address the specific type or types of illegality of which the plaintiffs were complaining. The issue would not be whether the platform acted reasonably in a specific case, but rather if, as a general matter, it had been acting reasonably to address the type of illegality at issue.[6] The proposal would encourage platforms to adopt reasonable content moderation practices writ large, along the lines of the Good Samaritan blocking and filtering imagined by Cox and Wyden when they drafted Section 230.

When I presented our reasonable steps approach before the House Permanent Select Committee on Intelligence in 2019, Congressman Devin Nunes asked me to respond to the objection that reasonableness was a vague and unworkable standard. As I explained, reasonableness would require evidence of a site's content moderation practices, but a reasonableness approach is neither unclear nor impractical.[7] Reasonableness is the lifeblood of the law, including civil rights law. Since the passage of the Americans with Disabilities Act in 1990, judges have assessed if hotels, schools, and workplaces have provided "reasonable accommodations" for disabled individuals. Courts have determined the reasonableness of practices in various fields, including tort law and the Fourth Amendment's ban on "unreasonable searches and seizures." They are not only adept at developing different standards for different contexts, but they are also skilled and experienced in adapting those standards to changing technologies and evolving wrongs and harms.[8]

When it comes to the reasonableness of content moderation practices, decision-makers won't have to design the practices from scratch because norms in this field have been evolving. In my more than ten years of working with tech companies, I have witnessed firsthand, and played a role in developing, best practices for content moderation. An entire industry is now devoted to content moderation; it has a professional organization, the Trust and Safety Professional Association, that provides guidance on these norms. These norms are advisory right now—no one can enforce them due to Section 230. But if we adopt my reform proposal, then they would provide guidance on the question of whether platforms acted reasonably to address intimate privacy violations or other types of illegality.

In revising Section 230, Congress should include illustrations of reasonable steps to address illegality online. Some norms are well established and widely applicable. For instance, platforms should have clear policies about the kinds of speech activity and conduct that they don't tolerate, and those policies should be continually updated to account for evolving threats and illegality that they are seeing on their platforms. They should clearly explain their policies, including what activities are prohibited, why they are prohibited, and how certain actions violate those policies. When platforms discover that their services are being used for illegal activities causing serious harm, then they should respond with a plan of action designed to combat such illegality. They should provide easy-to-use methods by which users can report policy violations. They should have established processes to address reports of policy violations. They should hire people to oversee content moderation and regularly train those content moderators about their policies. They should consider using technologies that help them flag or remove certain types of illegal content, bearing in mind that AI and other machine-learning techniques are more accurate in some contexts than in others. (See Chapter 9 for more about algorithmic moderation.) They should have clear channels of accountability where their responses to reports of abuse are explained. Upon receiving notice that victims intend to sue perpetrators, platforms should retain identifying information, such as IP addresses of posters. They should issue regular transparency bulletins that disclose to the public the number of reports about different types of illegality that they have received and the resolution of those reports.[9]

Although basic norms around transparency and accountability are clear, the details are not, and that is a good thing. The reasonable steps approach is valuable precisely because it is flexible. As technology and content moderation practices evolve, so, too, will the reasonableness and efficacy of certain policies and practices. As new kinds of privacy violations inevitably emerge, so will new strategies for tackling them. A reasonable steps approach pressures platforms to keep up with best practices—and even pushes them to devise innovative strategies—instead of sitting on their laurels. As *Wired* technology writer and lawyer Gilad Edelman noted in commending our recommendation, a reasonable steps approach would encourage companies to "get rich by making the internet less toxic."[10]

A reasonable steps approach wouldn't just benefit Americans facing intimate privacy violations. Recall that nonconsensual intimate image sites hosted in the United States can be viewed around the globe; the hosted images can feature people from every nation and region. Incentives to take reasonable steps would mean that sites would have legal reasons to respond to reported instances of nonconsensual intimate images. They might be less inclined to get into the business of nonconsensual intimate images because they would have to internalize the costs that they currently externalize.

Some argue that the reasonable steps approach favors the dominant platforms because they already have content moderation policies, processes, and staff in place and can afford to update their practices, whereas startups would struggle to pay for any of it. It is a fair point, but it over-looks the fact that a reasonable steps approach anticipates differentiation between online actors. A site with a handful of comments a day is differently situated than a dating app with thousands a day—what is a reasonable approach for one may not be what is reasonable for the other. A large social network faces different types of illegality and challenges than a small specialty humor site—what is reasonable for the former will be different from what is reasonable for the latter.

Sites that solicit nonconsensual intimate images and ignore victims' requests to remove their intimate images would not be able to show that they took reasonable steps to address intimate privacy violations (they are instigators, after all). Any objective view of their activities would find that they were not acting as responsible guardians—they would not receive immunity from liability. (Of course, the loss of the legal shield would not mean that platforms would be automatically liable—plaintiffs would have to bring cognizable claims against them and prove those claims.) By contrast, platforms that not only have policies that are transparent, tailored to particular illegality, and reasonably executed for their size and type of business but that follow practices that include effective modes of accountability should enjoy immunity from liability.

An alternative approach is a notice-and-takedown regime, which we see in the copyright arena under the Digital Millennium Copyright Act. I've been hesitant about that approach because platforms would be incentivized to do one thing and one thing only—to remove content after it has been reported, end of story (and responsibility). The law instead should obligate platforms to spend resources developing reasonable steps to address different types of illegality causing serious harms. Deleting content may be important, but it isn't everything; a notice-and-takedown regime would not obligate platforms to develop best practices, whether policies or technological approaches, to protect intimate privacy. It would not encourage sites to adopt solutions to protect victims, including preventing the posting of intimate privacy violations in the first place.

Critics argue that my Section 230 reform proposal would inevitably undermine free expression. But, as my research and work has shown, the status quo chills valuable speech. By doing nothing, we are saying that we are fine with intimate privacy violations that chase victims offline and inhibit their self-expression. A reasonable steps approach would reduce the opportunities for perpetrators to silence individuals with intimate privacy violations. It would encourage people to speak by making clear that companies have a duty to protect against illegality, rather than a free reign to monetize it. As legal scholar and social scientist Jonathon Penney and I have been studying, Section 230 reform has great potential to free us to speak.

Along similar lines, some argue that tech companies should not be making any decisions about online content because that power lets them censor speech that they do not like (as senators Cruz and Hawley have argued). In their view, social media platforms should be required to treat all content alike, as a telephone company does—hands off. But I am confident that you would not want to visit sites or join social networks under those circumstances. Without content moderation, they would be awash in spam, hate speech, and online abuse. (And the First Amendment likely would prevent law from prohibiting most private platforms from deciding what kinds of speech that they want to associate with.)

We can learn valuable lessons from our experience with Title VII of the Civil Rights Act of 1964. When courts began recognizing claims under Title VII for sexually hostile work environments in the late 1970s, employers argued that the cost of liability would ruin the free-flowing conversations and camaraderie of workspaces. History has taught us otherwise. Rather than chilling discussions amongst colleagues, Title VII has meant that workplace speech has thrived on- and offline. Thanks to Title VII, there is now less abuse to silence vulnerable people and thus more expression. Although we still have a way to go, we have come a long way in the past (nearly) 60 years. The same should be true for virtual spaces.

Consider what would have happened had a reasonable steps approach been adopted at the time Matthew Herrick (whom you met in Chapter 5) sued Grindr for the app's defective design. Recall that the company could not block abusers of its services—not even Herrick's ex, who incessantly impersonated him and posted his nude photos. Grindr designed its platform so it could not ban users, and it affirmatively chose not to change this aspect of its design, which would have been straightforward to do. Even smaller dating apps like Scruff have the capacity to ban bad actors. Grindr seemingly had no processes in place to respond to complaints about abuse. Of course, a judge also would have considered evidence offered by Grindr showing that it took reasonable steps to deal with privacy violations. But we never got to that question. Because of Section 230, Herrick's suit was dismissed before Grindr even had to answer his claims.

We are seeing parallel reform efforts in the United Kingdom. Under the UK's proposed Online Safety Bill, online services hosting user-generated content would have a "duty of care" to improve online safety. The bill would require online platforms to have appropriate systems and processes in place to protect users, including clear terms of service, mechanisms for accountability, and regularly issued transparency reports. Companies' duties of care would be tailored to their size and activities. The country's communications regulator, the Office of Communications (Ofcom), could issue fines of up to 10% of a company's annual global turnover; courts could order offending companies to cease operations in the United Kingdom.[11] If passed, the bill would apply to US tech companies providing services and apps to UK citizens. To return to Grindr, it would surely risk fines if it did nothing to address complaints from UK subscribers facing harmful impersonation and privacy violations on the app (similar to its mistreatment of Herrick). The European Commission's proposed Digital Services Act has similar provisions.[12]

Congress could move in this direction by giving a federal agency the authority to issue guidance on the reasonable steps approach that I have suggested. An expert agency would have the virtue of speaking in one voice versus the judiciary's many voices. It might issue guidance more quickly than courts, which depend upon plaintiffs to bring lawsuits; defendants to move to dismiss; and rulings on what constitutes reasonable steps in particular contexts and whether defendants meet the standard.[13] Courts could rely on the agency's guidance in assessing motions to dismiss, which would reduce the time and cost of litigation. The FTC would be a wise choice—the agency's career staff are some of the smartest and most dedicated privacy professionals in the country. The FTC has been ably providing guidance on reasonable data security practices through reports, press releases, blog posts, and enforcement actions under its UDAP authority.[14] Congress would need to commit to providing sufficient resources so the FTC could hire staff and technologists to formulate and—crucially—revise reasonable steps approaches, tailored to parties of certain sizes, subscriber populations, and types of illegality at hand. Right now, the FTC has 1,000 overtaxed employees with extensive privacy, fraud, and antitrust duties.

Section 230 reform is critical, but Congress must do more. It should adopt comprehensive federal privacy legislation to protect the right to intimate privacy.

COMPREHENSIVE FEDERAL PRIVACY LAW

Congress should adopt privacy legislation that obligates entities to act as data guardians. Rather than trying to cover every possible basis for reform, I suggest four critical rules that can be fleshed out and supplemented. My recommendations provide the foundation for treating entities as data guardians.

Under the first rule (Rule #1), entities may not collect intimate data (data about our bodies, health, sex, gender, sexual orientation, close relationships, online searches, reading habits, and private communications) unless doing so would serve a legitimate purpose (a core fair information practice principle) and would not pose a significant risk to intimate privacy. Under Rule #1, intimate data should not be collected if the risks to intimate privacy outweigh the potential benefits. Rule #1 would apply to private and public entities. It would rein in the massive over-collection of intimate data without substantially impeding valuable activity.

Limiting the handling of personal data to protect civil rights and civil liberties is a well-trod path. The Supreme Court ruled, in 1958, that the Alabama legislature could not require a local NAACP chapter to produce its membership list given the risk of bigoted harassment of the group's members, including "economic reprisal, loss of employment, threat of physical coercion, and other manifestations of public hostility." The state's demand—the collection of the group's membership list— would have deterred people from joining the NAACP, chilling their constitutionally protected right to free association.[15] The Privacy Act of 1974 bans federal agencies from collecting personal data related exclusively to someone's First Amendment activities.[16] Under the Genetic Information Nondiscrimination Act of 2008, employers cannot ask job applicants for their genetic histories given the risk of discrimination.[17]

Sites hosting nonconsensual intimate images would have a straightforward answer. Simply put, they don't have a legitimate business reason to host intimate images. Rule #1 would present a categorical ban to the collection of intimate images that have been obtained or shared without consent.

Of course, not every situation has such obvious answers. Recall Chapter 1's sex toy companies, whose apps collect video recordings and texts that subscribers share with each other. Those companies might have a legitimate reason to collect the private communications (say, to give subscribers the option of reliving those communications), but the risk to intimate privacy is undoubtedly significant. If the companies fail to protect the confidentiality of those communications, people might lose their jobs, face blackmail, and refrain from sexual expression in the future.

There is a strong argument that those private communications should not be collected on the grounds that the risks to intimate privacy are not worth the benefits. If individuals want to store the communications on their phones or computers, they are free to do so.

What if some people want sex toy companies to store private communications, despite those risks? Anita Allen has explored the legitimacy of laws that enforce what she calls "unpopular privacy." As an example of a privacy law that might not be popular with its intended beneficiaries (minors), Allen points to the federal Children's Online Privacy Protection Act (COPPA). Under COPPA, children under 13 years of age can't consent to the disclosure of their information online; only their parents and guardians can make that choice. The law's position is that privacy is "too important to be left to the judgment of minors." In Allen's view, COPPA rightfully protects the long-term autonomy and dignity of minors, even if it arbitrarily draws the line at 13 years of age.[18]

Rule #1 is morally and legally justified, even if it might be unpopular with some people. Entities should not collect intimate data if it does not serve a legitimate purpose and poses a significant risk to intimate privacy, even if some people would prefer such collection. This rule would reduce the incidence of data breaches leaking intimate data to blackmailers, extorters, and reputation destroyers. It would cut down on discriminatory uses of intimate data. The bottom line is that when the benefits of data collection are small and the long-term risks are grave, entities should not collect intimate data.

State and federal governments would be bound by Rule #1. Federal agencies already face some restraints on the collection of personal data. Under the Privacy Act of 1974, every federal agency must "maintain in its records only such information about individuals as is relevant and necessary to accomplish a purpose of the agency," as required by law or Executive Order of the President.[19] Courts have recognized a constitutional right to information privacy when governments have inappropriately disclosed individuals' intimate data.[20] In the only decision on that point that

I could find, a court held that a police department violated a female job applicant's constitutional right to information privacy in demanding to know if she ever had an abortion because it had no connection to a "legitimate state interest."[21]

Let's consider the impact of Rule #1 on state regulations related to publicly funded health care. Recall from Chapter 2 the nurse's demand to know about Erica's past abortions, rapes, and prostitution as a condition of publicly funded prenatal care. Rule #1 would call into question the New York State regulation requiring the collection of that data. Courts would assess if the collection of that intimate data serves a legitimate governmental purpose without posing a significant risk to intimate privacy. There, the risk to intimate privacy was profound—the state's data collection profoundly damaged human dignity in suggesting that poor women like Erica typically have such histories. And it wasn't clear that the state's goals—notably, a healthy pregnancy—would be advanced by the collection of that information.

The second rule (Rule #2) restricts the private collection of intimate *and* non-intimate data. Under that rule, businesses may only collect personal data if, first, it would serve a legitimate business purpose that isn't outweighed by a significant risk to intimate privacy, and second, those businesses have secured individuals' meaningful consent to collect their data.

The gold standard of consent, borrowed from bioethics, is informed, voluntary, and clearly manifested. To inform individuals, requests for consent must explain what data will be collected, how it will be used, with whom it will be shared, and how long it will be retained. The risks must be laid out in concrete and vivid language. To be voluntary, requests must be as easy to reject as they are to accept.[22] Crucially, "take it or leave it" requests are not voluntary. People must be able to say no and still be able to use the service (presumably, at some charge) unless the service cannot be provided without the collection of that data. People must convey their permission in a clear and unmistakable manner.

How is it possible to convey a real choice if we are constantly bombarded by requests? If people click "I Agree" just to get rid of the question, then they are not conveying their wishes; they are yielding to the pressure of being hassled. You might recall that as soon as the EU's data protection regulation went into effect in May 2018, you were inundated with emails from companies letting you know that they were collecting your data and asking you to click a box. No doubt, you clicked because you wanted to clear your inbox, not because you really agreed to the handling of your data. No doubt, meaningful consent at scale is hard. But where there is a will, companies will find a way. Much as my Section 230 reform proposal would hopefully result in companies getting rich by innovating to make the internet less toxic, as *Wired*'s Edelman put it, companies would also develop solutions for meaningful consent. I am all for that.

Why include *non-intimate* data in Rule #2? Because with enough non-intimate data, companies can infer intimate data with a high degree of accuracy.[23] As privacy scholar Ryan Calo puts it, "AI is increasingly capable of deriving the intimate from the available." Even if you never shared your sexual fantasies with a company, it might extract those details from prosaic personal information. Unless collection rules are formulated with that eventuality in mind, companies will simply hoard innocuous, non-intimate personal data (like favorite clothing brands or frequent fruit purchases), figuring that it will be revealing someday. We cannot let data collection become a shell game, a way to divert attention as lots of personal data is amassed to eventually infer intimate information. We can't let legal loopholes become gaping chasms.

The third rule (Rule #3) holds companies to duties of *non-discrimination* and *loyalty*. The duty of non-discrimination would reinforce today's civil rights laws. It would prohibit companies from using intimate data as a proxy for sex, gender, sexual orientation, race, disability, or religion in making decisions about important opportunities, including employment, insurance, housing, education, professional certification, credit, and the provision of health care. Under a federal privacy bill proposed by Senator Kirsten Gillibrand in 2021, companies would have a duty of nondiscrimination in their handling of personal data. This duty would cover both different treatment of individuals based on their membership in a protected class and data practices that have a disparate impact on protected classes.[24]

The duty of loyalty would mean that companies would have to prioritize people's well-being when handling their intimate data. As Neil Richards and Woodrow Hartzog have elegantly and carefully argued, "the core idea animating a duty of loyalty is that trusted parties must make their own interests subservient to those made vulnerable through the extension of trust." Once intimate information is properly collected, it should be used, shared, and stored in ways that serves *people's* best interests. The law needs to step in and require that duty of loyalty, since companies won't advance our interests over theirs without such a requirement. Under Rule #3, companies would not be permitted to handle intimate data to advantage themselves and disadvantage us. They would be barred from retaining intimate data just because maybe someday it might be valuable to them. They would be prohibited from using our intimate data to manipulate us, exploit our irrationalities, and leverage our vulnerabilities to get us to take actions that benefit them and hurt us.[25]

Rule #3 would provide meaningful, substantive protections to individuals and their intimate privacy. It would depart from data protection laws that leave the determination of *how* personal data is processed in theory to individuals based on some version of notice and consent (strong under the GDPR, weak in the United States), but in practice to companies that set the terms on which consent is sought. It would require companies to handle intimate data in ways that serve people's well-being rather than the current largely "anything-goes" approach.[26]

Let's return to period-tracking apps discussed in Chapter 1. The fertility-tracking app FEMM showed women false information about abortion without ever telling them about the app's pro-life agenda. It did not prioritize subscribers' interests—what the women using the app wanted was not part of the app's calculus when it showed subscribers false information. When Grindr collected subscribers' HIV status, doctors lauded the development because it would help start conversations about safe sex. Grindr's move was in their subscribers' best interest. But when Grindr shared people's HIV status with analytics firms, subscribers' interests were not advanced. The only party benefiting was Grindr. There, Grindr would be understood to have violated subscribers' duty of loyalty.

The fourth rule (Rule #4) would ban the sharing of intimate data with third parties. Businesses with which we have relationships—the sites that we visit, the apps that we use, the companies that sell us home devices—are our data guardians. They should not sell our intimate data to parties with whom we have no relationship. Full stop, end of story. Dating apps, porn sites, and social media companies should not share intimate data with advertisers and data brokers. That means that those companies, sites, and apps can't ask us for permission to do so.

To be sure, the rule is prophylactic and paternalistic, but it is necessary and valuable. Intimate data reveals our vulnerabilities—things that leave us open to coercion, manipulation, and discrimination. It should not be shared or sold to businesses with which we have no relationship. Because we don't have direct connections with those third parties (they're called "third parties" for a reason), we can neither control nor even know what they will do with our intimate data.

None of this means that we shouldn't be able to sell our intimate data directly to those parties ourselves. (Hence, this approach isn't as paternalistic as it might seem.)[27] Advertisers would have to bargain for our meaningful permission to collect our intimate data themselves. Advertising is a legitimate business reason; it can be conducted in a way that does not pose a significant risk to intimate privacy. Advertisers would have to persuade *us* to hand over our data. So long as their request is not mediated through other businesses and so long as they have gotten our meaningful consent (see Rule #2), we can say yes.

Rule #4 would establish a direct relationship between individuals and companies, allowing individuals to hold companies accountable for their practices. We give our written consent to our doctors to collect our personal data under HIPAA's Privacy Rule; that rule lets us complain about our doctors' practices to the Department of Health and Human Services (HHS) if they betray our trust or break their promises. We need similar mechanisms of transparency and accountability for advertisers and data brokers.

These rules, taken together, would change the value proposition for many online services. At present, many businesses don't (and don't need to) charge fees for their services because they earn revenue by selling access to intimate data to third parties. It's true that prohibiting these third-party sales may lead to new subscription fees, which a nontrivial number of people might be unable to afford. Nonprofit organizations could help offset these costs. Reproductive justice organizations could develop or provide funding to period-tracking apps that protect intimate privacy. LGBTQ advocacy groups could hire technologists to create secure dating apps for community members. Even when such alternatives are not feasible, protecting intimate privacy remains the priority. The unavailability of services to some is worth the benefit to all.

Of course, strong rules require strong remedies. To start, we need enough enforcers on the beat. State attorneys general and the FTC should be given power to enforce these rules and to seek civil penalties; but given their limited resources, they need individuals' help. Individuals should be able to bring lawsuits against companies that fail to adhere to those rules via "private rights of action." To incentivize their involvement, successful plaintiffs should be able to recover attorney's fees and financial rewards for themselves. Those financial awards should be limited so as not to bankrupt companies; they should be designed to deter rule violations.

Congress should also make clear that courts have the power to order companies to halt the collection, use, or sharing of intimate data until they comply with the law. Judges should be able to order companies to delete personal data obtained in violation of the law. If businesses fail to heed these orders, then courts should be able to impose what I have described as a "data death penalty," an order to permanently stop a business from handling intimate data.[28]

Injunctive relief of this sort is par for the course for countries bound by the GDPR. Article 58 gives DPAs the authority to impose temporary or permanent bans on the collection, use, or sharing of personal data. In 2021, the Norwegian DPA ordered Grindr to delete all personal data that had been illegally collected—which included sensitive data related to sexual orientation, health, or sexual activity for which Grindr had not gotten explicit consent to collect—in addition to the monetary penalties discussed in Chapter 5.[29] In 2019, the Hamburg Commissioner for Data Protection and Freedom of Information started an administrative procedure to stop Google employees and contractors from listening to voice recordings of home-device subscribers; Google responded by pledging not to transcribe voice recordings collected from its devices.[30] US courts should be allowed to issue similar orders.

Individuals should have the right to ask companies to delete their intimate data. In California and Virginia, for instance, residents have the right to ask companies of a certain size to delete or to stop selling their personal data.[31] Those rights, if shared by everyone, would be meaningful and powerful *if* we could make those decisions at scale. People cannot possibly contact all companies that collect and store their intimate data. We need a one-stop shop for deletion. The law should secure the ability to make a deletion request that would reach every company holding intimate data. Telephone privacy laws provide a model for facilitating such requests. Administered and enforced by the Federal Communications Commission (FCC), the FTC, and state attorneys general, Do Not Call registries let people opt out of telemarketing and robocalls with a single request. Congress should follow the path laid out in telephone privacy laws so that the FTC, FCC, and state attorneys general can facilitate deletion at scale for companies amassing intimate data. The United States needs a "Do Not Sell My Intimate Data" registry. Data protection laws like the GDPR do not facilitate such a registry, and they should.

No doubt, companies will marshal their lobbying power to defeat my proposals. They will not want to ask us for permission. They won't want any friction between us and their data grabs. Consider the response of social media companies to the proposal that nude images should not be posted online without people's written consent. When Franks and I pitched that idea to social media executives, they flatly rejected it, even though their own companies *banned* nonconsensual porn in their terms of service. We were surprised because their policy would be better served with roadblocks to the posting of nonconsensual images. But we got the message: companies would deal with problems after people engaged with their sites and added to their lucrative data stockpiles. They wanted nothing to do with policies that might interfere with the data-collection imperative.

Perhaps we can convince companies that these rules are not the end of the world. There are smart privacy scholars and advocates (indeed, some of my closest friends) who argue that strong privacy rules benefit companies in the long run by naturally enhancing the trust that we as consumers place in our commercial relationships and transactions. They argue that restrictions would reassure us that our personal data is being used to better serve us and assuage our fears that we are being exploited for someone else's private gain.[32] Corporate leaders like Apple CEO Tim Cook appreciate that "privacy and markets" are a "love story," as Ryan Calo has astutely put it.[33] Taking the long view, companies might reap the financial benefits of earning people's trust—having loyal customers. But even if collection restrictions just reduce corporate profits with no benefit whatsoever to companies, a civil right to intimate privacy is more important. Companies must adhere to these rules for the good of all of us.

RESPONDING TO FIRST AMENDMENT CHALLENGES

Regulating the surveillance of intimate life with no-collection zones, consent requirements, and duties of loyalty and antidiscrimination would not chill self-expression, but rather secure the conditions necessary for self-expression. If people could trust firms to put their intimate privacy first, then they would be more willing to use those services to experiment with ideas and forge close relationships. My proposals also relate to "purely private matters," which do not raise the same constitutional concerns as laws restricting speech on matters of public interest.[34]

My proposals restricting the handling of intimate information would not run afoul of the First Amendment. Courts have upheld laws, such as the Fair Credit Reporting Act (FCRA), requiring informed consent before entities can collect personal data. Employers cannot avoid liability under FCRA by arguing that they are just trying to learn about people so they should not have to ask for permission to see people's credit reports.[35] Countless laws restrict certain uses of personal information, from state and federal antidiscrimination laws and trade secret laws to census rules. The Supreme Court has explained that prohibitions on the use of the contents of an illegally intercepted phone call is a "regulation of conduct," whereas the prohibition of the disclosure or publication of information is a regulation of speech.[36]

Sorrell v. IMS Health, which held that a state law restricting the sale, use, and disclosure of records indicating doctors' prescribing practices violated the First Amendment, does not cast doubt on the constitutionality of my proposals. At the heart of the *Sorrell* case was the world of drug "detailing." Pharmaceutical companies pay hefty sums to obtain data about doctors' prescriptions so that their representatives can follow up and get them to prescribe their drugs. Health data miners serve as the conduits, gathering lists of the drugs that individual doctors prescribe; the dossiers have no patient data, just doctors' information. Doctors did not like the practice because it gave drug representatives the upper hand in their dealings; states weren't fond of it either, because doctors often felt pressure to prescribe brand-name drugs rather than equally effective generics, which added to Medicaid and Medicare expenditures. Vermont passed a law to address these practices, banning pharmacies, health insurers, and similar entities from disclosing doctors' prescription data for marketing purposes, and pharmaceutical companies and health data brokers from using doctors' prescription data for marketing purposes, without the doctors' consent. Data brokers and an association of pharmaceutical companies challenged the law on the grounds that it violated their free speech rights.

The Supreme Court struck down the law on First Amendment grounds. Under First Amendment doctrine, discrimination against particular speakers or messages—known as "viewpoint-based discrimination"—is "presumptively invalid." The court found that the Vermont law did exactly that: it "impose[d] a burden based on the content of the speech and the identity of the speaker." The law told pharmacies that they could not sell or give away prescription data for marketing purposes, but that they could sell or give it away for non-marketing reasons like medical research. The court identified the problem as the state's burdening of some speakers (data brokers and pharmaceutical companies), and not others, because it found those speakers too persuasive for its liking. The majority rejected the state's argument that the consent provision insulated the law's use restriction from constitutional concerns because it gave doctors "a contrived choice: Either consent, which will allow your . . . information to be disseminated and used without constraint; or, withhold consent, which will allow your information to be used by those speakers whose message the State supports." The majority explained that privacy could be chosen only if it "acquiesced in the State's goal of burdening disfavored speech by disfavored speakers."[37]

The court held that the state failed to provide a sufficiently compelling reason to justify the law because it only protected medical privacy some of the time, leaving it unprotected in non-marketing settings. The majority went out of its way to say that its finding did not spell the end of all privacy law. Justice Kennedy explained that if Vermont had "advanced its asserted privacy interest by allowing the information's sale or disclosure in only a few narrow and well-justified circumstances" as in HIPAA, the law would have been constitutional. As privacy scholar Neil Richards explains, the court made clear that the "statute would have been less problematic if it had imposed greater duties of confidentiality" on the data.[38] So if the limits on the collection and sharing of personal data are made tighter, then it follows that the law is less problematic, which is precisely what I am suggesting in my reform proposals.

———

LAW IS A blunt instrument. It takes time to adopt and enforce. It can't address every aspect or violation of intimate privacy. And we wouldn't want it to—legal overreach has costs. Social norms have a crucial role to play as well. If we all work to protect intimate privacy, we can have a freer and more just society. Along with the legal commitments I've outlined here, voluntary efforts form the heart of a new whole-society approach for intimate privacy. Imagine a Silicon Valley whose engineers, privacy and safety teams, and funders share the life experiences of all of us, including people from marginalized groups. We can chart a path for a better future if we adopt products and services that secure intimate privacy, teach lessons that help us respect the boundaries around intimate life, and support organizations that help remove nonconsensual intimate images from the internet.

9

The New Compact for Social Norms

MUTALE NKONDE, FOUNDER OF AI FOR THE PEOPLE, HAS AN AMBI-
tious agenda for Silicon Valley. She wants tech companies to achieve
racial and gender diversity in their workforce by 2030. With passion and
her characteristic brilliance, former journalist Nkonde has taken her case
to social media companies, academics, and journalists. She argues that
the people building digital technologies must look like *everyone*—not
only like white and Asian men—so that their life experiences allow them
to see and address concerns of traditionally marginalized communities
before bias gets baked into products and services. Nkonde's proposals
aim not just to protect equality and intimate privacy in the present—
though her proposals will do that—but to secure equality and intimate
privacy for the future as well. After all, when children from diverse backgrounds can see themselves in technologists, they can set their sights on
becoming them.[1]

If inertia holds, tech companies and venture capital (VC) firms will
keep hiring and funding people from their own networks, effectively
reproducing themselves. As Nkonde and advocacy groups like Color for

Change argue, companies should begin by devoting time and money to diversifying their engineering and product teams. Tremendous power resides in the hands of those teams. Technologists build the systems that collect, use, share, and store intimate data, so they can choose to minimize the handling of that data, or they can choose to maximize it. They select the data sets on which algorithms are trained, giving them the power to either protect against the entrenchment of invidious attitudes and practices at scale or ignore the existence of such attitudes and practices (thus further perpetuating them). It's simple: they can either make a conscious effort to build in guardrails for equality and intimate privacy, or not.

Employees who set policy for privacy, content moderation, and online abuse would also benefit from diversity initiatives. There have been some notable efforts. When I first met Sarah Hoyle in 2014, she was working for Twitter's Trust and Safety team. Along with Del Harvey, Hoyle helped develop the company's rules around hate speech, threats, stalking, and privacy invasions. Because Hoyle understood the gendered, racialized, and homophobic nature of online abuse (my book about cyberstalking was assigned reading for her team), she deliberately hired people from impacted communities. When she joined Spotify in 2019 to lead its Trust and Safety team, she continued this approach to hiring. As Hoyle has told me, the diversity of her team has made all the difference, particularly by bringing to the fore issues that would have otherwise been overlooked; varied inputs and perspectives have made for better-informed decisions.

Funders of tech startups have taken some modest steps in this direction, too. After Black Lives Matter protests swept the world in the wake of Minneapolis police officer Derek Chauvin's killing of George Floyd, high-profile venture capital firms tweeted statements pledging to invest in Black-owned businesses. But activists criticized the tweets as "diversity theater" and pressed VC firms for results. Soon after, in June 2020, Softbank launched a 100-million-dollar fund dedicated to investing in minority-owned businesses. Andreessen Horowitz, Google, and Collab Capital have spearheaded similar efforts. VC firms introduced standard language into term sheets requiring that companies and lead investors endeavor to include at least one underrepresented minority business as a co-investor.[2] The National Venture Capital Association, the industry's lobbying group, launched Venture Forward, a nonprofit devoted to supporting diversity.[3]

But VC firms should do more to overcome structural barriers to diversity. Equal opportunity is in their interest. According to researchers, diversity significantly increases overall fund returns and investment profits. VC firms that increased the number of female partners by 10% had 9.7% more profitable investments.[4] These firms should pursue a variety of strategies, including setting aside time to meet with Black, female, and other underrepresented entrepreneurs; hiring women and minorities to senior positions; setting targets for investing in female- and minority-owned businesses; conducting *regular* unconscious-bias training (not just one-and-done); and reporting diversity metrics.[5] Firms following diversity and inclusion best practices will receive a mark of approval from the nonprofit organization Diversity VC.[6]

But intimate privacy requires another kind of diversity, one that involves the categories of employees involved in everything from developing new products to setting policy. Most tech companies don't have in-house civil rights experts, but they should—if only for their own sake. Only after Facebook faced severe public criticism for enabling discriminatory employment and housing ads in 2021 did the tech giant hire civil rights leader Roy Austin as its first-ever Vice President of Civil Rights and Deputy General Counsel.[7] Austin told *Black Enterprise* that he is building a team of civil rights experts to make sure the company is addressing hate speech and "not doubling down on historic discrimination," and tackling 125 issues raised in a civil rights audit conducted by an outside law firm.[8]

Engineers and privacy and safety teams tend to work in separate divisions. Only *after* engineers have already devoted substantial time and effort to making plans, selecting data sets, and designing software and hardware are privacy and safety experts asked for their feedback. This must change; it is not effective to simply tack on protections after the design stage. Rather, intimate privacy experts should work with engineers *while* they develop products and services, not after the fact. Intimate privacy and equality considerations should be integral to product development.

I encountered this problem as a member of Twitter's Trust and Safety Council. Twitter employees asked the Council for its advice on features set for release. On one occasion, CCRI and other Council members expressed deep reservations about a feature due to the significant risk it posed to intimate privacy. Twitter rolled out the feature shortly thereafter. The real problem, we suspected, was the company's internal processes. The product team likely asked privacy and trust and safety officials for feedback *after* the feature had been designed, so there was little that anyone, let alone the Council, could do. The company's privacy and safety leaders should have been consulted way before it got to the rollout phase. After CCRI pushed back on the Council's limited ability to help, Twitter changed its approach, and it now consults the Council earlier in the process, though it is unclear whether the timing means the feedback will actually make a difference.

Once companies have sunk resources into building a given product or service, they are averse to abandoning it when the risk of liability is negligible (which it almost always is, given Section 230), the people at risk of harm have little power, and estimated profits exceed reputational costs. Consider Facebook Live. After its release in April 2016, CEO Mark Zuckerberg praised Facebook Live as "the most personal and emotional and raw and visceral" way to communicate.[9] It didn't take long for people to use the feature to livestream crimes like sexual assaults—effectively amounting to a live version of rape videos, as discussed in Chapter 2. In January 2017, three Swedish men livestreamed themselves raping a woman as most of the 60 viewers cheered and joked in real time.[10] In March 2017, teenage boys in Chicago livestreamed their brutal sexual assault of a 15-year-old girl. None of the 40 viewers contacted the police.[11] Because neither of these rapes were reported to Facebook at the time, the videos proceeded without interruption. Against the advice of Facebook's safety researchers, Zuckerberg refused to shut the service down. Instead, he hired 3,000 additional employees to review video content (presumably to deal with complaints rather than to proactively monitor feeds).[12] This was like building up a reserve of Band-Aids to deal with stabbings. The service is alive and well on the platform.

Businesses might integrate intimate privacy into the design phase *if* venture funding was predicated on its protection. Australia's e-Safety Commissioner Julie Grant has designed a toolkit for VC firms so that they only invest in social media startups that take intimate privacy invasions seriously. As Grant explained to me, the toolkit is a "safety impact assessment" of sorts. It urges investors to press startups for how they plan on dealing with and mitigating the damage of intimate privacy violations. Grant hopes that it will become an integral part of VC firms' due diligence.[13]

Diversifying the tech ecosystem is a crucial step to protect intimate privacy. Another is the development of privacy-securing technologies.

CAUTIOUS TECHNOLOGICAL OPTIMISM

In the analog age, if people wanted to access racy literature, they had to go to a store to buy it. People who were embarrassed to be seen purchasing adult magazines either abandoned the idea or dipped into someone else's porn stash. In the digital age, there are no clerks or customers nearby to give us sideways glances as we search adult sites.

While the privacy calculus has shifted, it's not necessarily a win for individuals. Store clerks and customers no longer know what we're reading, but Spying Inc. does, and it monitors and shares the details. In this way, digital technologies afford new opportunities for protecting intimate privacy even as they undermine it in other ways. They shift privacy risks from the eyes of store clerks and customers to the databases of countless advertisers and data brokers—from mere fleeting moments to indelible digital memories.

We need to encourage the development of privacy-enhancing technologies. But before embracing any technological solutions, we must ensure that they don't generate more privacy problems than they solve. New technologies won't inevitably create more or better intimate privacy, so before adopting any we must assess each one critically, with a view toward the long-term.

I have spent more than a decade working with companies on their content moderation practices. Over time, automation has made it easier to detect, block, and remove privacy invasions. In some instances, such automation has been the right—if not the ideal—response, offering upsides at the expense of few downsides. Yet context is crucial for the successful deployment of algorithmic tools to protect intimate privacy.

When it comes to combating child pornography, hash technology is the "killer app." Hashing is a "mathematical operation that takes a long stream of data of arbitrary length, like a video clip or string of DNA, and assigns it a specific value of a fixed length, known as a hash. The same files or DNA strings will be given the same hash, allowing computers to quickly and easily spot duplicates."[4] In essence, hashes are digital fingerprints, each one unique. In conjunction with Microsoft, Hany Farid developed PhotoDNA hash technology, which blocks, filters, and removes content that matches hashes.

In the United States, the National Center of Missing and Exploited Children (NCMEC) collects hashes of child sexual abuse material (CSAM), storing them in a centralized database. With access to the NCMEC database, tech companies can filter or block online content containing hashed images. NCMEC ensures that only CSAM is included in its database. Tech companies avail themselves of the database largely out of self-interest: recall that federal criminal law is exempted from Section

230 immunity, which means that CSAM hosts run the risk of federal criminal liability for publishing child pornography. That makes a considerable difference, and it's why you won't find CSAM on popular social media sites.

Hashing techniques are now being used to tackle nonconsensual pornography. Facebook has banned nonconsensual intimate images in its terms-of-service agreement (TOS) since 2014 (a development that I will discuss in detail in Chapter 10). As is true of all TOS violations, the ban's enforcement needs users to report violations to work successfully. The company responds to each user-submitted report and removes images when appropriate. Unfortunately, in the early years of this initiative, abusers often simply reposted nonconsensual intimate images, perpetuating a cycle of repeated reporting and removal. For that reason, Franks and I urged Facebook to adopt a hashing program.[15] Eventually, Facebook listened. Since April 2017, individuals have submitted reports of nonconsensual intimate images in the same manner as before, but the company's specially trained representatives also have designated images for hashing if the content violates the company's ban, allowing photo-matching technology to prevent the images from reappearing on Facebook and Instagram.

This particular Facebook program mitigates the damage that victims suffer. It ensures that friends, families, and coworkers will not repeatedly see victims' intimate images on Facebook and Instagram. Facebook's storage of the hashed images poses little risk to intimate privacy. After a particular image is hashed, the hashes are the only remnant of that process; Facebook removes and destroys the intimate image. As computer scientists explain, it is exceptionally difficult to reverse-engineer a hash back to the original image.

Facebook's next step, however, received substantial pushback from privacy advocates and journalists. In November 2017, the company announced a program that would allow actual or potential victims of nonconsensual porn to send special representatives images that they feared would be posted without their consent but that had not yet been circulated in this way. The idea was to preemptively hash images to ensure that Facebook (and Instagram) would automatically filter them out on their platforms. This initiative grew out of the work of Facebook's Non-consensual Intimate Imagery Task Force, led by Facebook's Global Head of Safety, Antigone Davis, and its Global Safety Policy Director, Karuna Nain. Franks and I served on the task force along with representatives from the National Network to End Domestic Violence (NNEDV) and Australia's e-Safety Commissioner, Julie Grant (who created the safety assessment tool kit). Task force members knew from working with victims that abusers routinely threaten to post nude images online. The existing hashing program was helpful, but it could not prevent the initial publication of a given image—the initial privacy violation.[16] Members of the task force strongly supported the pilot program, knowing that it would help allay some of the fear and anxiety that victims experience. It couldn't assuage all of their concerns—after all, it only applied to Facebook and Instagram—but it would be a good start.

Davis and Nain worked with the company's head of cybersecurity and Grant to design and implement a pilot program in Australia. Under the pilot program, individuals notified Grant's office about the threat. It then vetted the situation to ensure that it involved a genuine threat of nonconsensual pornography (rather than anti-pornography groups using the company's TOS for their own ends). Then, the e-Safety office notified Facebook, which sent the person a one-time link to share the intimate image so that the operations team could hash it. As soon as the hashing process was finished, the image was destroyed.

The public's initial reaction to the program was negative. Information security experts warned that transmitting intimate images to Facebook entailed security risks.[17] Civil liberties groups mocked the effort as a privacy disaster.[18] Journalists asked why anyone should trust Facebook after the Cambridge Analytica fiasco.[19] Admittedly, *if* Facebook failed to secure the transmission of intimate images or to delete the images after hashing them, hackers could obtain the images and post them online. It was also true that the image submission process could be attacked by phishing schemes that would put intimate images into the hands of criminals. Despite these criticisms, the pilot program went forward. Davis and Nain assured the task force that intimate images were immediately destroyed after the hashing process and that the cybersecurity team was prepared to deal with phishing schemes and other potential vulnerabilities.

The hash pilot program was a win for intimate privacy. That was not guaranteed: Facebook's Davis and Nain made it so with careful oversight. They hosted in-house training sessions to help content moderators learn to distinguish legitimate from illegitimate (i.e., reports of images that do not constitute nonconsensual pornography) claims. They worked with victims' organizations like CCRI and NNEDV to continue improvements to their training efforts.

The pilot program has been extended beyond Australia to include Brazil, Canada, Italy, Pakistan, the United Kingdom, and the United States, with trusted partners in those countries working with Facebook, including CCRI.[20] As far as I know, there have been no security breaches. The biggest problem, however, was victims not using the program as much as advocates expected. As journalists had warned, and as had seemed to be true, Facebook had lost people's trust.[21]

Facebook isn't the only company trying to protect intimate privacy. The female-focused dating app Bumble has taken steps to ensure that daters are not forced to look at unwelcome intimate images, most notably dick pics. The app uses an AI tool called "Private Detector" that finds images with nudity, blurs them, and asks recipients to decide whether to view or block "unwelcome junk." If recipients want to block the images, they are given the option to block the sender. Bumble sends a message to the senders: "If you are sending someone a photo that is suspected of lewd imagery, the Private Detector will remind you that sending such an image may lead to you being reported. Consent is crucial. If you send an unsolicited lewd photo and are reported, you will be blocked from using the app."[22]

Bumble's technological solution reduces the risk of receiving unwanted intimate images in texts sent in the app. It does not invade the sender's privacy beyond what the sender intended. Indeed, it could minimize a sender's potential risk by ensuring that their photos don't end up in the hands of someone who did not want to see them and might use them in privacy-invasive ways.

Of course, not every technological solution protects privacy. We should be particularly wary of technical solutions that promise quick fixes to hard problems. The "there's an app for that" response often overpromises and under-delivers. Sometimes, what seems too good to be true is, sadly, precisely that. "Consent" apps have proven especially disappointing.

According to their creators, consent apps help facilitate healthy sexual interactions, including the exchange of intimate images. The Legal-Fling app lets subscribers form agreements that "stipulate sexual dos and don'ts as well as rules on the use of condoms, disclosure of sexually transmitted diseases, and the taking of photos and videos." Subscribers can designate a monetary penalty for sharing nude footage in violation of the agreement.[23] We-Consent, ConsentAmour, uConsent, and Yes to Sex are a few examples of the latter.[24]

Getting people to talk about what they do and don't want in sexual encounters is generally a good thing. Founders of the apps say that they want to encourage partners to clarify their expectations about sex and sexual expression. Yes to Sex founder Wendy Mandell Geller explained her hope that her app will "make it easier to talk about sexually transmitted diseases, protection, and boundaries." uConsent app founder Cody Swann explained that his software will get people to communicate, enhancing intimacy and forging a "digital handshake."[25]

But there is no guarantee that sober, coercion-free discussions will ensue. Consent apps paint a picture of digital handshakes made with clear heads, and imply that all sexual interactions and sexual expression

that follow will be consensual from start to finish, but there is little reason to think that is the case. Apps can't guarantee that consent in one
moment amounts to consent in another. An app that memorializes someone's permission to have their nude photo taken captures just one piece of
a complex, ongoing consent puzzle that cannot be reduced to a one-time
yes-or-no answer. Not captured is the person's permission for the recipient to share or keep the image, or the person's withdrawal of permission.
If "you can coerce someone into having sex with you, there is nothing to
stop you from being able to coerce somebody into using an application
that makes it seem like you consented."[26]

Consider how the ConsentAmour app described its mission when
I first wrote about consent apps in 2020. The company claimed that its
app would end "'he-said-she-said' scenarios" and "false accusations of
sexual misconduct." "False accusations . . . are [made] against innocent
guys every day. That's where ConsentAmour App comes in. Just a few
clicks away, the ConsentAmour App is there when you need it. When
your girl accepts your request, you have proof of mutual consent."[27] The
premise of the ConsentAmour app's pitch was that *women*—it only said
women—were not capable of seeing sex that they have had as consensual and that *men* must get them on the record. The entire project oozed
preconceived gender scripts and troubling assumptions. (Seemingly in
response to criticism about its retrograde marketing, ConsentAmour
changed its message, emphasizing that "Women will have the Proof
they need when they say NO—No means NO. Men also will have
Proof should the need arise."[28])

We should encourage the development of technological solutions,
but we have to be wary of tools offering but not delivering privacy. Even
well-designed privacy-enhancing technologies may not suffice. There are
no silver-bullet answers. (If there were, do you really think I'd be writing
this book?) Instead, we face a far harder task: people—all people—need
to be taught about the importance of intimate privacy; they need to learn
to value and appreciate it and to protect not only their own, but that of

others, too. Coupled with technological solutions, education can ensure that intimate privacy becomes our default position—the law within us.

EDUCATING US

In 2021, on the floor of the House of Representatives, Congressman Matt Gaetz took aside male colleagues to show them nude photos of women with whom he had sex. Gaetz didn't do it once or twice, but many, many times. He kept doing it because his colleagues seemingly did not express their disapproval. As *Washington Post* writer Alexandra Petri observed, the "accumulation of little assents" normalized the invasions of intimate privacy. If "just one person, one guy in a locker room, or around a campfire, or even on the floor of Congress, sa[id], uncomfortably, 'What?' or, 'Why would you *show* someone that?' . . . it could reshape this whole place, if it happened enough."[29]

Amen to that. Changing troubling social attitudes won't be easy no matter what, but it has even less of a chance if people don't start standing up for intimate privacy. People need to tell the Gaetzes of the world to knock it off, to cut it out. Advocacy groups like CCRI devote considerable energy to highlighting intimate privacy's centrality to our lives, and the damage inflicted upon its denial. But it can't be up to those groups alone; we must each play a role in teaching our friends, colleagues, and family members.

Education efforts must confront the cultural denigration of the bodies of women, nonwhites, and sexual and gender minorities. Legal philosopher Martha Nussbaum has explored how the "culture of gender-based objectification" stems from our education of boys. All over the globe, young men are often taught that a "real man" is "never weak, never dependent, always in control." Psychologists explain that boys brought up in that tradition eschew "trust, empathy, and relationships" and instead embrace cruelty, humiliation, and aggression. Especially when it comes to sex: peer culture tells boys that sex is all about domination.[30]

Families should teach boys and girls to devalue aggression and dominance, prioritize empathy and connection, and treat others with respect and dignity. As Nussbaum puts it, families must confront the "culture of maleness that teaches that any status short of total control is weak and shameful." For those messages to stick, families need society's help, including that of educators.[31] Schools have a long way to go on this score. In the United States, the curriculum on sexual education is often outdated and incomplete. Most students don't learn about consent, and they hardly ever spend time talking about sexting, online abuse, and nonconsensual porn. Nonprofit organizations like Schools Consent Project lead workshops in schools in the United Kingdom that focus on the legal definitions of consent and invasions of intimate privacy. Founder Kate Parker explains: "We want young people to appreciate that consent is the bedrock to any sexual interaction; it distinguishes a sexual act from a sexual crime."[32]

In teaching young people about intimate privacy and consent, we should acknowledge the forces that bring out the worst in us online. We should talk about human frailties that lead us to post and share nude images without subjects' consent, so that we can guard against them. In the spring of 2021 as the COVID pandemic raged, I taught a seminar on Zoom: "Free Speech in a Digital Age." One of my students astutely asked: "What if people had to get a license before using the internet [to] learn about the harm that they can cause online? We do it with cars; why not the internet?" The student was only partly joking. She asked the class to consider the good that could result if everyone were taught about the harms of online abuse. What would we teach them before giving them their internet learner's permits?

When my daughters were in middle and high school, I talked to local schools (including theirs, bless their patience) in Baltimore, where we lived at the time. I focused on the dynamics that make it easy for us to forget our shared humanity online. Young or old, middle age or teenage, we act impulsively. We like, click, link, and share without thinking. In front of a screen, we feel anonymous. The feeling of anonymity emboldens us to defy norms, making it easier for us to do and say things we would never do and never say if people were standing in front of us. People's facial expressions, body language, and tone of voice remind us to keep our behavior in check. Online, we don't have those cues, so we are more inclined to pivot to cruelty. We can resist those tendencies so long as we remain conscious of them and endeavor to combat them.

Now more than ever, we need to talk to kids about the blending of personal and professional lives online. During the COVID pandemic, home computers became our schools and workplaces. At times, people forgot that the computers they were using provided other people with a window into their lives. They brought their laptops into the bathroom without muting the audio on online conference calls; they masturbated in front of their computers, without turning off their video camera on Zoom, which allowed colleagues to see. Kids and adults need to talk about these lessons, since our workplaces show no sign of fully returning to physical offices.

In my talks to students, I urged them to see themselves as digital citizens. I explained that everyone depends on networked tools for friendship, education, networking, careers, and expression, so they need to wield those tools responsibly. They, and everyone else, deserve the chance to enjoy all they can from online engagement—to reap its benefits and evade its ills.

Young people often think that no one besides their close friends cares about or pays attention to what they say or do online. They're wrong. Once information is posted online or shared via email or text, it can spread far beyond its intended—and expected—audience. I urge young people to check their privacy settings because the default ones tend to relinquish essentially all privacy. I also encourage them—actually, everyone—to cover their computer cameras when not using them. (I have included more detail about self-help efforts at the end of this book.)

As for their responsibility toward others, I talk about how harmful it is to post, text, or forward nude or sexually explicit images. I share the story of a 15-year-old boy from Enschede, Netherlands who jumped off an apartment building after discovering that a nude photo he sent to a girl at school was posted on Instagram.[33] I talk about how college freshman Tyler Clementi committed suicide after his freshman roommate secretly streamed his sexual encounter with a man and watched with his friends. And I talk about how Audrie Pott hanged herself approximately a week after three 16-year-old boys sexually assaulted her while she was unconscious and posted nude photos of her online.

Schools need to do better. At best, they devote a few hours to teaching responsible online behavior (which often includes guest speakers). They need to integrate these lessons into a broader civics education. I interviewed Amy Enright, who spearheads the Center for Community and Civic Engagement at the Rivers School in Weston, Massachusetts. The Rivers School is a wealthy private school, and even with considerable funds and curricular freedom, it does not routinely teach students about online abuse. As Enright explained to me, her courses focus on helping students discern reliable, newsworthy information online and appreciate the breadth and depth of disinformation online. It took a lot for her to convince the school to spend resources and classroom time on digital citizenship. Even when she succeeded, the school's conception of digital citizenship centered on media literacy, political engagements, and elections. There was no discussion of online abuse, sexting, and other ways that teenagers can undermine their peers' ability to become digital citizens. Enright noted that her initiative was unusual: most schools don't spend any sustained time on civics, online literacy and engagement, or bullying beyond an annual one-and-done speaker about online safety.

It is crucial for schools to discuss violations of intimate privacy in their own communities—they occur more often than most people realize. Administrators and parents normally don't call me until they get wind that a student has violated another's intimate privacy. The story is often a variation on a theme: student A secretly taped classmates B and

C having sex, and then A shared the video with friends who shared it with other friends, until seemingly every student in the community had it. "What should we do?" the administrators inevitably ask.

Ever ready with my pitch, I say that teachers should gather small groups of students together to talk about intimate privacy. No shaming, no naming; just discuss intimate privacy's importance and their obligation to protect it. Admittedly, this is a challenging task. Victims won't want to partake in the discussion; addressing the violations (that everyone is pretending to ignore) might make matters worse. The key is to ensure that community members respect the privacy of both the victims and the privacy violators. In truth, the community is already talking about what happened behind the victims' backs yet with no context or guidance for how to move forward to heal and to protect intimate privacy.

Regrettably, school administrators avoid those teaching moments, doing everything possible to sweep incidents under the rug. Perhaps they check on students B and C, who were the subjects of the video, to make sure that they are "okay"; perhaps they suspend student A, who took the video and shared it without consent, as if doing so would miraculously erase the video from students' phones, computers, and minds; perhaps they hold meetings with the parents or guardians of students A, B, and C to discuss what happened. They may ask me to talk to the parents or guardians of student A, and I oblige. Regrettably, parents or guardians often deny that their children did anything wrong, or if they did, they claim, someone else was to blame. I can't tell you how many times I have had to bite my tongue or, at the very least, stop myself from going ballistic.

On that note, what about teaching intimate privacy to adults? This is a difficult task, especially because there's no easy way to reach them—they don't have to sit in classrooms or auditoriums. Social media companies, however, can help us: their subscribers are a captive audience. They leverage that audience for ads; why not for education?

Sociologist Sudhir Venkatesh, who led Facebook's research team on trust and safety from 2018 to 2020, championed that idea. He believed that when people signed up for Facebook, they should undergo an onboarding process where they would learn about the company's rules and why certain practices are banned. (That process sounds a little like what my student was proposing.) Teaching them would make a difference, since most users know very little about the rules, Venkatesh explained on his podcast, *Sudhir Breaks the Internet*. Matt Radha, who served on Venkatesh's team, had experience discussing the rules with users whose accounts had been suspended; he found that his mini-lessons worked—the individuals followed the rules from then onward. When Venkatesh and Radha pitched the teaching idea to Facebook executives, the response was a hard no. Executives considered teaching efforts a waste of money. In their view, people's minds could not be changed, so users would do what they wanted to do no matter what Facebook said. Although Venkatesh's research and Radha's experience had proven those assumptions wrong, there was nothing that the two colleagues could do about it at the time.[34]

That was then; this is now. Social media companies should create teaching modules for users to view before they can access their accounts. We ask people, young and old, to study the rules of the road before they can get their driver's licenses, just as my student wisely noted. Companies should insist upon the same. They should follow up with regular reminders about commitments to intimate privacy and refresher courses. We need to give people a reason to treat social networks as communities to which they owe responsible behavior. Social media companies purport to be all about forging social connection; they should put their efforts where their mouths (and PR) are. Those lessons might carry over into other online activities in a virtuous cycle.

Teaching people about intimate privacy and their privacy-related duties would help them be better and more informed digital citizens. It would be neither easy nor cheap, but it would be a worthwhile long-term investment in growing into the type of society we aspire to be. Other efforts—international efforts—to help victims minimize the damage wrought by intimate privacy violations may have more immediate payoffs.

INTERNATIONAL COOPERATION

The Internet Watch Foundation (IWF), a nonprofit organization located in London, has been combatting the spread of child sexual abuse material (CSAM) since 1996. Its operations encompass a vast array of activities. These include identifying CSAM online, reporting it to law enforcement, and issuing takedown orders to internet service providers (ISPs). IWF also maintains a hotline that allows people to report CSAM, and the organization even helps locate victims so that law enforcement can rescue those individuals. Although some financial assistance comes from the UK government, the group's funding primarily comes from internet companies.

IWF's reach is now global. In 2015, IWF teamed up with Microsoft's cloud service to enable the sharing of a hash list of CSAM images with online platforms like Twitter, Google, Facebook, and Yahoo. Images come from reports to the hotline, the group's own research, and the UK Home Office's Child Abuse Image Database.[35] IWF has 43 "portals" in Europe, Asia, Africa, and the Americas so countries and companies can report CSAM for inclusion in the hash list.[36] IWF's analysts assess reported material to confirm that it is CSAM before hashing it. As IWF says of its mission: "We have to act quickly. The longer an image stays live, the more opportunity there is for offenders to view and share it, and more harm is caused to victims. In partnership with the online industry, we push to secure the rapid removal of content."[37]

In 2016, IWF helped remove 57,335 web pages hosted in the Netherlands (37%), the United States (22%), Canada (15%), France (11%), and Russia (7%).[38] In 2020, IWF helped remove three times as much

CSAM—resulting from 153,383 reports—from around the world. Almost 44% of those pages—approximately 68,000—were created by children themselves; most were girls between the ages of 11 and 13. According to IWF, self-generated images were the result of predator pressure, bullying, or coercion. (This accords with the discussion of sextortion in Chapter 2.)

IWF has continued to innovate. It has created a web crawler that targets suspicious areas of the internet, comparing images in its database to locate duplicates. At present, the organization is working to improve its web crawler so it can find images online that have not yet been identified; once implemented, the web crawler will forward those images to analysts tasked with assessing whether the images should be included in the hash list.[39] It uses machine learning technology to signal which reports most likely contain CSAM, thereby helping human analysts prioritize the most urgent work. IWF also has a tool that protects analysts from looking at the same image twice, in an effort to preserve employee well-being.[40]

We need an IWF-like effort to combat intimate privacy violations. Online platforms should have access to a hash list of nonconsensual imagery so that they can filter, remove, and block such images. Such an effort would scale up what victims want most: for friends, colleagues, clients, and loved ones not to see their intimate images. Of course, reviewers would need facts suggesting that an intimate image's subject did not consent to its disclosure. They also would need to make sure that images do not involve a matter of *legitimate* public interest. That determination can be straightforward: no one needs to see intimate images of nonconsenting private individuals. But in cases involving public officials, that isn't always the case—though most often it is (as I think it was for Katie Hill). The public might have a legitimate interest in seeing a nude photo (or at least part of it) in cases where it documents an official engaged in a crime (and blurs others' faces and bodies).

The organization running such a hash list should follow trust and safety best practices, as detailed in Chapter 8. The organization would have to ensure that its efforts do not impair the legal system. They would need to preserve the images and all relevant metadata (data about data), such as the name of the content's author, the date it was created, and any other data about the poster. This would borrow from the IWF and the NCMEC model—both entities have a legal right to indefinitely possess such material about CSAM to support prosecutions.[41]

What can we do about sites that have neither the interest nor the legal incentive to participate in a nonconsensual intimate image hash list? Safety officials in Australia and South Korea have told me that their biggest frustration is nonconsensual pornography of their citizens hosted in the United States and the Netherlands. Yes, those officials could ask service providers in their own countries to block web pages or sites from being accessed (and they do, as I will discuss in Chapter 10), but victims still have relatives and friends in the United States or the Netherlands who may see their images on such pages. Companies involved in other parts of the internet's infrastructure—for example, web domain registrars or credit card companies—could voluntarily refuse to provide their services to those platforms. In 2021, after payment processors like Visa threatened to pull their services, Pornhub agreed to step up its removal of nonconsensual porn and permit only verified users to upload content. But without Section 230 reform, sites that make money from nonconsensual intimate images won't cooperate. There are limits to norms—that is why we need law and norms to work together.

10

Hope and Change

CHANGE DOESN'T JUST HAPPEN. POLICYMAKERS AND COMPANIES likely won't decide to protect intimate privacy on their own. Facebook and Bumble stepped up because doing so buoyed their brands. But will the ad-tech ecosystem or sites specializing in nonconsensual intimate images change their ways? Will Congress pass comprehensive privacy law along the lines of my proposal in Chapter 8? I'm a hopeful person, perhaps even a bit of a Pollyanna, but I'm not that naïve.

Change *has* occurred in the past decade. Reform efforts to protect intimate privacy have evolved in different ways. Officials and advocates were the key to progress in some cases, whereas everyday people led the charge in others. Individuals charted the work of coalitions in some cases, whereas surges of interest became forces of their own in others. In all cases, a shared purpose was evident. A passage from Antoine de Saint-Exupéry's *Wind, Sand, and Stars* comes to mind: "Love is not just looking at each other, but in looking outward together in the same direction." I have seen, and been part of, coalitions of victims, attorneys, academics, and advocacy groups pressing for reform. Members of those coalitions tweeted, petitioned, and marched. They wrote op-eds and articles. They worked with corporate and legislative staff, showing them that reform served their principals' interests. With some luck and fortuitous political developments, important steps have been taken to protect intimate privacy. Change isn't an academic fantasy. It is a real thing, and it is in reach.

THE CYBER EXPLOITATION TASK FORCE

"Good afternoon, I am contacting you on behalf of the Executive team in the office of the California Attorney General Kamala D. Harris." The email asked if I might talk to the executive team about online abuse. The timing could not have been more perfect. My book about cyberstalking, *Hate Crimes in Cyberspace*, had just been released. Mary Anne Franks and I were helping a Maryland lawmaker draft a bill to criminalize nonconsensual porn—we had just coauthored the first law review article on the topic. A year before, with Holly Jacobs, we had founded CCRI, a nonprofit devoted to defending civil rights and liberties that focuses on the nonconsensual posting of intimate images. Of course, I wanted to help.

On our call, the California AG's privacy and tech guru Jeffrey Rabkin explained that they were sketching out a strategy to combat online abuse. AG Harris had prosecuted site operators who extorted California women for considerable sums in exchange for removing their nude images, but she wanted to do more. Might I join them in creating a task force to combat the nonconsensual posting of intimate images?

Lucky for me, I had a work trip in San Francisco scheduled for the next month, so I flew in a day early to meet with the executive team, including California Solicitor General Ed Dumont and California DOJ attorneys in Sacramento and Los Angeles (who joined us via video conference). We spent the morning of November 5, 2014 working through the privacy, civil rights, and public safety implications of the abuse of intimate images.

That afternoon, I sat down with AG Harris and her chief of policy Daniel Suvor. As Harris explained, combating the exploitation of the vulnerable had long been her priority. She wanted to stop or at the very least minimize the damage wrought by the unwanted posting of intimate images. She had seen firsthand that women and minorities were the primary targets of cyber exploitation (as she was calling the nonconsensual disclosure of intimate images). She wanted my advice on where she should focus her energies. I suggested four areas: encouraging industry best practices; educating law enforcement; changing public attitudes; and working on legislative proposals.

The more we talked, the more it became clear that our work would start with a "convening" of stakeholders. Convenings were one of AG Harris's specialties. In 2012, she brought together six companies whose platforms hosted the majority of mobile apps to see how they could encourage app developers to post privacy policies. At the time, three-quarters of mobile apps lacked privacy policies, which violated California law.[1] After the convening, the companies announced a joint statement of principles, including changes that would prompt apps to post privacy policies. By June 2012, the "number of free Apple Store apps with a privacy policy doubled, from 40 percent to 84 percent."[2] AG Harris had accomplished her goal by encouraging collaboration, rather than by filing lawsuits.

During our meeting, AG Harris shared her view of convenings. They reflected her policy preference for carrots (incentivizing cooperation) versus sticks (coercive action like enforcement activity). She wanted companies to see that eliminating cyber exploitation from their platforms served *them*. She heeded the civil rights–era insight that constitutional law and critical race scholar Derrick Bell theorized as interest convergence: that progress is far more likely when it aligns with the self-interest of the powerful. By the end of the meeting, she asked me to spend the next months and my forthcoming sabbatical advising her team. I was all in.

November 2014 was an auspicious time to begin our work. Actor Jennifer Lawrence had just broken her silence about the nonconsensual posting of her and other celebrities' nude images in the summer's so-called "Fappening." In an interview in *Vanity Fair*, Lawrence condemned sites profiting from the "sexual exploitation" of her body *and* the people viewing her intimate images without permission. She was clear in her rebuke: "I didn't tell you that you could look at my naked body."[3] Such a statement from a beloved California star gave tech company officials, law enforcement leaders, and lawmakers all the more reason for them to accept the AG's invitation to join the convening.

On February 4, 2015, we gathered in a conference room in the basement of the San Francisco office of the California Department of Justice. At a long table in the front of the room sat the speakers, including AG Harris, myself, a state lawmaker, a victims' rights attorney, and chief safety or cybersecurity executives of Twitter (Del Harvey, whom I had worked with since 2009), Facebook (Joseph Sullivan), and Microsoft (Claudia Gregoire). The room was packed. Attendees included state legislators, law enforcement leaders, academics, and representatives of Pinterest, Yahoo, Google, YouTube, Tumblr, Secret, and other tech companies. Victim advocates Elisa D'Amico, Mary Anne Franks, and Carrie Goldberg flew in from Florida and New York. Leaders of the Anti-Defamation League and other advocacy groups were there. Although the room was dingy and dimly lit, the star power made it feel electric.

At 1:00 p.m., AG Harris kicked off the meeting. She urged everyone to reject the term "revenge porn" because it insinuated that victims played a blameworthy role or deserved retribution. The wrongdoers were the people who exploited intimate images without subjects' consent. She spoke about her prosecution of Kevin Bollaert, who operated a site called UGotPosted that urged people to post ex-lovers' nude photos and then charged $350 for their removal. Bollaert's site was just one of thousands that exploited the bodies of women and girls. The scale of the problem was vast; the damage was profound. AG Harris asked for help from people in the room.[4]

My job was to convey the extent of the damage, especially in comparison to the meager state of the law. I talked about how no one would help Holly Jacobs after her ex plastered the internet with her nude images. Law enforcement said that she should turn off her computer and buy a gun; sites ignored her requests to remove the photos; and Google did nothing either. At the time, Jacobs was getting her PhD and teaching undergraduate students. On the advice of her dean, she changed her name so students and employers would not find her nude images in online searches. She had to extinguish her identity to have a chance at work, love, and safety. Jacobs founded CCRI with Franks and me to help others whose intimate images had been exploited. I argued that victims like Jacobs needed tech companies, advocacy groups, law enforcers, and lawmakers in the fight for intimate privacy.

The meeting covered considerable ground. Victim advocate Erica Johnstone emphasized the prohibitive cost of tort suits and the scarcity of counsel able and willing to represent victims. As she explained, average attorney's fees ranged from $10,000 to $60,000—far out of reach for most victims to afford, especially since there were rarely deep pockets to recover from and no laws mandating that defendants cover attorney's fees when they lose. Assemblyman Mike Gatto discussed his legislative efforts, including a bill that would allow law enforcement to obtain warrants in cyber exploitation cases. Tech companies' safety and cybersecurity officers discussed their approaches to addressing nonconsensual intimate images and their work with law enforcement on child sexual abuse material.

The convening set the stage for reform. We ended the meeting confident that attendees would want to join our effort. And they did—in droves. Tech companies, victims' groups, and law enforcement leaders joined AG Harris's official Cyber Exploitation Task Force. Deputy Attorney General Venus Johnson led the charge, creating subcommittees to tackle different issues. For instance, one group drafted industry best practices and policies, while another created resources for victims so they could better understand their rights. A third group developed tools to help law enforcement investigate cyber exploitation cases.

Within six months, we made our work available to the public. The AG's website featured a cyber exploitation hub with the resources that we had created. It had a cheat sheet for police officers so they would know how to proceed when victims reported cyber exploitation. It had resources for victims, including an explanation of their rights and a list of groups that could help. It had a discussion of the relevant laws.

On October 14, 2015, AG Harris held a press conference in Los Angeles, at which I spoke, to discuss the task force's work. She applauded the tech companies for their efforts. As AG Harris explained, task force participants Google, Twitter, Microsoft, Pinterest, Tumblr, and Yahoo developed best practices and policies for the cyber exploitation hub.[5] Equally important were tech companies' internal reforms. Consider Google's change in its policy toward search results. Its longstanding mantra was that search was sacred. Search results could not be changed, Google insisted, because its search engine was neutral. This was Google's position in 2011 when I began working with company officials in connection with the Anti Cyberhate Coalition, led by the Anti-Defamation League. This was its position in early 2015 when we formed the task force. Google was adamant: no tinkering with search results, not then, not ever. (Never mind the fact that the company was tinkering with search results to protect social security or stolen credit card numbers.)

That shifted after the task force began its work. On June 18, 2015, I got word that Google had changed its mind, first from a company executive and then from *USA Today*'s tech reporter Jessica Guynn, who had an exclusive on the story. Google would treat nonconsensual intimate images like social security numbers and honor requests to remove links to the images from search results in people's names.[6] Franks and I had urged search engines to honor victims' requests to remove links to intimate images in searches of their names in our 2014 law review article; Franks gave a talk with just that theme at Google—and now they embraced it. I vividly recall talking to Guynn about the news. I was speaking at a National Association of Attorneys General meeting in San Diego, so I had to step outside to take her call. I will never forget the joy that I felt. (I might have jumped up and down.) Victims could finally get their nude images de-indexed from search results of their names. If only Jacobs had had that option before she changed her name.

Of course, it was not just the task force; no single factor instigated Google's policy change. The company has 154 offices around the world, including 40 in Europe. Google's terms of service operate globally, and it reacts to pressures accordingly. Developments in the EU surely played a role in nudging the company to agree to de-index nonconsensual porn in searches of people's names. Recall that in 2014, the Court of Justice of the European Union had recognized the "right to be forgotten," ruling that Google had to de-index from search results stories in which the public had no interest because they included "no longer relevant" personal information, like news about a person's decades-old bankruptcy.[7] Agreeing to de-index nonconsensual intimate images would comport with the CJEU's ruling *and* the task force's goals. In all likelihood, both contributed to Google's momentous decision.

Google wasn't the only tech company that changed its policies during the six months that the task force was doing its work. Right after Google's announcement, Microsoft's Bing and Yahoo followed suit and agreed to de-index nonconsensually posted nude or sexually explicit images in searches of people's names. Twitter and Tumblr altered their policies at the outset of our work, changing their global terms of service to ban nonconsensual intimate images. Microsoft also pledged to block links to intimate content on its Xbox Live gaming service.[8]

With these positive developments behind us, the reform coalition continued its work. Erica Johnson and Colette Vogel's nonprofit organization Without My Consent created an online hub with resources for victims, including a survey of the laws surrounding whether victims could bring suits pseudonymously. CCRI's Holly Jacobs bravely talked about her experience with the press and wrote op-eds. Franks, Goldberg, and I continued to work with lawmakers to criminalize the nonconsensual posting of intimate images. In 2015, only a handful of states banned non-consensual pornography. By 2021, 48 states, the District of Columbia, and Guam criminalized the practice.

The task force began in Silicon Valley and continued its work on Capitol Hill when Harris was elected to the Senate in 2016. At the time, Franks was working closely with Congresswoman Jackie Speier's staff to draft a bill criminalizing nonconsensual pornography.[9] I advised then-senator Harris, who served as the cosponsor of the Senate's version of the bill.[10] That bill was incorporated into the Violence Against Women Reauthorization Act of 2021, which would renew and enhance federal protections against gender-based violence. The House passed that version of the VAWA Reauthorization Act in March 2021. Unfortunately, the Senate's version, which passed in February 2022, did not include the bill. This was disappointing news, but Franks and I are not giving up. Some steps forward, and a few back—onward we go.

No doubt, the insider status of the task force's leader helped build a robust coalition that made strides in the fight against nonconsensual intimate imagery. But, as we will see, political outsiders can make a huge difference too.

THE VICTIM ACTIVIST, THE LAWYER, AND THE CONSTITUENTS

On July 8, 2017, Gina Martin and her sister went to hear a band play at an outdoor concert at Hyde Park in London. A group of men standing behind them tried to get their attention. After Martin politely conveyed their disinterest, she heard one man laughing loudly. When she glanced around, she saw that the man had taken a photograph up her skirt. On his phone was a photo of her thighs, buttocks, pubic hair, and genitals covered by her underwear.[11]

Martin grabbed the phone out of the man's hand and screamed, "You've got a picture of my vagina. *What is wrong with you!?*" Just a "picture of the stage," he shot back. Martin took the phone and ran. She quickly found a police officer and explained what happened. The officer was sympathetic. He said, "You should be able to go to a concert without being worried about someone taking a photo up your skirt." But after consulting with a colleague, he told Martin that nothing could be done. UK law did not cover up-skirt photos. The officer gave the man back his phone and told him to delete the photo.[12]

As Martin told me, she was mortified that the man treated her like she was "just a crotch." She was depressed that women had to choose between their safety and their autonomy. And she was furious—not because she didn't prevent the man from taking the up-skirt photo, but because it was apparently her responsibility to make sure that he could not take such a photo. She hadn't done something wrong—*he* had—but the law did not recognize his actions as wrongful.[13]

Enough was enough. Martin worked as a copywriter at an advertising firm, so she knew how to use social media to make a point. On Facebook, Martin posted a selfie that she took with her sister right before the incident. The photo featured two of the men in the background. In her post, Martin explained what happened. She asked for help identifying the men (whose faces she circled) so she could follow up with the police. Perhaps there was something that could be done. After the post went viral, Facebook took it down. Why? Because, Facebook explained, her post constituted "harassment." It was the irony of all ironies: "Posting a photograph of these men's faces was harassment, but apparently them taking photos of my crotch, without my consent, was not."[14]

Martin's work in advertising had prepared her for quite a bit, but not a legislative campaign. So she did what any of us might do—she googled "how to change the law." The results weren't terribly helpful, but she sat down and sketched out a plan to make up-skirting a crime in England and Wales. With the hashtag #StopSkirtingtheIssue, Martin called for legislative reform on various social media platforms. She sponsored Facebook ads that asked, "Why is up-skirting not a sexual offense?" She pitched the idea to journalists, and some covered it for their outlets. She did a live television debate with police officers who said the solution was easy—"just wear trousers." Martin knew that she had lots of minds to change on the topic.

As soon as the online campaign began attracting attention, Martin faced a torrent of abuse on Twitter and email (rape threats, doxing, sexist slurs, you name it). The harassment did not stop her, but it made her realize that she needed help. Her first objective was finding a lawyer to help her draft legislation, though she couldn't afford legal fees. Ryan Whelan, a lawyer at a fancy white-shoe firm, agreed to take her on as a pro bono client to help her navigate the legislative process.

Martin and Whelan spent the next 18 months lobbying MPs to criminalize the nonconsensual taking or recording of images up people's skirts. At first, lawmakers dismissed the suggestion. That was no surprise, given the way that the television debate had gone. Martin understood that social attitudes would be tough to overcome. Nearly two-thirds of the MPs were privately educated men. Martin worried that they would not sympathize with a working-class woman and would see themselves in the rowdy young men at the concert, not as a target of sexual violence. She was right to be concerned: while some MPs brushed her off by saying that they did not want to pass more criminal laws, a few intimated that her "low-class behavior" was to blame. This was an elitist twist on the "short skirt" narrative, which blames female victims for gendered harms. One MP made his misogyny explicit, refusing to help because he was "not a feminist."[15]

While MPs risked little in turning away an up-skirt victim and her lawyer, constituencies were a different matter. Martin and Whelan knew that they needed voters to convey support for their effort. Likes and shares on posts were one thing, but concrete support from voters mattered more. Martin and Whelan created an online petition calling for legal change. More than 7,000 people in the United Kingdom signed the petition, which sent MPs prewritten emails from their constituents showing their support for the campaign. That amounted to an average of 10 emails per MP.

The political climate bolstered the case for reform. Public sentiment was growing in favor of the #MeToo movement. Just as women were talking about their experiences with sexual harassment, Martin was drawing attention to up-skirting. Martin's posts made the case that up-skirt photos were akin to the sexual assault of women and girls. When I interviewed Martin in 2020, I asked her if she had considered discussing up-skirt images as a violation of intimate privacy *and* an affront to gender equality. She agreed that up-skirt photos violated the "human right to privacy," but given the attention to the #MeToo movement, gender inequality made the most practical sense for the campaign.

The last piece of the puzzle was getting MPs to see that criminalizing up-skirt photos was in their interest. Martin and Whelan found the hook in interest-convergence theory, just as AG Harris had. A male teacher at an elite girls' school was caught taking photographs up students' skirts. After some of the parents expressed support for the #StopSkirtingtheIssue campaign, MPs started to change their tune. This made perfect sense to Martin—many of those MPs had children or grandchildren in schools that required girls to wear skirts as part of their uniforms. "The MPs could not blame the kids for wearing those skirts as they had blamed me," she explained to me.

Less than a year after Martin started calling for reform, MP Wera Hobhouse introduced a bill to criminalize up-skirting. The UK Ministry of Justice backed the bill, a promising sign. But in early June 2018, MP Christopher Chope blocked the bill, a move that quickly backfired on him. MPs and constituents draped underwear across his London office in protest. Tweets showed photos of women's underwear hung outside his door. One woman's tweet said: "I've made a small protest of knicker bunting outside my MP Christopher Chope's constituency office #Up-skirting #Chope #knickerstochope #Up-skirting bill 'no one should be able to photo my pants unless I want them to.'" The tweet went viral: it was retweeted more than 10,000 times and had 669 comments.[16]

On July 6, 2018, Martin and Whelan stood in the chamber as the House of Commons passed the bill to criminalize up-skirt photos. The House of Lords approved it in April 2019.[17] As Black Lives Matter co-organizer Alicia Garza has said: "Hashtags don't make movements. People do."[18] Martin showed that to be true, though on a smaller scale. She may have started the reform effort, but she succeeded with help from Whelan, volunteers, and constituents who signed online petitions.

The campaign was successful on another level. It sparked a re-examination of the UK's exploitation of intimate image laws. In 2020, the country's Ministry of Justice formed a law commission to assess the efficacy of criminal laws related to "intimate image abuse." The commission spent months consulting with victims like Martin, advocacy groups, and experts, including me. In February 2021, the commission issued a comprehensive report that conceptualized the wrongful behavior as both a violation of intimate privacy and a denial of equal opportunity for women and girls. It recommended a comprehensive criminal response to various types of image-based abuse, which, if adopted, would lead to meaningful change in the law—precisely what my proposal for a civil right to intimate privacy aims to do.[19]

While some coalitions are led by a small group of people, others have emerged in a less coordinated fashion. That is the story of South Korea.

MASS PROTESTS AND ACTIVISM

"My life is not your porn." That sentence was chanted over and over again by thousands of people who gathered in the streets of Seoul to protest the secret recording of women and girls in bathroom stalls, and sites devoted to hosting those videos. The protests were sparked by the May 2018 announcement of a 10-month jail sentence for a woman who posted her male classmate's nude photo online. She had secretly photographed the man as he posed nude for art class and posted the photo on a feminist website.[20] The woman was arrested, convicted, and sentenced within a month's time. The speed of the prosecution and the severity of the punishment stood in painful contrast to the state's lackluster response to male perpetrators:[21] only 2% of 5,437 suspects arrested for secretly recording women in 2017 were prosecuted.[22]

In five jam-packed protests in 2018, in ever-increasing numbers, demonstrators showed that they were fed up.[23] The first rally (May 19, 2018) had 12,000 protestors. The second rally (June 9) had 45,000; the third (July 7) had 60,000; and the fourth (August 4) had 70,000. During the fifth protest (December 22), more than 110,000 people marched in freezing temperatures.[24] Here was a reform coalition of thousands of women and their supporters.[25] Their protests were called "Uncomfortable Courage."[26]

The demonstrations reflected women's long-simmering concerns about nonconsensual intimate imagery. Ever since 2003, cell phones sold in the country have been designed to make a loud shutter noise whenever a photograph is taken. But, as with all things internet, technical solution soon met technical evasion and apps that silenced the shutter sound became available. In response, advocates focused on raising awareness about the prevalence of cameras hidden in public restrooms and changing rooms. Twitter accounts like @ProjReset and @DigitalCrimeKRS shared warnings about hidden cameras and circulated petitions about intimate privacy invasions.

Much like CCRI, activists in South Korea sought to rename the problem. In 2015, 22-year-old Soo-Yeu Park started the nonprofit organization Digital Sex Crime Out. The public referred to the nonconsensual taping of women in public bathrooms as "molka," the title of a television show about hidden-camera pranks.[27] But in the view of activists like

Park, the term "molka" trivialized the perpetrators' actions by equating their actions with playful pranks. Park described the mission of Digital Sex Crime Out as stamping out not "molka" but digital sex crime, just as CCRI rejected the term "revenge porn" in favor of "nonconsensual pornography." The organization's volunteers have been working with victims since 2017. (Park was named one of the BBC's 100 Women of 2018.)

Advocates also pressed law enforcement to prosecute perpetrators. Recall the "Nth Room" sextortion ring discussed in Chapter 2, where perpetrators extorted young girls and women to perform sexually explicit acts on camera and charged men to view the "slave" videos. Two female college journalists collected evidence about the sextortion ring and brought it to law enforcement. They got *five million* people to sign a petition calling on the South Korean president to arrest the perpetrators.[28] They have continued to investigate sextortion and other intimate privacy invasions on a popular YouTube channel.[29]

The 2018 protests—which brought the concerns of activists to the streets in ways that lawmakers could not ignore—resulted in promising reforms. The South Korean government's approach has been holistic. The first step was to embrace the approach of activists in using the term "digital sex crime information." Officials hope that the shift to DSCI will change attitudes regarding intimate privacy invasions.[30] Along these lines, city officials have supported training programs around DSCI for elementary and middle school students.[31]

The second step involved direct aid to victims. In 2019, the South Korean government established the Digital Sex Crime Information Bureau (DSCIB). Won-mo Lee, DSCIB's director general, explained that the government recognized the steep financial and emotional costs associated with digital sex crime information. Now, with the bureau's help, victims can obtain publicly funded counseling and support for housing and essentials.[32] From September to December 2019, 990 individuals reported DSCI to the Review Board and 880 received counseling and other services. In 2020, 6,313 individuals reported DSCI and 2,926 received counseling.[33]

Another aspect of the bureau's work is helping to get victims' intimate images taken down. DSCIB has the authority to ask sites to take down intimate images and, for internet service providers, to block access to pages coming from outside South Korea. DSCIB also maintains a digital sex crime information hash database, along the lines of the United States's NCMEC hash database that I discussed in Chapter 9. South Korean platforms have access to the hash database—they are not required to use it, but many do. In 2020, DSCIB issued 35,603 formal requests to block digital sex crime information, and nearly all Korean-based platforms complied with those requests (35,550).[34] Sites located "overseas over which [his] agency has no jurisdiction" remain an intractable problem for Lee and the bureau.[35]

Platforms now have legal obligations to address nonconsensual intimate images. In May 2020, a law was passed imposing duties of care on platforms so that they address harmful online activity, somewhat akin to my Section 230 reform proposal discussed in Chapter 8. Under South Korean law, platforms of a certain size must respond to complaints involving digital sex crime information. They must assign a point of contact for addressing those complaints. They have to issue regular transparency bulletins that detail the number of digital sex crime information complaints and their response to those complaints.[36]

Lawmakers have also focused on criminalizing digital sex crime information. Now, the nation's criminal law covers the nonconsensual taking, recording, manipulation (deepfake sex content), and disclosure of intimate images. Perpetrators face up to five years in prison rather than fines and probation. The law has enhanced penalties for sextortion. The DSCIB has called upon the police to enforce the law, though only time will tell if officers change their views and practices.[37] The city of Seoul has also increased the number of municipal employees checking for spy cameras in public bathrooms from 50 to 8,000.[38]

We have seen a change in the severity of criminal sentences in sextortion cases. In 2020, police arrested 245 men in connection with the Nth

Room sextortion scheme, including the ring leaders. Prosecutors sought life sentences for the individuals who ran the ring. In April 2021, one of the ring leaders, architecture student Moon Hyeong-wook, was sentenced to 34 years in prison. Another ring leader, Cho Joo-bin, was sentenced to 40 years in prison. On the day of the sentencing, victim advocates held a rally demanding maximum sentences for the defendants.[39]

Although these reforms are important, they are no cure-all for cultures like South Korea's that are steeped in misogyny and gender norms. No surprise that there has been resistance to reform measures aimed at protecting intimate privacy and combating gender inequality. As legislator Jung Choun-Sook has remarked, it has been "hard" for the "women's movement in South Korea to get victims of sexual assault to be properly seen as 'victims' and not 'flower snakes' (a term similar to gold digger)."[40]

The attitudes of law enforcement and the judiciary may be difficult to dislodge. After an international investigation of the world's largest child porn site on the dark web, in July 2020 the site's mastermind Son Jong-woo received an 18-month sentence—the same sentence given to a man convicted of stealing 18 eggs.[41]

Attitudes that trivialize the intimate privacy of women and minorities aren't unique to South Korea. Whereas societal attitudes and cultures differ in countless ways, misogyny and other forms of subordination are regrettable constants. And while reform has happened in several countries, it is all the more difficult where stereotypes and bigoted attitudes are more entrenched.

Attitudes are one thing; lobbyists are another. The reforms explored in this chapter did not threaten the business models of powerful companies. In fact, combating nonconsensual porn may be good business, as Facebook and Bumble see it (unless, of course, that is your business model). When individual perpetrators use social media platforms to violate the intimate privacy of women, nonwhites, or LGBTQ individuals, people from those groups will feel less safe. If people don't trust sites to keep them safe and protect their intimate privacy, they will leave when alternatives emerge. Remember MySpace? It was popular, until it wasn't. Although network efforts make it difficult to leave popular social media sites, the market will supply alternatives. Companies need to prepare for that eventuality. Protecting intimate privacy can help cement trust and loyalty.

Recall that Google changed its policy to de-index nonconsensual porn in 2015 during the work of the Cyber Exploitation Task Force. The company made the change in part because it already had to process European residents' "right to be forgotten" requests. Nonconsensual porn is precisely the sort of personal information that should be "forgotten"— indeed, it was never meant to escape the private sphere; it was never meant to be known publicly in the first place; the public has little to no legitimate interest in viewing it; and indeed, its subjects never permitted its consumption.

———

WHILE WE HAVE miles to walk across states, countries, and continents to protect intimate privacy, we have made progress. I am going to count that as a win, no matter how much work we have before us.

Epilogue

THE FIGHT CONTINUES

FOR LISA PAGE, THERE IS A BEFORE AND AN AFTER. BEFORE THE violation of her intimate privacy at the hands of the DOJ and President Trump, she was a highly regarded government lawyer, unknown to the public—to be exact, a GS15 lawyer (civil servant–speak for the highest rung on the federal pay scale). Page started at the DOJ in 2006 right after law school, joining the Honors Program, a coveted spot for law graduates. For years, she worked on organized crime cases. In 2012, she moved to the FBI to work on counterintelligence. Throughout her career as a government lawyer, Page was "anonymous by design." She had no online presence. She avoided posting anything online that could be exploited against her and her employer, the People of the United States.

Then came the after: the DOJ's release of her texts with Peter Strzok, President Trump's weaponization of those texts, and the never-ending cascade of discussion of the texts and her intimate life on Fox News, OANN, and Twitter. The after: a world in which the US government exploited her intimate privacy against her, the very government for whom she had maintained anonymity to avoid such exploitation. The after: resignation from her job and likely banishment from federal service, a role that defined how she saw herself (public servant) and filled her life with deep meaning. The after: suing her professional home (DOJ) for violating the Privacy Act, something she did only at the last second (two days before the time would run out for her to do so) because it was the last thing that she wanted to do. The after: an online identity (her Google CV) defined by her extramarital relationship and texts and sullied by online comments that labeled her a slut, coup plotter, and traitor and falsely accused her of sleeping with her former boss at the FBI, Andy McCabe. The after: being unable to see her former boss—her mentor—lest the cyber mob render that proof of her nonexistent affair.

When people ask Page if she wishes that the violation of her intimate privacy never happened, she thinks that "it is like imagining life as a choose-your-own-adventure game. It does not work like that." She would never wish the years of ongoing trauma on anyone—the constant heartache, the fear of crowds, the serious difficulty regaining her professional footing, the time spent reporting vile comments on Twitter. She would never wish on anyone those moments when she wasn't sure if she could survive the humiliation and the loss of her life's work.

But, as Page told me, the simple truth is that she is a different person now. The experience is "integral to who I am," Page explained. Others may define her by that experience, but she won't let it define her. She refuses to give power to the shame that others want her to feel—she has suffered enough. She should not be ashamed about her texts with Strzok; the public should never have read about them. It was all a "hard and terrible lesson."

What *is* the lesson for us? Should Page, already very careful, have lived her life assuming *anything* she ever wrote, said, texted, whispered, or confided, even in the most private of spaces or relationships, could become public and weaponized against her at any moment? Would that really be a life worth living?

Not by my lights. Not for Page or for anyone else. No one should have to tolerate the steady erosion of intimate privacy to get the most out of life in a digital age. We can delete apps from our phone and ask companies not to sell our data (to the extent that they let us), but the reality is that online services and products are part of our lives, and we need to ensure that they give us what we want and deserve, including intimate privacy.

Intimate privacy can be ours. Securing that future is a project that must begin now. We need to use every tool at our disposal, beginning with the law. Law is a mirror into our values and ideals. It reveals the future selves, society, and democracy that we want. The legal agenda set out in this book would make clear that intimate privacy—and the respect, love, equality, and democracy that it enables—is a moral imperative. With law's lessons in view, Spying Inc. and governments would come to see themselves as data guardians, rather than as data exploiters; individuals would come to treat others' bodies and confidences with respect and discretion, rather than with cruelty and contempt. With law informing social attitudes and practices, protecting intimate privacy would become something that we all just do, as natural to us as getting up in the morning and as important to us as the defense of other crucial rights and liberties.

I am amazed at how far we have come in only a decade. In 2009, I was told that any suggestion to hold content platforms responsible would "break the internet," that my suggestion that companies had to serve as the guardians of our intimate data was off the wall. Well, those skeptical attitudes don't rule the day anymore. Now, lawmakers and companies are taking these ideas seriously. And I have seen legal change both inside and outside the United States. In the United States, we have seen the passage of state laws criminalizing nonconsensual pornography, imperfect though they are. Globally, we have witnessed South Korea make important strides to support victims of intimate privacy and to penalize intimate privacy violations; and the United Kingdom take steps to address intimate image abuse in a comprehensive manner. These developments show me that we can take the next step and recognize intimate privacy as a civil right.

Of course, law won't change overnight. We need to reform our practices now. Here is where moral suasion comes in. Companies aren't incentivized to change their practices on their own, so we must persuade them to stop the over-collection of intimate information and to avoid the perils that follow. We need to press companies to hire more diverse teams to fund, conceive, and build the next generation's products and services so that tackling concerns about harms to women and minorities are part of the design process. We need to convince them to spearhead projects to protect intimate privacy because everyone's flourishing is on the line, because such protections would engender trust, and because they would secure a world where we could get the most out of digital technologies without fear that our intimate data might be used against us. It isn't too late for pressure campaigns. In the face of public pushback, companies have placed limits on their facial recognition systems. Facebook (now Meta) said that it will shut down the system it used to identify people in images posted on the social network (though it won't dispose of the system's algorithms). Microsoft and Amazon.com have restricted the use of their systems by law enforcement agencies. Today's products and services have great promise to supply knowledge and enable expression necessary for developing authentic identities, healthy esteem, and close relationships. I want us to get the most out of these tools, but we need to recognize that all the good they promise can only be realized if we protect intimate privacy.

If we don't create a world that assiduously protects privacy, more and more of us will suffer. We need to combat our cultures of violation. We need to flip the script so that what is normal and inevitable is the protection of intimate privacy, rather than its exploitation. Education, in all various and sundry forms, must be part of that effort. Parents, teachers, and students should discuss the fight for intimate privacy as *their* fight, not something far away or someone else's problem. The United States could make a different name for itself—as a legal and social culture where intimate privacy is respected and protected. Change in the United States might inspire legal and social change elsewhere. And if US products were designed with intimate privacy in mind, then its protection would be there from the start, for the good of subscribers everywhere.

I'm hopeful that as my daughters' and niece's generation comes of age, we will see that world come to fruition. It's a world worth fighting for.

Acknowledgments

FINDING THE RIGHT WORDS TO THANK THE PEOPLE WHO HELPED me as I wrote this book is a difficult task. Though I won't be able to fully capture the depth of my gratitude, I will try.

I have had a dream team of women behind me—my editors at W. W. Norton and Penguin Vintage UK, Melanie Tortoroli and Poppy Hampson, and my agent, Lucy Cleland. They believed in the project and helped me every step of the way. They are brilliant and thoughtful, full of inspiration and encouragement. Elizabeth Knoll, my editor for *Hate Crimes in Cyberspace*, provided helpful advice before introducing me to Lucy, who in turn connected me to Melanie and Poppy—an amazing group. The Norton team was fantastic—ever grateful to Jodi Beder, Steve Colca, Mo Crist, Renata Mitchell, and Rachel Salzman.

Over the years, so many individuals trusted me with their experiences. They sought my advice, but they taught me far more. I am indebted to them for letting me into their lives, for helping me understand the depth and breadth of their experiences, and for keeping me posted on how they were doing. I cherish them.

As I was formulating my ideas for this book in 2019, I had the honor of receiving a MacArthur Fellowship. The John D. and Cathe-rine T. MacArthur Foundation's support enabled me to take off a year from teaching, which gave me space and time to write the manuscript. It shored up my confidence. I will never forget that day in September 2019 when John Palfrey and Cecilia Conrad called to tell me the news, and Martha Minow's lunch on the day of the public announcement and her advice and friendship ever since. The Knight Foundation also gener-ously supported a study that Jonathon Penney, Alexis Shore, and I have been conducting about the impact of intimate privacy legal reform and platform self-regulation on our willingness to speak and engage in other key life opportunities. John Sands made that grant happen, and I am ever grateful.

The privacy and tech law community was uniquely supportive. Julia Angwin, Ryan Calo, Julie Cohen, Hany Farid, Barry Friedman, Sue Glueck, Woody Hartzog, Neil Richards, Paul Schwartz, Dan Solove, and Ari Waldman read drafts, workshopped chapters via Zoom, and nudged me to make this book the best that it could be. (Bless Ari and Barry for reading every chapter, above and beyond the call of duty!) Our group texts and emails kept me going. We lost Ian Kerr and Joel Reidenberg just as I began this work—I miss them terribly. Jon Penney and Alexis Shore have been extraordinary research partners—our work has been key to my thinking, and I am excited to share our findings when they are ready. Deep thanks to my colleagues at the Cyber Civil Rights Initiative: Hany Farid, Mary Anne Franks, Michelle Gonzalez, Holly Jacobs, Safiya Umoja Noble, and Ari Waldman. David Bateman, Elisa D'Amico, Car-rie Goldberg, and Erica Johnstone taught me about the reality of client representation while inspiring me (and everyone else who knows them). Alan Butler, John Davisson, and Caitriona Fitzgerald of the Electronic Privacy Information Center provided helpful insights; Chris Wolf, Kirk Nahra, Jules Polonetsky, and the late Kurt Wimmer modeled mentor-ship. I wasn't able to fulfill my promise to present this book to Kurt's practice at Covington—he died as I was completing the manuscript. The privacy community feels the loss of his support and leadership in deep and incalculable ways.

My mentors are many, but these scholars have had an indelible mark on my thinking: Anita Allen, Michele Goodwin, Linda McClain, Martha Nussbaum, Jana Singer, Geoffrey Stone, Robin West, and Benjamin Zipursky.

As I worked on different aspects of this project, I got fantastic feedback from Wael Abd-Almageed, Marc Blitz, Khiara Bridges, Susan Brison, Gian Marco Caletti, Ali Cooper-Ponte, Stacey Dogan, Amy Enright, Lisa Fairfax, Matthew Ferraro, James Fleming, Mike Fox, Rachel Goldbrenner, Leigh Goodmark, Michele Goodwin, Yasmin Green, Leslie Meltzer Henry, William Hitchcock, Clare Huntington, Rebecca Ingber, Margot Kaminski, David Kaye, Daphne Keller, Cam Kerry, Jeff Kosseff, Robin Lenhardt, Mark McKenna, Roger McNamee, Helen Norton, Nick Nugent, David Pozen, Amanda Pustilnik, Tara Roslin, David Rossman, Andrew Selbst, Jessica Silbey, Kate Silbaugh, Scott Skinner-Thompson, Daniel Sokol, Lior Strahelivitz, Peter Swire, Olivier Sylvain, Matthew Tokson, and Jonathan Zittrain. Students and faculty at American University School of Law, University of California, Berkeley School of Law, Boston University School of Law, Emory University School of Law, Gonzaga School of Law, New York University School of Law, UC Davis School of Law, University of Southern California's Visual Intelligence Lab, University of Virginia School of Law and Vanderbilt University School of Law provided terrific feedback.

I am indebted to my coauthors on various projects—our conversations and scholarship inspired me. Endless thanks to Bobby Chesney, Hany Farid, Mary Anne Franks, Barry Friedman, David Gray, Quinta Jurecic, Spencer Overton, Frank Pasquale, Jon Penney, Neil Richards, Daniel Solove, and Benjamin Wittes.

As I started my writing in earnest, I was lucky to join the University of Virginia School of Law's faculty. Ken Abraham, Risa Goluboff, Debbie Hellman, Leslie Kendrick, and Ted White provided extraordinarily helpful comments and suggestions. Richard Schragger, Payvand Ahdout, and Rachel Bayefsky advised me as I worked through ideas—they, along with Anne Coughlin, Charles Barzun, John Duffy, Kristen Eichensehr, Thomas Frampton, Andrew Hayashi, Kim Krawiec, Mitu Gulati, Cathy Hwang, Dan Ortiz, and Micah Schwartzman, provided serious cheer during the editing process. My dean Risa Goluboff is the exemplar of a scholar-mentor, and my former deans Angela Onwuachi-Willig of Boston University School of Law and Donald Tobin of University of Maryland School of Law supported me along the way.

This project benefited from the insights of lawmakers, law enforcers, career staff in the public and private sector, journalists, and activists. Vice President Kamala Harris was a north star. Michael Atleson, Emily Bazelon, Lauren Moxley Beatty, Sarah Cable, Julia Dahl, Antigone Davis, Ed Dumont, Gilad Edelman, Julie Grant, Rachel Haas, Drew Harwell, Kashmir Hill, Sarah Hoyle, Leah Juliett, Ryan Krieger, Won-mo Lee, Nadia Manzoor, Gina Martin, Rafi Martina, Karuna Nain, Jeffrey Rabkin, Stacey Schesser, and Mona Sedky were wonderful advisors and sounding boards.

Behind any scholarly effort is a group of intrepid librarians and research assistants. Shira Megerman and Leslie Ashbrook are librarians extraordinaire—they found me abundant resources, and Shira helped structure work for my research assistants. My research assistants at Boston University School of Law and the University of Virginia School of Law—as well as my daughters Ellie and Julia Jean—were superb. Their research was comprehensive, and I was buoyed by their ideas and good cheer. Thank you to Matt Atha, Jackson Barnett, Ross Chapman, Bao Chau, Olivia Coleman, Court Dierkes, Laura Faas, Micki Frai, Sarah Guinee, Rebecca Gutterman, Emily Hockett, Caroline Hopland, Peter Kaplan, Shweta Kumar, Jehanne McCollough, Michaela Rosen, Rachel Samuels, Julia Schur, Felicity Slater, and Rebecca Weitzel. Serious thanks to all of the LawTech Fellows at UVA Law. I also had the help of wonderful undergraduate students, Ali Ostad and Fiona

Richards. Rebecca Klaff, Billi Jo Morningstar, and Karen Sowers of the University of Virginia were enormously helpful—there is nothing they can't do.

My family: I could not have done any of this without my husband, Lou, and daughters, JJ and Ellie. They talked to me about this work all of the time; supported me; made me laugh; gave reassuring hugs; and helped in immeasurable ways (including research and editing!). My sister and best friend, Dr. Jeanine Morris-Rush, was a constant interlocutor and companion; as an ob-gyn, she provided insights about intimate privacy that made an indelible mark on these pages. My father, Dr. Joel Jean Morris, is with me every day; though he died more than 25 years ago, I feel his kindness, love, and support. My mother, Mary Lee Morris, stepdad, Bob Kaczorowski, brother-in-law, Greg Rush, mother-in-law, Cokie Citron, niece and nephews, Olivia, Landon, James, and Luke, and adopted family member Andrew Hudak gave great hugs and inspired me. And of course Patsy "Pizzle" Bean, whose love is unconditional. Through my relationships with them, I have come to understand the meaning of love.

Appendix

TIPS FOR EVERYDAY INTERACTIONS

WHEN IT COMES to your digital communications and interactions, you can take a number of steps to protect your accounts, communications, and activities. These suggestions are admittedly modest—the risks to our intimate privacy are systemic, so individuals can only do so much to protect themselves. Here's what I try to do.

Tip #1: Have strong and varied passwords.

A GOOD PASSWORD can go a long way. Having different passwords for your accounts isn't easy, but it is worth the effort. Here are some ideas for keeping track of your passwords. Consider using a password manager, which saves and encrypts lists of your passwords. Most password managers require a master password, which increases the safety of your stored passwords, as the managers of the services do not retain your master password. Some examples of password managers include LastPass, Dashlane, and iCloud Keychain (for Apple users). When using a password manager, lock it with a strong password. Passwords should not be easy to guess and should not contain any identifiable information.

Tip #2: Work on the privacy of your communications and online activities.

YOU CAN TAKE steps to protect the privacy of your online communications. To send and make private messages and calls, download encrypted apps like Signal. You can use PGP encryption to protect your email. This is basically an added layer of privacy and authentication. PGP encryption can be used on most online communications, though one of its most common uses is email. And cover up the camera on your laptop or desktop computer when you are not using the camera—this prevents hackers from seeing, hearing, and recording you when you don't want to be seen, heard, and recorded.

Tip #3: There are ways to help you avoid tracking from advertisers.

PLUG-IN BROWSER EXTENSIONS are a good way to block ads and limit tracking. Privacy Badger and uBlock Origin are examples. For some services like Facebook, Google, Reddit, and Twitter, you may not be able to fully disable ads. For others, you can cut down the frequency of ads. Look for opt-outs within the settings tabs.

Tip #4: Add an extra layer of privacy control.

USE MULTIFACTOR AUTHENTICATION (MFA). When you input a username and password to log into an online account, MFA can add an extra component of security. With MFA, you will not be able to get into your account simply with a username and password. Rather, you will need to use two or more authentication methods. Authentication methods vary widely, but they are all easy to use and accessible—and difficult to hack into. Some examples of authentication methods are security questions, fingerprints, and codes sent to your cell phone.*

---

* "What Is Multi-Factor Authentication (MFA), and How Does It Work?," OneLogin, accessed July 27, 2021, https://www.onelogin.com/learn/what-is-mfa.

Tip #5: Avoid using public Wi-Fi—it can prevent hacking into your mobile device.

I MADE THIS mistake while riding the Amtrak train—and regretted it as I watched someone erase all of my work emails. We all make mistakes!

Tip #6: Think before you click, view, and share.

CONSIDER THE ETHICS of your digital engagement. Ask yourself if you really want to click on sites known for sharing nonconsensual intimate images. Those sites don't deserve your attention. Nor do links that someone sends you that suggests that you are looking or watching something that someone did not want others to see or hear. Ethical consumption matters because it conveys to producers of content that they have an audience. Don't give them that impression.

TIPS FOR APP USERS

Tip #1: Check the privacy settings on your mobile device to see if there are things that you can do to cut down on an app's collection of your data.

YOU MIGHT BE able to switch the defaults to decrease the amount of personal data that is being collected and shared. Consider limiting which apps have access to your location and reset the defaults so your location information is only collected when you are using the app (if indeed the app needs your location to operate)

Tip #2: You are not obligated to share intimate information.

IF YOUR APP requires you to share information about yourself that you don't really want to share and won't let you skip that step, reconsider using the app. Apps will try to get you to disclose far more personal information than they need. Don't fall into that trap. If the app lets you skip providing that information, pay attention to your gut and skip sharing it.

Tip #3: Consider using a burner email (not your primary email) when you sign up for apps.

THIS ADDS AN extra barrier of security between your personal life and your app life. You can make a separate email account that you use solely for apps.

Tip #4: If you are not going to use an app anymore, delete the account and the app.

THIS PREVENTS THE app from obtaining unwanted access to your phone, location, etc.

TIPS FOR HOME DEVICES AND OTHER TOOLS

Tip #1: Create your own username.
OFTENTIMES, WHEN YOU first set up your home device, a default username is selected. To secure your privacy, change the username to something unique.

Tip #2: Disable functions that you do not need.
HOME DEVICES OFTEN offer a myriad of functions, like tapping into information from other devices. If you don't need such features, disable them.

Tip #3: If your manufacturer suggests a software update, do not avoid it.
SOFTWARE UPDATES HELP solve and avoid security flaws.

Tip #4: If you are using a home device that uses a "wake word" (a word that enables activation), change the word to something not in your day-to-day lexicon—it may cut down on the over-collection of your data.

Tip #5: If you want to delete data stored in a home device, you may be able to access and clear your home device's history within the settings.

Tip #6: Replace outdated home routers.

GUIDANCE FOR PARENTS AND GUARDIANS

YOU MIGHT THINK that when it comes to digital technologies, kids are better at it than you, smarter than you, and savvier than you. But truth be told, they are not, at least not in the ways that count. As a parent, you can take several precautions to protect a child's privacy and safety online.

Tip #1: Your teenagers need your help protecting their privacy.

AFTER THE KIDS in your lives turn 13, they are no longer protected by the federal child privacy law. So, the tips that apply to adults also apply to teenagers. An important area that teenagers will confront are educational tools used by their school. Vendors provide those tools—check out what your school and the vendor are saying about collection, storage, and sharing of personal data. You may be able to limit the over-collection of that data and help educate teachers.

Tip #2: Start the conversation and keep talking (and talking).

TALK TO YOUR kids about intimate privacy and why it is so important. Discuss how they can protect themselves and others—often left out of the conversation is the responsibility that teenagers have for their peers and friends. Explain that privacy for thee *is* privacy for me. We are social beings. Keeping a friend's texts private also protects lots of other people and not only the people in the chain of conversation. What is practical is also moral and ethical.

WHEN YOU FEEL lost in these conversations, you can consult *The Connected Parent: An Expert Guide to Parenting in a Digital World*. This book, my favorite resource, is written by tech expert-lawyer-educators John Palfrey (president of the MacArthur Foundation, former head of Phillips Academy Andover) and Urs Gasser (law professor).

Tip #3: Consider reading books and watching movies (with your kids) that explore privacy generally and intimate privacy specifically.

THERE IS OFTEN nothing better than a great book or movie to kickstart conversations about the risks to intimate privacy posed by networked tools. For older kids, I suggest Julia Dahl's *The Missing Hours*, a thriller about the recording and sharing of a college student's sexual assault and the fallout. The book is valuable for the conversations that it will generate about the harms of intimate privacy invasions and sexual assault and the perils of taking the law into one's own hands. The movie *The Lives of Others*, about the Stasi regime of East Germany, will hopefully spark conversations about what it is like living in a surveillance state. For much younger kids, Daniel J. Solove has written *The Eyemonger*, the first children's fiction book about privacy, and it is delightful. It combines catchy rhymes and beautiful illustrations that tease out why privacy matters for creativity. It debunks the notion that the only people who need privacy are those with something to hide.

TIPS FOR INTIMATE PARTNERS

TALK TO ANYONE with whom you become intimate—physically or emotionally—about your expectations about intimate privacy. Make clear what you want and expect. Talk about intimate images. This is true whether you are with a longtime partner or someone you have just met and with whom you plan on having some form of sex.

GUIDANCE FOR VICTIMS

IF YOUR INTIMATE privacy has been violated, here are some important first steps to take.

Tip #1: Make a record of what has happened.

THIS IS HARD for victims to hear because they just want the privacy violation to disappear. But you should create a record of what is happening to you. Take screenshots. Keep emails and texts. Do a Reverse Image Search to help catch all instances of image posting.

Tip #2: Report intimate privacy violations to the site or content platform on which it is posted.

YOU MAY BE able to report certain intimate privacy invasions like nonconsensual pornography and deepfake sex videos as terms of service violations. Keep a record of your reports and the outcomes.

Tip #3: Ask Google, Yahoo!, and Bing to de-link nonconsensual pornography and deepfake sex videos in searches of your name.

GO TO A search engine's help page. There, you will find a link to start a request for the removal of nonconsensual intimate images in a search of your name. In its help page, Google explains that you or someone who is authorized to speak on your behalf can submit a request to remove links to the images. You or your representative reviews the URLs to determine if the images included in the link violate the policy banning nonconsensual intimate personal images. Google explains that it will provide notice about any action that it takes in response to the request.

Tip #4: Think about seeing a victim advocate or social worker in your area.

IN THE UNITED States, victim advocates can be found in police stations, rape crisis centers, domestic violence prevention centers, and state or local offices (office of the state attorney general, sheriff's office, and county offices).* Also, advocacy groups like Cyber Civil Rights Initiative (US) and Revenge Porn Helpline (UK) connect victims with helpline services that provide advice.

Tip #5: Consider seeing a therapist or health professional.

OF COURSE, THERAPY isn't for everyone, nor is it available to everyone. But victims have told me time and time again how helpful it was to talk to someone with mental health expertise about their anxiety, PTSD, and depression related to violations of intimate privacy.

Tip #6: Try to connect with supportive online communities.

LOOK FOR ONLINE communities that you can join to talk about the abuse. Check out HeartMob, an online support site for individuals experiencing online harassment.

Tip #7: Find a lawyer.

THERE IS NOTHING better than finding an attorney who gets what you have gone through and wants to help you navigate the legal system.

---

* "Get Help," Cyber Civil Rights Initiative, accessed July 27, 2021, https://www
.cybercivilrights.org/faqs-usvictims/.

HOW TO GET INVOLVED WITH ADVOCACY EFFORTS

THERE ARE MYRIAD ways you can get involved in advocacy efforts, both to increase online safety and to support victims of intimate privacy violations.

Tip #1: Support nonprofit organizations devoted to fostering intimate privacy and equal opportunity online.

1. Cyber Civil Rights Initiative (CCRI) is a nonprofit organization that fights online abuses that threaten civil right and liberties. They serve thousands of victims around the world, and work to impact law, policy, and technological innovation and implementations that can increase and ensure intimate privacy. You can support CCRI through volunteering, legal support, or donations.
2. March Against Revenge Porn is a nonprofit devoted to raising awareness about intimate privacy violations. It has begun a legal defense fund that aims to provide mini-grants to individuals who have faced the posting of their intimate images online and who come from "marginalized backgrounds or face unique socioeconomic barriers to justice."
3. #iCANHELP works to empower kids and young adults to create positive online communities. To get involved with them, you can donate, become a sponsor, or bring one of their workshops to your workplace.
4. Take Back the Tech! is a campaign project working to empower women and girls to take control of the technological space to end violence against women. Their website offers ways to enter their campaign in your own area.
5. Revenge Porn Helpline is a UK-funded service that supports adults (18+) living in the UK who are experiencing intimate

privacy violations. The Helpline provides advice, helps with the reporting of online content, and maintains a relationship with a legal advice center.

6. VOIC.org.uk is run by a UK survivor of intimate image abuse. The site provides stories from victim survivors.

Tip #2: Get involved with legal reform.

CONTACT YOUR REPRESENTATIVE to push for the passage of laws to protect intimate privacy.

Tip #3: If you are an attorney, try to get your practice involved in representing victims on a pro bono or low-cost basis.

IF YOU ARE interested in offering pro- or low-bono services to victims, you can send your contact information to the Cyber Civil Rights Initiative so you can be included in our roster of attorneys. CCRI's website has more specific information regarding legal involvement and representation.

Notes

INTRODUCTION: INTIMACY IN THE TWENTY-FIRST CENTURY

1. Samuel D. Warren and Louis D. Brandeis, "The Right to Privacy," *Harvard Law Review* 4 (1890): 193–99.
2. Iris Marion Young, *Intersecting Voices: Dilemmas of Gender, Political Philosophy, and Policy* (Princeton, NJ: Princeton University Press, 1997).
3. Charles Fried, *An Anatomy of Values* (Cambridge, MA: Harvard University Press, 1970), 140.
4. John G. Holmes and John K. Rempel, "Trust in Close Relationships," in *Close Relationships*, ed. Clyde Hendrick (Thousand Oaks, CA: SAGE Publications, 1989), 187, 190.
5. Julie Cohen, *Between Truth and Power* (New York: Oxford University Press, 2019), 5. Shoshana Zuboff has memorably described it as "surveillance capitalism." Shoshana Zuboff, *The Age of Surveillance Capitalism* (New York: PublicAffairs, 2020).
6. FBI, "Online Extortion Scams Increasing During the COVID-19 Crisis," August 20, 2020, https://www.ic3.gov/media/2020/200420.aspx.
7. Suthentira Govender, "Bored South Africans Increasingly Falling Prey to 'Sextortion' during Lockdown," *Times Live (South Africa)*, April 20, 2020, https://www.timeslive.co.za/news/south-africa/2020-04-20-bored-south-africans-increasingly-falling-prey-to-sextortion-during-lockdown/; Fight the New Drug, "'Sextortion' Scams Dramatically Increase Since COVID-19 Quarantines Began,'" June 19, 2020, https://fightthenewdrug.org/sextortion-scams-increase-since-covid-19-quarantines-began/.
8. Yanet Ruvalcaba and Asia A. Eaton, "Nonconsensual Pornography among U.S. Adults: A Sexual Scripts Framework on Victimization, Perpetration, and Health Correlates for Women and Men," *Journal of Psychology of Violence* (2019), https://www.esafety.gov.au/sites/default/files/2019-07/Image-based-abuse-national-survey-summary-report-2017.pdf (women under 45 more likely to face nonconsensual porn than older women).

9. Ruvalcaba and Eaton, "Nonconsensual Pornography." Ari Waldman found that gay and bisexual male users of dating apps are more frequently victims of nonconsensual pornography than both the general population and the broader lesbian, gay, and bisexual communities. Ari Waldman, "Law, Privacy, and Online Dating: 'Revenge Porn' in Gay Online Communities," *Law and Social Inquiry* 44 (2019).

CHAPTER 1: SPYING INC.

1. Dieter Bonn, "Amazon Announces Halo, a Fitness Band and App that Scans Your Body and Voice," *The Verge*, August 27, 2020, https://www.theverge.com/2020 /8/27/21402493/amazon-halo-band-health-fitness-body-scan-tone-emotion -activity-sleep; Adrienne So, "Wrist Watchers: No matter how hard you're working out, or just walking, monitor your progress with a smart new fitness tracker," *Wired* (magazine), December 10, 2021, https://www.wired.com/gallery/best-fitness -tracker/.

2. Forbrukerradet, "Out of Control," January 14, 2020, https://www.forbrukerradet.no/ undersokelse/no-undersokelsekategori/report-out-of-control/; Judith Duportail, "I Asked Tinder for My Data. It Sent Me 800 Pages of My Deepest, Darkest Secrets," *The Guardian*, September 26, 2017, https://www.theguardian.com/technology/2017/ sep/26/tinder-personal-data-dating-app-messages-hacked-sold.

3. Kashmir Hill, "I Got Access to My Secret Consumer Score. Now You Can Get Yours Too," *New York Times*, November 4, 2019, https://www.nytimes.com/2019/11/04/ business/secret-consumer-score-access.html.

4. Aleecia M. McDonald and Lorrie Cranor, "The Cost of Reading Privacy Policies," *I/S: A Journal of Law and Policy for the Information Society* 4 (2008–9): 540–61.

5. Joseph Turow, Lauren Feldman, and Kimberly Meltzer, "Open to Exploitation: American Shoppers Online and Offline," Report from the Annenberg Public Policy Center of the University of Pennsylvania, 2005, https://repository.upenn.edu/cgi/viewcontent .cgi?article=1035&context=asc_papers.

6. Woodrow Hartzog, *Privacy's Blueprint* (Cambridge, MA: Harvard University Press, 2018), 211.

7. Pinelopi Troullinou, "Exploring the Subjective Experience of Everyday Surveillance: The Case of Smartphone Devices as Means of Facilitating 'Seductive' Surveillance," PhD thesis, the Open University, http://oro.open.ac.uk/52613/2/thesis_PT_library_ submission.pdf.

8. Anna Altman, "Mommy and Data," *The New Republic*, January 14, 2019, https:// newrepublic.com/article/152693/femtech-companies-alleviate-exploit-female-anxiety.

9. Joseph Turow, *The Voice Catchers* (New Haven, CT: Yale University Press, 2021).

10. Woodrow Hartzog, *Privacy's Blueprint* (Cambridge, MA: Harvard University Press, 2018), 162.

11. Laura Stampler, "Inside Tinder: Meet the Guys Who Turned Dating into an Addiction," *Time* (magazine), February 6, 2014, https://time.com/4837/tinder-meet-the -guys-who-turned-dating-into-an-addiction/.

12. Nancy Jo Sales, *Nothing Personal: My Secret Life in the Dating App Inferno* (New York: Hatchette Book Group, 2021), 11.

13. Allen St. John, "Smart Speakers That Listen When They Shouldn't," *Consumer Reports*, August 29, 2019, https://www.consumerreports.org/smart-speakers/smart -speakers-that-listen-when-they-shouldnt/.

14. Jeb Su, "Confirmed: Apple Caught In Siri Privacy Scandal, Let Contractors Listen to Private Recordings," *Forbes*, July 30, 2019, https://www.forbes.com/sites/ jeanbaptiste/2019/07/30/confirmed-apple-caught-in-siri-privacy-scandal-let -contractors-listen-to-private-voice-recordings/?sh=3422d3317314.

15. Turow, *The Voice Catchers*.

16. SEC Consult, "Internet of Dildos: A Long Way to a Vibrant Future—from IoT to IoD," January 2, 2018, https://sec-consult.com/en/blog/2018/02/internet-of-dildos-a -long-way-to-a-vibrant-future-from-iot-to-iod/index.html.

17. Grand View Research, "Sex Toys Market Size, Share and Trends Analysis Report by Type (Male, Female), by Distribution Channel (E-commerce, Specialty Stores, Mass Merchandizers), by Region, and Segment Forecasts, 2021–2028," *Market Analysis Report*, January 2021, https://www.grandviewresearch.com/industry-analysis/sex-toys -market.

18. Kyle Taylor and Laura Silver, "Smartphone Ownership Is Growing Rapidly around the World, but Not Always Equally," Pew Research Center, February 5, 2019, https://www .pewresearch.org/global/wp-content/uploads/sites/2/2019/02/Pew-Research-Center_ Global-Technology-Use-2018_2019-02-05.pdf.

19. Elena Maris, Timothy Libert, and Jennifer Henrichsen, "Tracking Sex: The Implications of Widespread Sexual Data Leakage and Tracking on Porn Websites," *New Media and Society* 22, no. 11 (July 2019), https://doi.org/10.1177/1461444820924632.

20. Natasha Lomas, "GDPR Adtech Complaints Keep Stacking Up in Europe," *Tech-Crunch*, May 20, 2019, https://techcrunch.com/2019/05/20/gdpr-adtech-complaints -keep-stacking-up-in-europe/.

21. Maris, Libert, and Henrichsen, "Tracking Sex."

22. Pelayo Vallina et al., "Tales from the Porn: A Comprehensive Privacy Analysis of the Web Porn Ecosystem," *Proceedings of the Internet Measurement Conference,* October 2019, https://doi.org/10.1145/3355369.3355583.

23. Charlie Warzel, "Facebook and Google Trackers Are Showing Up on Porn Sites," *New York Times*, July 17, 2019, https://www.nytimes.com/2019/07/17/opinion/google -facebook-sex-websites.html.

24. Sebastian Meineck, "Here's How Much Pornhub Knows about You," *VICE*, September 5, 2019, https://www.vice.com/en/article/kzmmpa/pornhub-xhamster-data-about -you.

25. Daniel Zwerdling, "Your Digital Trail: Private Company Access," *NPR*, October 1, 2013, https://www.npr.org/sections/alltechconsidered/2013/10/01/227776072/your-digital -trail-private-company-access.

26. Natasha Singer and Aaron Krolik, "Grindr and OkCupid Spread Personal Details,

Study Says," *New York Times*, January 13, 2020, https://www.nytimes.com/2020/01/13/technology/grindr-apps-dating-data-tracking.html.

27. Singer and Krolik, "Grindr and OkCupid Spread Personal Details."

28. Kit Huckvale, John Torous, and Mark Larsen, "Assessment of the Data Sharing and Privacy Practices of Smartphone Apps for Depression and Smoking Cessation, JAMA Network Open, April 19, 2019; see also Rachel Becker, "That Mental Health App Might Share Your Data without Telling You," *The Verge*, April 20, 2019, https://www.theverge.com/2019/4/20/18508382/apps-mental-health-smoking-cessation-data-sharing-privacy-facebook-google-advertising.

29. Becker, "That Mental Health App," note 32.

30. Julia Angwin, *Dragnet Nation: A Quest for Privacy, Security, and Freedom in a World of Relentless Surveillance* (New York: St. Martin's Griffin, 2014).

31. Michelle Boorstein, Marisa Iati, and Annys Shin, "Top U.S. Catholic Church Official Resigns After Cellphone Data Used to Track Him on Grindr and to Gay Bars," *Washington Post*, July 21, 2021, https://www.washingtonpost.com/religion/2021/07/20/bishop-misconduct-resign-burrill/.

32. Joseph Cox, "Inside the Industry that Unmasks People at Scale," *Vice Motherboard*, July 14, 2021, https://www.vice.com/en/article/epnmvz/industry-unmasks-at-scale-maid-to-pii.

33. Alfred Ng and Maddy Varner, "The Little-Known Data Broker Industry Is Spending Big Bucks Lobbying Congress," *The Markup*, April 1, 2021, https://themarkup.org/privacy/2021/04/01/the-little-known-data-broker-industry-is-spending-big-bucks-lobbying-congress.

34. Daniel J. Solove, *The Digital Person* (New York: New York University Press, 2004).

35. Lois Beckett, "Everything We Know about What Data Brokers Know about You," *ProPublica*, June 13, 2014, https://www.propublica.org/article/everything-we-know-about-what-data-brokers-know-about-you; Steve Kroft, "The Data Brokers: Selling Your Personal Information," *CBS 60 Minutes*, March 9, 2014, https://www.cbsnews.com/news/data-brokers-selling-personal-information-60-minutes/.

36. Aaron Rieke, Harlan Yu, David Robinson, and Joris von Hoboken, "Data Brokers in an Open Society," UpTurn Report, *Open Society Foundations*, 2016, https://www.opensocietyfoundations.org/uploads/42d529c7-a351-412e-a065-53770cf1d35e/data-brokers-in-an-open-society-20161121.pdf.

37. Natasha Singer, "The Scoreboards Where You Can't See Your Score," *New York Times*, December 27, 2014, https://www.nytimes.com/2014/12/28/technology/the-scoreboards-where-you-cant-see-your-score.html.

38. Jon Keegan and Alfred Ng, "There's a Multibillion-Dollar Market for Your Phone's Location Data," *The Markup*, September 30, 2021, https://themarkup.org/privacy/2021/09/30/theres-a-multibillion-dollar-market-for-your-phones-location-data; Jennifer Valentino-DeVries, Natasha Singer, Michael H. Keller, and Aaron Krolik, "Your Apps Know Where You Were Last Night, and They're Not

Keeping It a Secret," *New York Times*, December 10, 2018, https://www.nytimes.com/interactive/2018/12/10/business/location-data-privacy-apps.html.

39. Danielle Keats Citron and Frank Pasquale, "The Scored Society: Due Process for Automated Predictions," *Washington Law Review* 89 (2014).

40. Wolfie Christl, "Corporate Surveillance in Everyday Life," *CrackedLabs*, June 2017, https://crackedlabs.org/en/corporate-surveillance.

41. Christl, "Corporate Surveillance in Everyday Life."

42. Samantha Cole, "Shady Data Brokers Are Selling Online Dating Profiles by the Millions," *VICE*, November 12, 2018, https://www.vice.com/en/article/59vbp5/shady-data-brokers-are-selling-online-dating-profiles-by-the-millions.

43. Flint Duxfield and Scott Mitchell, "Personal Data of Thousands of Australians Sold for Just $60 US," *ABC News Australia*, May 30, 2019, https://www.abc.net.au/news/2019-05-31/online-privacy-personal-data-purchased-for-$us60-warning-experts/11157092.

44. BeenVerified does not list its prices on its site. I had to sign up for its services to get its pricing and information. I signed up for a month in 2021 (as I was writing the book) and then canceled the service.

45. Christl, "Corporate Surveillance in Everyday Life."

46. Lachlan Markay and Sam Stein, "Dems Are Buying 'Tens of Millions' of Cellphone Numbers in Huge Voter Contact Push," *Daily Beast*, January 29, 2020, https://www.thedailybeast.com/dems-are-buying-tens-of-millions-of-cellphone-numbers-in-huge-voter-contact-push; Geoffrey A. Fowler, "How Politicians Target You: 3,000 Data Points on Every Voter, Including Your Phone Number," *Washington Post*, October 27, 2020, https://www.washingtonpost.com/technology/2020/10/27/political-campaign-data-targeting/.

47. Acxiom, "Acxiom Data," 2021, https://www.acxiom.com/customer-data/.

48. Julia Angwin, "Why Online Tracking Is Getting Creepier: The Merger of Online and Offline Data Is Bringing More Intrusive Tracking," *ProPublica*, June 12, 2014.

49. UK Information Commissioner's Office, "Investigation into Data Protection Compliance in the Direct Marketing Data Broking Sector," October 2020, https://ico.org.uk/media/action-weve-taken/2618470/investigation-into-data-protection-compliance-in-the-direct-marketing-data-broking-sector.pdf; UK Information Commissioner's Office, "ICO Takes Enforcement Action against Experian after Data Broking Investigation," October 27, 2020, https://ico.org.uk/about-the-ico/news-and-events/news-and-blogs/2020/10/ico-takes-enforcement-action-against-experian-after-data-broking-investigation/.

50. Becker, "That Mental Health App."

51. Michelle L. Moglia et al., "Evaluation of Smartphone Menstrual Cycle Tracking Applications Using an Adapted APPLICATIONS Scoring System," *Journal of Obstetrics and Gynecology* 127 (June 2016); Kaitlyn Tiffany, "Period-tracking Apps Are Not for Women," *Vox*, November 16, 2018, https://www.vox.com/the-goods/2018/11/13/18079458/menstrual-tracking-surveillance-glow-clue-apple-health.

52. Laura Shipp and Jorge Blasco, "How Private Is Your Period? A Systematic Analysis of Menstrual App Privacy Policies," in *Sciendo: Proceedings on Privacy Enhancing Technologies* 497–99 (2020).

53. Tiffany, "Period-Tracking Apps Are Not for Women."

54. Michelle L. Moglia et al., "Evaluation of Smartphone Menstrual Cycle Tracking Applications Using an Adapted APPLICATIONS Scoring System," *Journal of Obstetrics & Gynecology* 127 (June 2016).

55. Anna Altman, "Mommy and Data," *The New Republic*, January 14, 2019, https://newrepublic.com/article/152693/femtech-companies-alleviate-exploit-female-anxiety.

56. Olivia Sudjic, " 'I Felt Colossally Naïve': The Backlash against the Birth Control App," *The Guardian*, July 21, 2018, https://www.theguardian.com/society/2018/jul/21/colossally-naive-backlash-birth-control-app.

57. Natasha Singer, "Period-Tracking Apps Say You May Have a Disorder. What If They Are Wrong?," *New York Times*, October 27, 2019, https://www.nytimes.com/2019/10/27/technology/personaltech/health-apps-hormonal-disorder-pcos.html.

58. 45 C.F.R. § 164.514(b)(1) (allowing health professionals to trade sensitive information so long as they made the data unidentifiable).

59. Michelle Meyer, "Law, Ethics, and Science of Re-identification Demonstrations," Harvard Law Petrie Flom Center's Bill of Health, https://blog.petrieflom.law.harvard.edu/symposia/law-ethics-science-of-re-identification-demonstrations/.

60. Adam Tanner, "How Data Brokers Make Money off Your Medical Records," *Scientific American*, February 1, 2016, https://www.scientificamerican.com/article/how-data-brokers-make-money-off-your-medical-records/.

61. Paul Ohm, "Broken Promises of Privacy: Responding to the Surprising Failure of Anonymization," *UCLA Law Review* 57 (2010).

62. Naomi Kresge, Ilya Khrennikov, and David Ramli, "How Period-Tracking Apps Are Monetizing Women's Extremely Personal Data," *Bloomberg News*, January 24, 2019, https://www.bloomberg.com/news/articles/2019-01-24/how-period-tracking-apps-are-monetizing-women-s-extremely-personal-data.

63. Donna Rosato, "What Your Period Tracking App Knows about You," *Consumer Reports*, January 28, 2020, https://www.consumerreports.org/health-privacy/what-your-period-tracker-app-knows-about-you/.

64. Sam Schechner, "Eleven Popular Apps That Shared Data with Facebook," *Wall Street Journal*, February 24, 2019, https://www.wsj.com/articles/eleven-popular-apps-that-shared-data-with-facebook-11551055132.

65. Danielle Keats Citron, "Reservoirs of Danger: The Evolution of Public and Private Law at the Dawn of the Information Age," *Southern California Law Review* 80 (2007).

66. Renju Jose, "Australia Tracing Source of COVID-19 Case in Victoria State," *Reuters*, May 11, 2021, https://www.reuters.com/world/asia-pacific/australia-tracing-source-covid-19-case-victoria-state-2021-05-12/.

67. Danielle Citron and Geng Ngarmboonanant, "Be Very Wary of Trump's Health

Surveillance Plans," *Washington Post*, April 16, 2020, https://www.washingtonpost .com/opinions/2020/04/16/be-very-wary-trumps-health-surveillance-plans/.

68. Sadaf Khan, "Data Bleeding Everywhere: A Story of Period Trackers," *Medium*, June 7, 2019, https://deepdives.in/data-bleeding-everywhere-a-story-of-period-trackers-8766 dc6a1e00.

69. Deborah Lupton, *Data Selves* (Cambridge: Polity Press, 2020), 104.

70. Sarah Myers West, Meredith Whittacker, and Kate Crawford, "Discriminating Systems: Gender, Race, and Power in AI," *AI Now Institute*, April 2019, https:// ainowinstitute.org/discriminatingsystems.pdf.

71. Rebecca Heilweil, "Why Algorithms Can Be Racist and Sexist," *Vox's recode*, February 18, 2020, https://www.vox.com/recode/2020/2/18/21121286/algorithms-bias -discrimination-facial-recognition-transparency.

72. Julie Cohen, *Configuring the Networked Self* (New Haven, CT: Yale University Press, 2012), 144.

73. M. Ali et al., "Discrimination through Optimization: How Facebook's Ad Delivery Can Lead to Skewed Outcomes," *Proceedings of the ACM on Human-Computer Interaction* 3 (CSCW, November 2019).

74. Safiya Noble, *Algorithms of Oppression: How Search Engines Reinforce Racism* (New York: New York University Press, 2016).

75. "Period-Tracking Apps Are Monetizing Women's Extremely Personal Data," *Bloomberg Business*, January 24, 2019, https://www.bloomberg.com/news/ articles/2019-01-24/how-period-tracking-apps-are-monetizing-women-s -extremely-personal-data.

76. Drew Harwell, "Is Your Period App Sharing Your Intimate Data with Your Boss?," *Washington Post*, April 10, 2019, https://www.washingtonpost.com/technology /2019/04/10/tracking-your-pregnancy-an-app-may-be-more-public-than-you-think/.

77. Forbrukerradet, "Out of Control."

78. Drew Harwell, "Code Words and Fake Names: The Low-tech Ways Women Protect Their Privacy on Pregnancy Apps," *Washington Post*, April 25, 2019), https://www .washingtonpost.com/technology/2019/04/25/code-words-fake-names-low-tech-ways -women-protect-their-privacy-pregnancy-apps/.

CHAPTER 2: PRIVACY INVADERS

1. Myron Brenton, *The Privacy Invaders* (New York: Coward-McCann, 1964), 152–55.

2. Samuel Dash, *The Intruders: Unreasonable Searches and Seizures from King John to John Ashcroft* (New Brunswick: Rutgers University Press, 2004).

3. Dan Morse, "Chevy Chase Landlord Used Tiny Cameras to Peep on Tenants, Policy Say," *Washington Post*, February 16, 2013, https://www.washingtonpost .com/local/chevy-chase-landlord-used-tiny-cameras-to-peep-on-tenants-police -say/2013/02/16/022252cc-76c1-11e2-aa12-e6cf1d31106b_story.html.

4. Benjamin Wittes, Cody Poplin, and Quinta Jurecic, "Sextortion: Cybersecurity, Teenagers, and Remote Sexual Assault," Washington, DC: Brookings Institute, May 11, 2018,

https://www.brookings.edu/research/sextortion-cybersecurity-teenagers-and-remote
-sexual-assault/.

5. Richard B. Krueger and Meg S. Kaplan, "Noncontact Paraphilic Sexual Offenses,"
in *Sexual Offending*, (2016), https://www.researchgate.net/publication/301264280_
Noncontact_Paraphilic_Sexual_Offenses/link/5718cb3208ae986b8b7a9896/
download.

6. Danielle Keats Citron, "Cyber Mobs, Disinformation, and Death Videos: The Internet
As It Is (and As It Should Be)," *Michigan Law Review* 118 (2020): 1074.

7. Susan Sontag, *On Photography* (New York: Farrar, Straus and Giroux, 1978), 5.

8. Jenna Gibson, "K-Pop's Sexual Assault Scandal Is the Tip of the Iceberg," *Foreign
Policy*, March 21, 2019, https://foreignpolicy.com/2019/03/21/k-pops-sexual-assault
-scandal-is-the-tip-of-the-iceberg/; Adam Taylor and Min Joo Kim, "'My Life Is Not
Your Porn': South Korea's War against Spy Cameras and Sexual Harassment,'" *Independent*, July 31, 2018, https://www.independent.co.uk/news/world/asia/south-korea
-spy-cams-metoo-sexual-harassment-ahn-hee-jung-a8470771.html.

9. Justin McCurry and Nemo Kim, "'A Part of Daily Life': South Korea Confronts its
Voyeurism Epidemic," *The Guardian*, July 3, 2018, https://www.theguardian.com/
world/2018/jul/03/a-part-of-daily-life-south-korea-confronts-its-voyeurism-epidemic
-sexual-harassment; "South Korea Revenge Porn: Sora Owner Arrested," BBC, June
26, 2018, https://www.bbc.com/news/world-asia-44615303.

10. Juwon Park and Isabella Steger, "South Korean Women Aren't Safe in Public Bathrooms—or Their Homes—Because of Spy-cam Porn," *Quartz*, https://qz.com/1354304/
south-korean-women-dread-public-bathrooms-because-of-spy-cam-porn/.

11. Gary Robbins, "Is Someone Watching You through Your Webcam?," *San Diego Union-
Tribune*, September 24, 2016, https://www.sandiegouniontribune.com/news/science/
sd-me-webcam-hacking-20160920-story.html.

12. Nicola Henry, Clare McGlynn, Asher Flynn, Kelly Johnson, Anastasia Powell, and
Adrian J. Scott, *Image-Based Sexual Abuse: A Study on the Causes and Consequences of
Non-Consensual Nude or Sexual Imagery* (London: Routledge, 2020), 21.

13. Gabriela Resto-Montero, "Man Arrested for Hiding Camera in Office Urinal; Jeffrey
Larcade Charged with Video Voyeurism," *New York Daily News*, July 20, 2010, https://
www.nydailynews.com/news/national/man-arrested-hiding-camera-office-urinal
-jeffery-larcade-charged-video-voyeurism-article-1.159951;   http://www.thesmoking
gun.com/file/urinal-peeper?page=0.

14. Chris De Benedetti, "UC Berkeley: Police Arrest Man Suspected of Videotap-
ing Women in Dorm Bathroom," *Mercury News*, September 25, 2015, https://
www.mercurynews.com/2015/09/25/uc-berkeley-police-arrest-man-suspected-of
-videotaping-women-in-dorm-bathroom/.

15. Emily Raguso, "UC Berkeley Police Seek Help in 'Video Voyeurism' Case from Campus
Bathroom," *Berkeleyside*, May 14, 2019, https://www.berkeleyside.com/2019/05/14/uc
-berkeley-police-seek-help-in-video-voyeurism-case-from-campus-bathroom.

16. iTV, "Voyeur Admits Police Changing Room Spy Camera," March 3, 2014, https://

www.itv.com/news/update/2014-03-03/voyeur-admits-police-changing-room-spy
-camera/.

17. Louisa Tang, "Jail for Man Who Amassed 1,500 Obscene Files of Women, Minors over
13-year Period Using Spy Cams," *TODAY*, June 4, 2020, https://www.todayonline
.com/singapore/jail-man-who-amassed-1500-obscene-files-women-minors-over-13
-year-period-using-spy-cams.

18. Suzanne Rowan Kelleher, "Why You Should Start Screening for Hidden Spy Cameras When You Travel," *Forbes*, January 27, 2020, https://www.forbes.com/sites/
suzannerowankelleher/2020/01/27/why-you-should-start-screening-for-hidden-spy
-cameras-when-you-travel/amp/.

19. Sophie Jeong and James Griffiths, "Hundreds of Motel Guests Were Secretly Filmed and
Live-streamed Online," *CNN*, March 21, 2019, https://edition.cnn.com/2019/03/20/
asia/south-korea-hotel-spy-cam-intl/index.html.

20. *CBS*, "Hopkins to Pay $190 Million to Patients of Gynecologist Who Secretly Vid-
eotaped Women," July 21, 2014, https://www.cbsnews.com/news/johns-hopkins
-agrees-to-pay-190-million-to-patients-of-gynecologist-who-secretly-videotaped
-women/.

21. "Rabbi Who Spied on Women Taking Ritual Baths Released," *Associated Press*, April
2, 2020, https://wtop.com/local/2020/04/rabbi-who-spied-on-women-taking-ritual
-baths-released/.

22. Zhang Wanqing, "Viral Video Starts Discussion on Up-skirting and 'Safety Pants,'"
Sixth Tone, July 27, 2020, https://www.sixthtone.com/news/1005981/viral-video
-starts-discussion-on-up-skirting-and-safety-pants.

23. Alistair Charlton, "iPhone Cyber-flashing: What Is It and How to Stop It Happening
to You," *International Business Times*, August 14, 2015, https://www.ibtimes.co.uk/
iphone-cyber-flashing-what-it-how-stop-it-happening-you-1515440.

24. Polly Dunbar, "Cyberflashing in Schools: 'I Hate That This Was One Of Her First Sexual Experiences—Something 'She Didn't Want,'" *Grazia UK*, July 16, 2021, https://
graziadaily.co.uk/life/parenting/cyberflashing-campaign-schools-ofsted/.

25. The Economist, "A Sex-abuse Scandal Incenses Millions of South Koreans," March
26, 2020, https://www.economist.com/asia/2020/03/26/a-sex-abuse-scandal-incenses
-millions-of-south-koreans; Ron Kim, "Victim of Telegram Nth Room Case Speaks Up
about the Horrors She Faced as a Middle School Student," *Koreaboo*, March 24, 2020,
https://www.koreaboo.com/news/victim-telegram-nth-room-case-speaks-horrors
-faced-middle-school-student/.

26. Shim Kyu-Seok, "'God God' Claims He Had No Ties to Cho Ju-bin's Nth
Rooms," *Korea JoongAng Daily*, May 18, 2020, https://koreajoongangdaily.joins
.com/2020/05/18/socialAffairs/telegram-police-nth-room/20200518172500242.html.

27. Ryan Flores et al, "Sextortion in the Far East: Blackmail Goes Mobile," *Trend Micro*,
March 2015, https://www.trendmicro.com/vinfo/pl/security/news/cybercrime-and
-digital-threats/sextortion-in-the-far-east-blackmail-goes-mobile; Charles Hymas,
"Surge in 'Sextortion' Blackmailers Online Prompts Alert by National Crime

Agency," *Telegraph*, May 1, 2020, https://www.telegraph.co.uk/news/2020/05/01/surge-sextortion-blackmailers-online-prompts-alert-national/.

28. The Office of the eSafety Commissioner, "Michael's Story," https://www.esafety.gov.au/key-issues/image-based-abuse/stories/michael. Michael is a composite of men interviewed by the Australia eSafety Commissioner's office.

29. CNN, "Interview of Giancarlo Granda," aired at 8 a.m. EST, August 31, 2020; Carl Anthony, " 'Pool Boy' Spills the Beans on 'Sexual Predators' Jerry Falwell Jr and His Wife in CNN Interview,"*Daily Boulder*, August 31, 2020, https://dailyboulder.com/pool-boy-spills-the-beans-on-sexual-predators-jerry-falwell-jr-and-his-wife-in-cnn-interview/.

30. Nicole Hong, "R. Kelly Allies Accused of Trying to Threaten and Bribe Accusers," *New York Times,* August 12, 2020, https://www.nytimes.com/2020/08/12/nyregion/r-kelly-sexual-assault-arrest.html.

31. Quinta Jurecic, "A Turning Point for Sextortion," *The Atlantic*, May 1, 2020, https://www.telegraph.co.uk/news/2020/05/01/surge-sextortion-blackmailers-online-prompts-alert-national/.

32. Rebecca Rosenberg, " 'Beyond Humiliating': Woman Filmed by Banker during Sex," *New York Post*, June 30, 2014, https://nypost.com/2014/06/30/victims-speak-out-after-ex-banker-secretly-filmed-sex-romps/.

33. Nellie Bowles, "Thermostats, Locks and Lights: Digital Tools of Domestic Abuse," *New York Times*, June 23, 2018, https://www.nytimes.com/2018/06/23/technology/smart-home-devices-domestic-abuse.html.

34. Alexey Firsh, "Beware of Stalkerware," *Securelist*, April 3, 2019, https://securelist.com/beware-of-stalkerware/90264/.

35. Rahul Chatterjee et al., "The Spyware Used in Intimate Partner Violence," *2018 IEEE Symposium on Security and Privacy (SP)*, https://ieeexplore.ieee.org/stamp/stamp.jsp?tp=&arnumber=8418618.

36. Jason Koebler, " 'I See You': A Domestic Violence Survivor Talks About Being Surveilled By Her Ex," *VICE*, March 17, 2017, https://www.vice.com/en/article/bmbpvv/i-see-you-a-domestic-violence-survivor-talks-about-being-surveilled-by-her-ex.

37. National Network to End Domestic Violence, "Safety Net Technology Safety Survey, A Glimpse from the Field: How Abusers Are Misusing Technology," 2014, https://static1.squarespace.com/static/51dc541ce4b03ebab8c5c88c/t/54e3d1b6e4b08500fcb455a0/1424216502058/NNEDV_Glimpse+From+the+Field+-+2014.pdf.

38. Tara Seals, "Liverpool Voyeur used IM-RAT to Video Women at Home," *Threat Post*, January 8, 2020, https://threatpost.com/liverpool-voyeur-im-rat-video-women/151638/.

39. Kapersky, "The State of Stalkerware in 2019," *Securelist,* October 2, 2019, https://securelist.com/the-state-of-stalkerware-in-2019/93634/.

40. Almost 80% of people who disclose intimate imagery without consent do not do so out of an explicit desire to harm victims. Asia Eaton, Holly Jacobs, and Yanet Ruvalcaba, "2017 Nationwide Online Study of Nonconsensual Porn Victimization and

Perpetration," *Cyber Civil Rights Initiative*, June 2017, https://www.cybercivilrights
.org/wp-content/uploads/2017/06/CCRI-2017-Research-Report.pdf.

41. Nicola Henry et al., *Image-Based Sexual Abuse: A Study on the Causes and Consequences of Non-Consensual Nude or Sexual Imagery*, 25–26.

42. Rosemary Phago and Lesego Mkhize, "Local Woman's Nudes Leaked after She Lost Her Phone," *News24*, January 21, 2019, https://www.news24.com/drum/celebs/local-womans-nudes-leaked-after-she-lost-her-phone-20190121.

43. Henry et al., *Image-Based Sexual Abuse*.

44. Megha Mohan, "'I Was Raped at 14, and the Video Ended Up on a Porn Site,'" *BBC*, February 10, 2020, https://www.bbc.com/news/stories-51391981.

45. Jennifer Savin, "Pornhub Has Come under Fire for Allowing Real Rape Videos," *Cosmopolitan*, February 11, 2020, https://www.cosmopolitan.com/uk/reports/a30867324/pornhub-real-rape-videos/.

46. Emily Bazelon, "The Price of a Stolen Childhood," *New York Times*, January 24, 2013, https://www.nytimes.com/2013/01/27/magazine/how-much-can-restitution-help-victims-of-child-pornography.html.

47. Jon Porter, "Another Convincing Deepfake App Goes Viral Prompting Immediate Privacy Backlash," *The Verge*, September 2, 2019, https://www.theverge.com/2019/9/2/20844338/zao-deepfake-app-movie-tv-show-face-replace-privacy-policy-concerns.

48. Fun fact: Robert Chesney and I are included in the dictionary definition. Our blog post on Lawfare about deepfakes appears in the explanation of the word. Merriam-Webster, "Words We're Watching: 'Deepfake,'" https://www.merriam-webster.com/words-at-play/deepfake-slang-definition-examples.

49. Samantha Cole, "AI-Assisted Fake Porn Is Here and We're All Fucked," *VICE*, December 11, 2017, https://www.vice.com/en_us/article/gydydm/gal-gadot-fake-ai-porn.

50. Rob Toews, "Deepfakes Are Going to Wreak Havoc on Society. We Are Not Prepared," *Forbes*, May 25, 2020, https://www.forbes.com/sites/robtoews/2020/05/25/deepfakes-are-going-to-wreak-havoc-on-society-we-are-not-prepared/?sh=141b5fb47494.

51. Noelle Martin (as told to Daniella Scott), "Deepfake Porn Nearly Ruined My Life," *Elle* (magazine), June 2, 2020, https://www.elle.com/uk/life-and-culture/a30748079/deepfake-porn/.

52. McCurry and Kim, "A Part of Daily Life."

53. Matthew Smith, "Four in Ten Female Millennials Have Been Sent an Unsolicited Penis Photo," February 15, 2018, *YouGov*, https://yougov.co.uk/topics/politics/articles-reports/2018/02/16/four-ten-female-millennials-been-sent-dick-pic.

54. The Law Commission Reforming the Law, Intimate Image Abuse Consultation Paper 253, February 26, 2021, 2.22, https://s3-eu-west-2.amazonaws.com/lawcom-prod-storage-11jsxou24uy7q/uploads/2021/02/Intimate-image-abuse-consultation-paper.pdf.

55. Henry Ajder, Giorgio Patrini, Francesco Cavalli, and Laurence Cullen, "The State of Deepfakes," *Deeptrace*, September 2019, https://sensity.ai/reports/.

56. Law Commission, Intimate Image Abuse paper, 2.92–2.96.

57. Benjamin Wittes et al., "Sextortion: Cybersecurity, Teenagers, and Remote Sexual Assault."

58. Janis Wolak et al., "Sextortion of Minors: Characteristics and Dynamics," *Journal of Adolescent Health* 62 (October 18, 2017), https://doi.org/10.1016/j.jadohealth.2017.08 .014.

59. INTERPOL, "INTERPOL Report Shows Alarming Rate of Cyberattacks during Covid-19," August 4, 2020, https://www.interpol.int/en/News-and-Events/ News/2020/INTERPOL-report-shows-alarming-rate-of-cyberattacks-during -COVID-19.

60. Cyber Civil Rights Initiative, "End Revenge Porn: A Campaign of the Cyber Civil Rights Initiative," https://www.cybercivilrights.org/wp-content/uploads/2014/12/ RPStatistics.pdf.

61. Law Commission, "Intimate Image Abuse," 5.23.

62. Cyber Civil Rights Initiative, "End Revenge Porn."

63. Veronica Schmidt, "I Was Filmed in a Kmart Changing Room," *NZ Herald*, August 19, 2020, https://www.nzherald.co.nz/nz/news/article.cfm?c_id=1&objectid=123578 19#:~:text=When%20a%20stranger%20videoed%20Veronica,in%20front%20of%20 a%20judge.

64. Henry et al., *Image-Based Sexual Abuse*.

65. Cyber Civil Rights Initiative, "End Revenge Porn."

66. Danielle Keats Citron, *Hate Crimes in Cyberspace* (Cambridge, MA: Harvard University Press, 2014).

67. Miriam Berger, "Brazilian 17-Year-Old Commits Suicide After Revenge Porn Posted Online," *Buzzfeed*, November 20, 2013, https://www.buzzfeednews.com/article/ miriamberger/brazilian-17-year-old-commits-suicide-after-revenge-porn-pos.

68. Crystal Bonvillian, "Daisy Coleman of 'Audrie & Daisy' Netflix Documentary Dead of Suicide at 23," *KIRO7*, August 5, 2020, https://www.kiro7.com/ news/trending/daisy-coleman-audrie-daisy-netflix-documentary-dead-suicide -23/3BGN4KAUDBGZFB6T4JYCJV7ONQ/.

69. See Citron, *Hate Crimes in Cyberspace*; Asher Flynn, Nicola Henry, and Anastasia Powell, "More than Revenge: Addressing the Harms of Revenge Porn, Report of the More Than Revenge Roundtable," 5, ResearchGate, January 2016, https:// www.researchgate.net/publication/323078347_More_than_Revenge_Addressing_ the_Harms_of_Revenge_Pornography_Report_of_the_More_than_Revenge_ Roundtable.

70. Henry et al., *Image-Based Sexual Abuse*.

71. Elana Sztokman, "Video Voyeurism Is a Crime—Let's Treat It Like One," *Forward*, March 1, 2016, https://forward.com/sisterhood/334650/video-voyeurism-is-a -crimelets-treat-it-like-one/?gamp.

72. Martin, "Deepfake Porn Nearly Ruined My Life."

73. Law Commission, "Intimate Image Abuse," 5.75–5.77.

74. Mary Anne Franks, "How to Feel like a Woman, or Why Punishment Is a Drag," *UCLA Law Review* 61 (2014).

75. Daniel Victor, "Florida Fraternity Sued over Intimate Videos Shared on Facebook," *N.Y. Times*, June 14, 2018, https://www.nytimes.com/2018/06/14/us/delta-sigma-phi-revenge-porn.html.

76. Anna North, "Revenge Porn, Biphobia, and Alleged Relationships with Staffers: The Complicated Story around Rep. Katie Hill, Explained," *Vox*, October 28, 2019, https://www.vox.com/identities/2019/10/23/20928700/katie-hill-congresswoman-resigns-leaked-red-state.

77. Quinta Jurecic, "The Humiliation of Katie Hill Offers a Warning," *The Atlantic*, October 30, 2019, https://www.theatlantic.com/ideas/archive/2019/10/katie-hill-and-many-victims-revenge-porn/601198/.

78. Michael Finnegan and Matt Pearce, "GOP Enemies Wanted to Beat Katie Hill. Then They Got Her Nude Photos," *Los Angeles Times*, October 31, 2019, https://www.latimes.com/politics/story/2019-10-31/katie-hill-husband-revenge-porn-republicans.

79. Maureen Dowd, "Now Comes the Naked Truth," *New York Times*, November 2, 2019.

80. Abby Ohlheiser, "A Nude-photo Hoax Was Supposed to Silence Alexandria Ocasio-Cortez. Instead, She Turned Up the Volume," *Washington Post*, January 10, 2019, https://www.washingtonpost.com/technology/2019/01/10/nude-photo-hoax-was-supposed-silence-alexandria-ocasio-cortez-instead-she-turned-up-volume/.

81. Azmina Dhrodia, "Unsocial Media: Tracking Twitter Abuse against Women MPs," *Amnesty Global Insights*, 2017.

82. NATO Strategic Communications Centre of Excellence, "Abuse of Power: Coordinated Online Harassment of Finnish Government Ministers," November 2020, https://www.stratcomcoe.org/abuse-power-coordinated-online-harassment-finnish-government-ministers.

83. Leonie Cater, "Finland's Women-led Government Targeted by Online Harassment," *Politico.eu*, March 17, 2021, https://www.politico.eu/article/sanna-marin-finland-online-harassment-women-government-targeted/.

84. Cater, "Finland's Women-led Government."

85. Caroline Criado Perez, *Invisible Women: Data Bias in a World Designed for Men* (London: Penguin Vintage, 2019), 281.

86. Isabella Grullon Paz, "Women Running for Office Have to Worry about One More Thing: Their Phones," *New York Times*, November 9, 2019, https://www.nytimes.com/2019/11/09/us/politics/katie-hill-women-politics.html.

87. North, *Revenge Porn*.

88. Kim Willsher, "Paris Mayoral Candidate Drops Out over Sex Video Scandal," *The Guardian*, February 14, 2020.

89. Drew Harwell, "A Shadowy AI Service Has Transformed Thousands of Women's Photos into Fake Nudes: 'Make Fantasy a Reality,'" *Washington Post*, October 20, 2020, https://www.washingtonpost.com/technology/2020/10/20/deep-fake-nudes/.

90. I advised Sensity on the report.

91. Samantha Cole and Emanuel Maiberg, "Deepfake Porn Is Evolving to Give People Total Control Over Women's Bodies," *VICE*, December 6, 2019, https://www.vice.com/en_us/article/9keen8/deepfake-porn-is-evolving-to-give-people-total-control-over-womens-bodies.

CHAPTER 3: GOVERNMENT SPIES

1. David J. Garrows, "The Troubling Legacy of Martin Luther King," *Standpoint* (May 30, 2019).

2. https://www.cnn.com/2008/US/03/31/mlk.fbi.conspiracy/.

3. David A. Graham, "The Epistemic Quandry of the FBI and Trump," *The Atlantic*, January 24, 2018, https://www.theatlantic.com/politics/archive/2018/01/the-epistemic-quandary-of-the-fbi-and-trump/551276/.

4. Glenn Greenwald, Ryan Grim, and Ryan Gallagher, "Top-Secret Document Reveals NSA Spied on Porn Habits as Part of Plan to Discredit 'Radicalizers,'" *Huffington Post*, November 26, 2013, at https://www.huffpost.com/entry/nsa-porn-muslims_n_4346128?utm_hp_ref=politics+.

5. William Saletan, "'Osama Bin Lustin,'" *Slate*, May 17, 2011, https://slate.com/news-and-politics/2011/05/osama-bin-laden-s-porn-as-propaganda-is-it-more-damning-than-his-terrorism.html.

6. Caitlin Oprysko, "Lisa Page Sues DOJ and FBI Over Release of Her Text Messages," *Politico* (December 10, 2019).

7. I am serving as a pro bono expert for those officials (Lisa Page and Peter Strzok) in their separate lawsuits against the Department of Justice. None of the details included here are based on confidential conversations with either Page or Strzok or their counsel.

8. Complaint in Lisa Page v. U.S. Dept of Justice and FBI, filed in the US federal district court in the District of Columbia on December 10, 2019.

9. Complaint, *Page v. DOJ*, ¶ 79.

10. User Clip, "Trump Peter Strzok & Lisa Page," *C-SPAN*, October 10, 2019, https://www.c-span.org/video/?c4822026/user-clip-trump-peter-strzok-lisa-page.

11. Molly Jong-Fast, "Lisa Page Speaks: 'There's No Fathomable Way I Have Committed Any Crime at All,'" *The Daily Beast,* December 17, 2019, https://www.thedailybeast.com/lisa-page-speaks-theres-no-fathomable-way-i-have-committed-any-crime-at-all.

12. Jong-Fast, "Lisa Page Speaks."

13. Monica Lewinsky, "The Price of Shame," *TED Talks*, March 20, 2015, https://www.ted.com/talks/monica_lewinsky_the_price_of_shame?language=en

14. H. Keith Melton and Lieutenant Colonel Vladimir Alekseenko, *The Secret History of KGB Spycameras: 1945–1995* (Atglen, PA: Schiffer Publishing, 2018), 146–47.

15. Julia Ioffe, "How State-Sponsored Blackmail Works in Russia," *The Atlantic*, January 11, 2017, https://www.theatlantic.com/international/archive/2017/01/kompromat-trump-dossier/512891/

16. Hannah Beech and Sun Narin, "Threatened by Facebook Disinformation, a

Monk Flees Cambodia," *New York Times* (August 23, 2020), https://www.nytimes
.com/2020/08/23/world/asia/cambodia-facebook-disinformation.html.

17. Bill Bostock, "The Russian Government Demanded Access to Everybody's Tinder User Data in Case Its Spies Want to Take a Look," *Business Insider*, June 3, 2019,
https://www.businessinsider.com/russia-demands-access-tinder-fsb-2019-6.

18. "Tinder Denies Sharing Russian Users' Data With FSB," *Moscow Times*, June 4, 2019,
https://www.themoscowtimes.com/2019/06/04/tinder-denies-sharing-russian-users
-data-with-fsb-a65864.

19. David E. Sanger, "Grindr Is Owned by a Chinese Firm and the U.S. Is Trying to Force
It to Sell," *New York Times*, March 28, 2019, https://www.nytimes.com/2019/03/28/
us/politics/grindr-china-national-security.html.

20. Casey Newton, "How Grindr Became a National Security Issue," *Verge*, March 28, 2019,
https://www.theverge.com/interface/2019/3/28/18285274/grindr-national-security
-cfius-china-kunlun-military.

21. Tim Fitzsimons, "Inside Grindr, Fears That China Wanted to Access User Data via
HIV Research," *NBC.com* (April 2, 2019), https://www.nbcnews.com/feature/nbc
-out/inside-grindr-fears-china-wanted-access-user-data-hiv-research-n989996.

22. Echo Wang et al, "Winning Bidder for Grindr has ties to Chinese owner," *Reuters*
(June 2, 2020), https://www.reuters.com/article/us-grindr-m-a-sanvicente-exclusive/
exclusive-winning-bidder-for-grindr-has-ties-to-chinese-owner-idUSKBN2391AI.

23. Press release, "UK: Europe's Top Court Rules UK Mass Surveillance Regime Violated
Human Rights," *Amnesty International*, May 25, 2021, https://www.amnesty.org/en/
latest/press-release/2021/05/uk-surveillance-gchq-ecthr-ruling/.

24. Case of Big Brother Watch and Others v. the United Kingdom, Applications no.
58170/13, 62322/14, 24960/15, Grand Chamber of the European Court of Human
Rights, May 25, 2021, https://hudoc.echr.coe.int/eng#{%22documentcollectionid2
%22:[%22GRANDCHAMBER%22,%22CHAMBER%22],%22itemid%22:[%22001
-210077%22]}: ¶425.

25. Danielle Keats Citron and Frank Pasquale, "Network Accountability for the Domestic Intelligence Apparatus," *Hastings Law Journal* 62 (2011): 1448–55.

26. Riekie et al., "Data Brokers in an Open Society."

27. Sarah Brayne, *Predict and Surveil: Data, Discretion, and the Future of Policing* (New
York: Oxford University Press, 2021), 40–41.

28. Brayne, *Predict and Surveil*, 49–52.

29. Citron and Pasquale, "Network Accountability for the Domestic Intelligence
Apparatus."

30. Citron and Pasquale, "Network Accountability for the Domestic Intelligence
Apparatus."

31. Andrew Ferguson, *The Rise of Big Data Policing: Surveillance, Race, and the Future of
Law Enforcement* (New York: New York University Press, 2017), 131–35.

32. Drew Harwell, "ICE Investigators Used a Private Utility Database Covering Millions
to Pursue Immigration Violations," *Washington Post*, February 26, 2021, https://www

.washingtonpost.com/technology/2021/02/26/ice-private-utility-data/; Heather Murphy and Mihir Zaveri, "Pentagon Warns Military Personnel against At-Home DNA Tests," *New York Times*, December 24, 2019, https://www.nytimes.com/2019/12/24/us/military-dna-tests.html.

33. Amanda Peacher, "Why Is the State of Oregon Conducting Intelligence Work?," *Oregon Public Broadcasting*, April 26, 2016, https://www.opb.org/news/article/oregon-department-of-justice-intelligence/.

34. Carolyn D. Walker, Oregon Department of Justice Investigation Report, April 6, 2016, https://www.opb.org/pdf/doj_investigation_report_-_final_redacted_report_pacfjh_1527195896547.pdf.

35. Nigel Jaquis, "Attorney General Took Her Time Addressing Allegations of Illegal Surveillance by Her Agency," *Willamette Week*, November 15, 2015, https://www.wweek.com/news/2015/11/18/attorney-general-ellen-rosenblum-took-her-time-addressing-allegations-of-illegal-surveillance-by-her-agency/

36. Will Parrish and Jason Wilson, "Revealed: Anti-terror Center Helped Police Track Environmental Activists," *The Guardian*, October 2, 2019, https://www.theguardian.com/us-news/2019/oct/02/oregon-pipelines-protests-monitoring-police-anti-terror-unit.

37. 28 CFR Part 23.

38. For the surveillance of human rights groups, peace activists, and death penalty opponents, including two Catholic nuns and Democratic candidate for local office, and mislabeling as terrorists, Nick Madigan, "Spying Uncovered," *Baltimore Sun*, July 18, 2008, 1A, https://www.baltimoresun.com/maryland/bal-te.md.spy18jul18-story.html; Ryan Singel, "Maryland Cops Put 53 Non-Violent Activists on Terrorist List," *Wired*, October 8, 2008, https://www.wired.com/2008/10/maryland-cops-p/. For spying on Muslim communities, U.S. Senate Permanent Subcommittee on Investigations, Joint Majority and Minority Staff Report, Federal Support for And Involvement in State and Local Fusion Centers (October 3, 2012), https://www.hsgac.senate.gov/imo/media/doc/10-3-2012%20PSI%20STAFF%20REPORT%20re%20FUSION%20CENTERS.2.pdf.

39. "National Network of Fusion Centers Fact Sheet," Department of Homeland Security, https://www.dhs.gov/national-network-fusion-centers-fact-sheet.

40. Erica's experience is drawn from interviews and discussion in Khiara M. Bridges, *The Poverty of Privacy Rights* (Stanford, CA: Stanford University Press, 2017), 2–4, 111–12.

41. Bridges, *The Poverty of Privacy Rights*, 9, 131.

42. Bridges, *The Poverty of Privacy Rights*, 9–10.

43. Charles Reich, "The New Property," *Yale Law Journal* 73 (1964): 761.

44. Bridges, *The Poverty of Privacy Rights*, 7–8, 113.

45. Anna North, "'Failed' Abortions, a Period-Tracking Spreadsheet, and the Last Clinic Standing: The Controversy in Missouri, Explained," *Vox*, October 31, 2019, https://www.vox.com/2019/10/31/20939890/missouri-abortion-clinic-hearing-periods-roe-wade.

46. Priscilla Alvarez, "House Judiciary Committee Asks Former ORR Director to Clarify Testimony on Pregnant Minors," *CNN*, March 22, 2019.

47. Carter Sherman, "Trump Officials Discussed 'Reversing' Abortion for Undocumented Teen," *VICE*, January 31, 2018, https://www.vice.com/en/article/yw5a5g/exclusive-trump-officials-discussed-reversing-abortion-for-undocumented-teen.

CHAPTER 4: THIS IS US

1. Barack Obama, Speech at the White House Summit on Cybersecurity, Stanford, California, February 13, 2015.

2. Yasha Levine, *Surveillance Valley: The Secret Military History of the Internet* (London: PublicAffairs, 2019), 116.

3. Fred Turner, *From Counterculture to Cyberculture: Steward Brand, the Whole Earth Network, and the Rise of Digital Utopianism* (Chicago: University of Chicago Press, 2006), 172.

4. Levine, *Surveillance Valley*, 133.

5. Margaret O'Mara, *The Code: Silicon Valley and the Remaking of America* (New York: Penguin Books, 2019), 288–89.

6. Telephone interview with Julia Angwin, April 10, 2021.

7. "The Clipper Chip," *Electronic Privacy Information Center Blog*, https://epic.org/crypto/clipper/.

8. Steven Levy, "Battle of the Clipper Chip," *New York Times*, June 12, 1994, 46, https://www.nytimes.com/1994/06/12/magazine/battle-of-the-clipper-chip.html.

9. See John Perry Barlow, "A Not Terribly Brief History of the Electronic Frontier Foundation," *EFF Blog*, https://www.eff.org/pages/not-terribly-brief-history-electronic-frontier-foundation; John Perry Barlow, "A Plain Text on Crypto Policy," *EFF Blog*, https://www.eff.org/pages/plain-text-crypto-policy.

10. O'Mara, *The Code*, 300.

11. Jerry Berman, "Policy Architecture and Internet Freedom," *The Recorder (CA)*, November 10, 2017.

12. Sam Colt, "John Doerr: The Greatest Tech Entrepreneurs Are 'White, Male, Nerds,'" *Business Insider*, March 4, 2015, https://www.businessinsider.com/john-doerr-the-greatest-tech-entrepreneurs-are-white-male-nerds-2015-3.

13. Cade Metz, "Who is Making Sure the A.I. Machines Aren't Racist?" *New York Times*, March 15, 2021, https://www.nytimes.com/2021/03/15/technology/artificial-intelligence-google-bias.html.

14. Michaela Dempsey, "Silicon Valley Is Where Women Go to Fail—Unless They Do These Three Things," *Fast Company*, July 24, 2019, https://www.fastcompany.com/90380422/silicon-valley-is-where-women-go-to-fail-unless-they-do-these-three-things.

15. Priyamvada Mathur, "Quarterly VC Funding for Female Founders Drops to Three-Year Low," *PitchBook*, October 8, 2020, https://pitchbook.com/news/articles/vc-funding-female-founders-drops-low.

16. Emily Chang, *Brotopia: Breaking Up the Boys' Club of Silicon Valley* (New York: Portfolio/Penguin, 2019), 210.

17. Chang, *Brotopia*, 124–25.

18. Chang, *Brotopia*, 50.

19. Chang, *Brotopia*, 54.

20. O'Mara, *The Code,* 75, 401–2.

21. O'Mara, *The Code,* 75, 401–2.

22. Lizzie O'Shea, "Tech Has Become Another Way for Men to Oppress Women," *The Guardian*, July 7, 2017.

23. Chang, *Brotopia*, 124–25.

24. Patricia Hill Collins, *Black Feminist Thought: Knowledge, Consciousness, and the Politics of Empowerment* (London: Routledge, 2000); Patricia Hill Collins, *Black Sexual Politics: African Americans, Gender, and the New Racism* (London: Taylor and Francis, 2004).

25. Joy Buolamwini and Timnit Gebru, "Gender Shades: Intersectional Accuracy Disparities in Commercial Gender Classification," *Proceedings of Machine Learning Research*, volume 81, 2018, http://proceedings.mlr.press/v81/buolamwini18a/buolamwini18a.pdf.

26. Leon Yin and Aaron Sankin, "Google Ad Portal Equated 'Black Girls' with Porn," *The Markup*, July 23, 2020, https://themarkup.org/google-the-giant/2020/07/23/google-advertising-keywords-black-girls.

27. Jeremy B. Merrill, "Google Has Been Allowing Advertisers to Exclude Nonbinary People from Seeing Job Ads," *The Markup*, February 11, 2021, https://themarkup.org/google-the-giant/2021/02/11/google-has-been-allowing-advertisers-to-exclude-nonbinary-people-from-seeing-job-ads.

28. Sara Wachter-Boettcher, *Technically Wrong: Sexist Apps, Biased Algorithms, and Other Threats to Toxic Tech* (New York: W.W. Norton, 2017), 30–31.

29. Michelle Ruiz, "Safiya Noble Knew the Algorithm Was Oppressive," *Vogue* (magazine), October 21, 2021, https://www.vogue.com/article/safiya-noble; Safiya Umoja Noble, "Google Search: Hyper-visibility as a Means of Rendering Black Women and Girls Invisible," *InVisible Culture: An Electronic Journal for Visual Culture*, issue 19 (published on October 29, 2013), https://ivc.lib.rochester.edu/google-search-hyper-visibility-as-a-means-of-rendering-black-women-and-girls-invisible/.

30. Citron, *Hate Crimes in Cyberspace*, 51. My research assistant obtained a list of nonconsensual porn sites that DMCA Defender has dealt with in trying to get nonconsensual porn taken down, and there were more than 9,000 sites on the list. Email from DMCA Defender to Julia Schur, December 10, 2019 (on file with author).

31. Joseph Cox, "Inside the Private Forums Where Men Illegally Trade Up-skirt Photos," *Motherboard* (May 8, 2018).

32. James Rodger, "Massive Hack Sees 180,000 The Candid Board Account Details Leaked," *Birmingham Mail (UK)*, January 26, 2017, https://www.birminghammail.co.uk/news/midlands-news/massive-hack-sees-180000-candid-12506027.

33. Law Commission, "Intimate Image Abuse," 2.25.

34. Harwell, "A Shadowy AI Service Has Transformed Thousands of Women's Photos."

35. Joseph Cox, "People Are Filming Creepshots of Women at BLM Protests," *VICE*, June 18, 2020, https://www.vice.com/en_us/article/akz33z/creepshots-up-skirts-black-lives-matter-protests.

36. Amanda Hess, "Inside AnonIB, Where Hacking Is a Sport and Women's Bodies the Prize," *Slate*, September 3, 2014, https://slate.com/human-interest/2014/09/anonib-nude-photo-site-where-hackers-and-users-treat-women-as-property.html.

37. Amanda Marcotte, "'The Fappening' and Revenge Porn Culture: Jennifer Lawrence and the Creepshots Epidemic," *The Daily Beast*, September 3, 2014, https://www.thedailybeast.com/the-fappening-and-revenge-porn-culture-jennifer-lawrence-and-the-creepshot-epidemic.

38. Bethan Kapur, "An Army of Women Are Waging War on the Web's Most Notorious Revenge Porn Site," *Mel*, 2021, https://melmagazine.com/en-us/story/anon-ib-revenge-porn-badass-army.

39. Jessica M. Goldstein, "Revenge Porn Was Already Commonplace, the Pandemic Has Made Things Worse," *Washington Post*, October 29, 2020, https://www.washingtonpost.com/lifestyle/style/revenge-porn-nonconsensual-porn/2020/10/28/603b88f4-dbf1-11ea-b205-ff838e15a9a6_story.html.

40. Asia A. Eaton, Holly Jacobs, and Yanet Ruvalcaba, *2017 Nationwide Online Study of Nonconsensual Porn Victimization and Perpetration* (June 2017).

41. Research@eSafety, "Understanding the Attitudes and Motivations of Adults who Engage in Image-based Abuse," eSafety Commissioner, September 12, 2019, https://www.esafety.gov.au/sites/default/files/2019-10/Research_Report_IBA_Perp_Motivations.pdf.

42. Park and Steger, "South Korean Women Aren't Safe in Public Bathrooms—or Their Homes—because of Spy-cam Porn," *Quartz*, https://qz.com/1354304/south-korean-women-dread-public-bathrooms-because-of-spy-cam-porn/.

43. Nicola Smith, "South Korean Women Demand Equal Justice for Internet Sex Crimes amid 'Spy-cam Porn Epidemic,'" *Telegraph (UK)*, May 21, 2018, https://www.telegraph.co.uk/news/2018/05/21/south-korean-women-demand-equal-justice-internet-sex-crimes/.

44. Brian Mullahy, "University of Utah Chief to Discipline 3 Officers over 'Explicit' Photos of Lauren McCluskey," *2KTUV.com*, August 5, 2020, https://kutv.com/news/local/u-of-u-chief-to-discipline-3-officers-over-explicit-photos-of-lauren-mccluskey.

45. Courtney Tanner, "Logan Police Fire Officer Miguel Deras for Showing Off Explicit Photos of Lauren McCluskey," *Salt Lake Tribune*, August 7, 2020, https://www.sltrib.com/news/education/2020/08/07/logan-police-fire-officer/.

46. Liza Zvi and Mally Shechory Bitton, "Perceptions of Victim and Offender Culpability in Non-consensual Distribution of Intimate Images," *Journal of Psychology, Crime and Law* (Sept. 2020), 27.

47. Research@eSafety, "National Survey: Image-Based Abuse," e-Safety Commissioner, October 2017, https://www.esafety.gov.au/sites/default/files/2019-07/Image-based-abuse-qualitative-research-summary-2017.pdf.

48. Law Commission, "Intimate Image Abuse," 1.41.

49. Research@e-Safety, "National Survey."

CHAPTER 5: LAW'S INADEQUACY

1. Graham Moomaw, "Bill to Ban 'Cyber Flashing' in Virginia Fails in Senate Committee," *Virginia Mercury*, February 18, 2021, https://www.virginiamercury .com/2021/02/18/bill-to-ban-cyber-flashing-in-virginia-fails-in-senate-committee/; Michael Pope, "Senate Kills Cyberflashing Bill," *Virginia Public Radio*, February 18, 2021, https://virginiapublicradio.org/2021/02/18/senate-committee-kills-cyber -flashing-bill/.

2. Sharon Otterman, "Sending Lewd Nudes to Strangers Could Mean a Year in Jail," *New York Times*, November 30, 2018, https://www.nytimes.com/2018/11/30/nyregion/ airdrop-sexual-harassment.html?smid=tw-nytimes&smtyp=cur.

3. Jeffrey Kosseff, *The 26 Words that Created the Internet* (Ithaca, NY: Cornell University Press 2019); Bryan Pietsch, Isobel Asher Hamilton, and Katie Canales, "The Facebook Whistleblower Told Congress It Should Amend Section 230, the Internet Law Hated by both Biden and Trump. Here Is How It Works," *Business Insider*, October 6, 2021, https://www.businessinsider.com/what-is-section-230-internet-law-communications -decency-act-explained-2020-5.

4. Stratton Oakmont v. Prodigy Services Co., No. 31063/94, 1995 WL 323710 (N.Y. Supreme Court, 1995).

5. Communications Decency Act, 47 U.S.C. § 230(c)(1)(2) (1996).

6. 47 U.S.C. § 230(e).

7. Alina Selyukh, "Section 230: A Key Legal Shield for Facebook, Google About to Change," *National Public Radio*, March 21, 2018, https://www.npr.org/sections/all techconsidered/2018/03/21/591622450/section-230-a-key-legal-shield-for-facebook -google-is-about-to-change.

8. Danielle Keats Citron and Benjamin Wittes, "The Internet Will Not Break: Denying Bad Samaritans § 230 Immunity," *Fordham Law Review* 86 (2017): 414 (discussing cases).

9. Jane Doe No. 1 v. Backpage.com LLC, 817 F.3d 12, 29 (1st Cir. 2016), cert. denied, 137 S. Ct. 622 (2017).

10. Mary Anne Franks, "The Lawless Internet? Myths and Misconceptions about CDA Section 230," *Huffington Post*, February 17, 2014, https://www.huffpost.com/entry/ section-230-the-lawless-internet_b_4455090.

11. Carrie Goldberg, "Herrick v. Grindr: Why Section 230 of the Communications Decency Act Must Be Fixed," *Lawfare*, August 14, 2019, https://www.lawfareblog .com/herrick-v-grindr-why-section-230-communications-decency-act-must-be-fixed.

12. Email from Carrie Goldberg to author, August 2, 2019.

13. Rebecca Tushnet, "Power without Responsibility: Intermediaries and the First Amendment," *George Washington Law Review* 76 (2008).

14. Article 19.17 of the U.S.-Mexico-Canada Agreement. This provision does not apply

to Mexico until July 1, 2023, https://ustr.gov/trade-agreements/free-trade-agreements/united-states-mexico-canada-agreement/agreement-between.

15. Securing the Protection of Our Enduring and Established Constitutional Heritage Act, 28 U.S.C. § 2201, Public Law 111–223.

16. E-Commerce Directive of 2000, 2000/31/EC; Digital Services Act.

17. The Act to Improve Enforcement of the Law in Social Networks (Network Enforcement Act, December 7, 2017), https://perma.cc/7UCW-AA3A.

18. The Defamation (Operators of Websites) Regulations 2013, https://www.legislation.gov.uk/ukdsi/2013/9780111104620.

19. David Bateman and Elisa D'Amico, address at Information Privacy Law class at Fordham Law School, September 12, 2018.

20. Interview with Elisa D'Amico, September 12, 2018.

21. Ari Waldman, "Cyber Abuse," draft on file with author.

22. Barbara Streisand v. Kenneth Adelman et al., No. SC077257, Superior Court of California, May, 20, 2003; Justin Parkinson, "The Perils of the Streisand Effect," *BBC News*, July 31, 2014, https://www.bbc.com/news/magazine-28562156.

23. MC and CM v. Jeffrey Geiger and John Doe, 2018 WL 6503582, U.S. District Court, Middle District Florida, December 11, 2018.

24. Ari Ezra Waldman, *Privacy as Trust* (Cambridge: Cambridge University Press 2018), 72.

25. Gary v. State, 790 S.E.2d 150 (Ga. Ct. App. 2016).

26. Benjamin Wittes et al., "Closing the Sextortion Sentencing Gap: A Legislative Proposal" (Washington, DC: Brookings, 2016), 4, https://www.brookings.edu/wp-content/uploads/2016/05/sextortion2.pdf.

27. Derek Hawkins, "His Massive Sextortion Scheme Snared 155 Boys. Now He's Going to Prison for Decades," *Washington Post,* November 30, 2016, https://www.washingtonpost.com/news/morning-mix/wp/2016/11/30/his-massive-sextortion-scheme-snared-155-teen-boys-now-hes-going-to-prison-for-decades/.

28. Department of Justice, Former U.S. State Department Employee Sentenced to 57 Months in Extensive Computer Hacking, Cyberstalking, and 'Sextortion' Scheme (March 21, 2016).

29. McCurry and Kim, "A Part of Daily Life."

30. Rebecca Rosenberg, "Banker Accused of Filming Romps Getting Sweetheart Deal," *New York Post,* August 29, 2016, https://nypost.com/2016/08/29/banker-accused-of-filming-romps-is-getting-a-sweetheart-deal/.

31. Class Action Complaint, Robert Bergeron v. Grindr, filed in U.S. District Court in the Southern District of New York, January 31, 2020.

32. Fair Credit Reporting Act of 1970, 15 U.S.C. § 1681 (2012); Health Insurance Portability and Accountability Act and the Health Information Technology for Economic and Clinical Health Act, 42 U.S.C. §§ 300jj; Children's Online Privacy Protection Rule, 16 C.F.R. § 312 (2012); Telephone Consumer Privacy Act, 47 U.S.C. § 227.

33. California was the first with the California Online Privacy Protection Act of 2003, California Business & Professional Code § 22575 (2016).

34. Letter to Attorney General Ken Paxton, "Norwegian Consumer Council's Report Demonstrates How the Adtech Industry Fails to Respect Consumers Rights and Preferences," January 14, 2020, https://www.citizen.org/wp-content/uploads/TX-AG-Out-of-Control-NCC-1.14.20.pdf.

35. The UK GDPR, Information Commissioner's Office, available at https://ico.org.uk/for-organisations/dp-at-the-end-of-the-transition-period/data-protection-and-the-eu-in-detail/the-uk-gdpr/.

36. European Data Protection Board, "Norwegian DPA: Intention to Issue € 10 Million Fine to Grindr LLC," January 26, 2021, https://edpb.europa.eu/news/national-news/2021/norwegian-dpa-intention-issue-eu-10-million-fine-grindr-llc_en.

37. European Data Protection Board, "Norwegian DPA Imposes Fine against Grindr LLC," December 21, 2021, https://edpb.europa.eu/news/national-news/2021/norwegian-dpa-imposes-fine-against-grindr-llc_en.

38. In the Matter of Flo Health, Agreement Containing Consent Order, January 13, 2021, https://www.ftc.gov/system/files/documents/cases/flo_health_order.pdf

39. Statement of the Commission, "On Breaches by Health Apps and Other Connected Devices," September 15, 2021, https://www.ftc.gov/system/files/documents/public_statements/1596364/statement_of_the_commission_on_breaches_by_health_apps_and_other_connected_devices.pdf

40. Vermont v. Ruby Corp, No. 730-12-16, Vermont Superior Court, December 14, 2016; Press release, FTC, Operators of AshleyMadison.com Settle FTC, State Charges Resulting from 2015 Data Breach that Exposed 36 Million Users' Profile Information, December 14, 2016, https://www.ftc.gov/news-events/press-releases/2016/12/operators-ashleymadisoncom-settle-ftc-state-charges-resulting.

41. Press release, "Operators of AshleyMadison.com Settle FTC, State Charges From 2015 Data Breach that Exposed 36 Million Users' Profile Information," Federal Trade Commission, December 14, 2016, https://www.ftc.gov/news-events/press-releases/2016/12/operators-ashleymadisoncom-settle-ftc-state-charges-resulting.

42. Complaint, In re Retina-X Studios, LLC, Federal Trade Commission, October 22, 2019; Decision and Order, In re Retina-X Studios, LLC, No. C-4711, March 26, 2020.

43. Press release, "FTC Bans SpyFone and CEO from Surveillance Business and Orders Company to Delete All Secretly Stolen Data," Federal Trade Commission, Sept. 1, 2021, https://www.ftc.gov/news-events/press-releases/2021/09/ftc-bans-spyfone-and-ceo-from-surveillance-business.

44. Julie Cohen, "How (Not) to Write a Privacy Law," *Knight First Amendment Institute*, April 2, 2021, https://knightcolumbia.org/content/how-not-to-write-a-privacy-law.

45. Dwyer v. American Express, 652 N.E.2d 1351, Illinois Appellate Court, 1995.

46. Sasha Romanosky et al., "Empirical Analysis of Data Breach Litigation," *Journal of Empirical Legal Studies*, volume 11, 2014.

47. Danielle Keats Citron and Daniel J. Solove, "Privacy Harms," *Boston University Law Review* (forthcoming).

CHAPTER 6: THE RIGHT TO INTIMATE PRIVACY

1. Press release, "Attorney General James Announces Settlement with Dating App for Failure to Secure Private and Nude Photos," June 28, 2019, https://ag.ny.gov/press -release/2019/attorney-general-james-announces-settlement-dating-app-failure-secure -private-and.

2. Remarks by Simone Browne, "Government Surveillance and Race," Color of Surveillance conference, April 8, 2016; https://www.c-span.org/video/?407901-1/discussion -racial-bias-government&event=407901&playEvent&auto; Simone Browne, *Dark Matters: On the Surveillance of Blackness* (Durham, NC: Duke University Press, 2015); Claudia Garcia-Rojas, "The Surveillance of Blackness: From the Trans-Atlantic Slave Trade to Contemporary Surveillance Technologies," *Truthout*, March 3, 2016, https://truthout.org/articles/the-surveillance-of-blackness-from-the-slave-trade-to -the-police/.

3. Alvaro M. Bedoya, "Privacy as Civil Right," *New Mexico Law Review* 50 (2020): 306.

4. Robin L. West, *Civil Rights: Rethinking their Natural Foundation* (Cambridge: Cambridge University Press, 2019), 49, 156–57, 171. In developing her argument, West relies on the influential "human capabilities" approach of philosophers Martha Nussbaum and Amartya Sen. Martha C. Nussbaum, *Women and Human Development: The Capabilities Approach* (Cambridge: Cambridge University Press, 2000); Amartya Sen, *Commodities and Capabilities* (New Delhi: Oxford University Press, 1999).

5. Mary Wollstonecraft, *A Vindication of the Rights of Woman: With Strictures on Political and Moral Subjects* (New York: W.W. Norton & Company, 2009) (first published in 1792); Thomas Paine, *Rights of Man, Common Sense and Other Political Writings* (Oxford: Oxford World Classics 1995) (Part I first published in 1791, Part II first published in 1792).

6. George A. Rutherglen, *Civil Rights in the Shadow of Slavery: The Constitution, Common Law, and the Civil Rights Act of 1866* (Oxford: Oxford University Press, 2012); G. Edward White, *Law in American History, Volume II: From Reconstruction Through the 1920s* (Oxford: Oxford University Press, 2016).

7. Risa Goluboff, *The Lost Promise of Civil Rights* (Cambridge, MA: Harvard University Press, 2007), 147.

8. Carol Anderson, *Eyes Off the Prize: The United Nations and the African American Struggle for Human Rights, 1944–1955* (Cambridge: Cambridge University Press, 2003).

9. Samantha Barbas, *Laws of Image: Privacy and Publicity in America* (Palo Alto, CA: Stanford University Press, 2015), 32.

10. "The Washington Society World. Marriage of Senator Bayard's Daughter—A Reception and Two Banquets," *New York Times*, January 26, 1883, 1.

11. Amy Gajda, "What If Samuel D. Warren Hadn't Married a Senator's Daughter?: Uncovering the Press Coverage That Led to the 'Right to Privacy,'" *Michigan State Law Review* 2008 (2008).

12. Charles E. Colman, "About Ned," *Harvard Law Review Forum* 129 (2016).

13. Samuel D. Warren and Louis D. Brandeis, "The Right to Privacy," *Harvard Law Review* 4 (1890).

14. Warren and Brandeis, "The Right to Privacy," 193–97, 201.

15. Dorothy J. Glancy, "The Invention of the Right to Privacy," *Arizona Law Review* 21 (1979); Alpheus Thomas Mason, *Brandeis: A Free Man's Life* (New York: NY, Viking, 1956), 70.

16. Neil M. Richards, "The Puzzle of Brandeis, Privacy, and Speech," *Vanderbilt Law Review* 63 (2013): 1295.

17. Pavesich v. New England Life Insurance Company, 50 S.E. 68 (Georgia Supreme Court 1905).

18. Jessica Lake, *The Face That Launched a Thousand Lawsuits: The American Women Who Forged a Right to Privacy* (New Haven, CT: Yale University Press, 2016), 57–69, 94–107, 126–27.

19. Maurice Merleau-Ponty, *The Phenomenology of Perception* (London: Routledge, 2014 English translation by Donald A. Landes).

20. Anita L. Allen, *Unpopular Privacy* (New York: Oxford University Press, 2011).

21. Iris Marion Young, *On the Female Body Experience: Throwing Like a Girl and Other Essays* (New York: Oxford University Press, 2005).

22. Hannah Arendt, *The Human Condition* (Chicago: University of Chicago Press, 1958).

23. Leslie Meltzer Henry, "The Jurisprudence of Dignity," *University of Pennsylvania Law Review* 160 (2011).

24. Robert C. Post, "The Social Foundations of Privacy: Community and Self in the Common Law Tort," *Yale Law Journal* 77 (1989).

25. Anna Lauren Hoffmann, "Data, Technology, and Gender: Thinking About (and from) Trans Lives," in *Spaces for the Future: A Companion to Philosophy of Technology* (London: Routledge, 2018), 3, 9.

26. Jean-Paul Sartre, *Being and Nothingness: A Phenomenological Essay on Ontology* (New York: Washington Square Press, 1956 English translation by Hazel E. Barnes), 384.

27. Jeffrey Rosen, *The Unwanted Gaze: The Destruction of Privacy in America* (New York: Vintage Books, 2000), 9.

28. Martha C. Nussbaum, *Political Emotions: Why Love Matters for Justice* (Cambridge, MA: Harvard University Press, 2013), 3.

29. Martha C. Nussbaum, *From Disgust to Humanity: Sexual Orientation and Constitutional Law* (New York: Oxford University Press, 2010).

30. Martin Buber, *Between Man and Man* (Boston: Beacon Press, 1947), 30.

31. Martin Buber, *I and Thou* (New York: Touchstone Press, 1970).

32. Charles Fried, Privacy, *Yale Law Journal* 77 (1968): 490.

33. John Holmes and John K. Rempel, "Trust in Close Relationships," in *Close Relationships: A Sourcebook* (Clyde Hendrick editor, Thousand Oaks, CA: Sage Publications, 1989).

34. Erving Goffman, *Stigma: Notes on the Management of a Spoiled Identity* (New York: Touchstone, 1963, 1986 resissue edition).

35. Holmes and Rempel, "Trust in Close Relationships."

36. Irwin Altman and Dalmas A. Taylor, *Social Penetration: The Development of Interpersonal Relationships* (New York, New York: Holt, Rinehart and Winston 1973).

37. Patricia Boling, *Privacy and the Politics of Intimate Life* (Ithaca, NY: Cornell University Press, 1996).

38. Waldman, *Privacy as Trust.*

39. Eric Wemple, "Just How Did Matt Lauer's Famous Desk Button Work?," *Washington Post*, May 11, 2018, https://www.washingtonpost.com/blogs/erik-wemple/wp/2018/05/11/just-how-did-matt-lauers-famous-desk-button-work/; Jodi Kantor and Megan Twokey, "Harvey Weinstein Paid Off Sexual Harassment Accusers for Decades," *New York Times*, October 5, 2017, https://www.nytimes.com/2017/10/05/us/harvey-weinstein-harassment-allegations.html.

40. Emily Steel, "How Bill O'Reilly Silenced His Accusers," *New York Times*, April 4, 2018, https://www.nytimes.com/2018/04/04/business/media/how-bill-oreilly-silenced-his-accusers.html.

41. Anita L. Allen, *Uneasy Access: Privacy for Women in a Free Society* (Totowa, NJ: Rowman & Littlefield, 1988).

42. John Stuart Mill, "The Subjection of Woman" (1869), in *On Liberty and Other Writings,* ed. Stefan Collini (Cambridge: Cambridge University Press, 1989).

43. Reva B. Siegel, "The Rule of Love: Wife Beating as Prerogative and Privacy," *Yale Law Journal* 105 (1996).

44. Catharine A. MacKinnon, *Feminism Unmodified: Discourses on Life and the Law* (Boston: Harvard University Press, 1987), 93, 101–2.

45. Allen, *Uneasy Access*, 180.

46. J. M. Balkin, *Cultural Software: A Theory of Ideology* (New Haven: Yale University Press, 1998), 14.

47. Barry Friedman, "The Lawless Fourth Amendment" (unpublished paper, draft on file with author).

48. Friedman, "The Lawless Fourth Amendment."

49. Frederick Schauer, "A Comment on the Structure of Rights," *Georgia Law Review* 27 (1993): 429.

50. Ronald Dworkin, *Taking Rights Seriously* (Cambridge, MA: Harvard University Press, 1977), 198.

51. Megha Mohan, "I Was Raped at 14, and the Video Ended Up on a Porn Site," *BBC News*, February 10, 2020, https://www.bbc.com/news/stories-51391981.

52. Case of Verlagsgruppe News GMBH and Bobi v. Austria, No. 59631/09, European Court of Human Rights, December 4, 2012.

53. European Convention on Human Rights, https://www.echr.coe.int/documents/convention_eng.pdf.

54. Söderman v. Sweden, No. 57806/08, European Court of Human Rights, https://hudoc.echr.coe.int/fre#{"itemid":["001-128043"]}; Fontevecchio D'Amico v. Argentina, https://www.corteidh.or.cr/docs/casos/articulos/seriec_238_ing.pdf; Alkaya

v. Turkey, No. 42811/06, https://hudoc.echr.coe.int/eng#{"itemid":["001-114031"]}; Cârstea v. Rumunia, No. 20531/06, https://sip.lex.pl/orzeczenia-i-pisma-urzedowe/orzeczenia-sadow/20531-06-carstea-v-rumunia-wyrok-europejskiego-521620431.

55. UNHRC, Report of the Special Rapporteur on Violence against Women, Its Causes and Consequences on Online Violence against Women and Girls from a Human Rights Perspective, June 14, 2018, https://documents-dds-ny.un.org/doc/UNDOC/GEN/G18/184/58/PDF/G1818458.pdf?OpenElement; UN Doc. CEDAQ/C/NOR/CO/9.

56. Report of the Special Rapporteur on the Right to Privacy, No. A/HRC/37/62, October 25, 2018.

57. Volodina v. Russia, No. 41261/17, European Court of Human Rights, July 9, 2019, https://hudoc.echr.coe.int/spa#{"itemid":["001-194321"]}.

58. Case of Khadija Ismayilova v. Azerbaijan, 65286/13, 27370/14, European Court of Human Rights, January 10, 2019, https://hudoc.echr.coe.int/spa#{%22itemid%22:[%22001-201340%22]}.

59. Final Judgment and Permanent Injunction, People of State of California v. Upward Labs Holdings and Glow, September 18, 2020, https://oag.ca.gov/sites/default/files/People%20v.%20Glow%20-%20Final%20Judgment%20and%20Permanent%20Injunction%20-%2007374856.pdf.

60. Elisa Jillson, "Aiming for Truth, Fairness, and Equity in Your Company's Use of AI," FTC Blog, April 19, 2021, https://www.ftc.gov/news-events/blogs/business-blog/2021/04/aiming-truth-fairness-equity-your-companys-use-ai.

61. Remarks of Acting Chairwoman Rebecca Kelly Slaughter, "Protecting Consumer Privacy in a Time of Crisis," February 10, 2021, https://www.ftc.gov/system/files/documents/public_statements/1587283/fpf_opening_remarks_210_.pdf.

62. Daniel J. Solove and Woodrow Hartzog, "The FTC and the New Common Law of Privacy," *Columbia Law Review* 114 (2014).

63. Orson Lucas and Steven Stein, "The New Imperative for Corporate Data Responsibility," KPMG Report, 2020, https://advisory.kpmg.us/content/dam/advisory/en/pdfs/2020/consumer-data-report-kpmg.pdf.

CHAPTER 7: A COMPREHENSIVE APPROACH TO INTIMATE PRIVACY VIOLATIONS

1. See Citron, *Hate Crimes in Cyberspace,* 80–83.

2. Mary Anne Franks, "Why We Need a Federal Criminal Response to Revenge Porn," *Concurring Opinions* blog, February 15, 2013; Danielle Keats Citron and Mary Anne Franks, "Criminalizing Revenge Porn," *Wake Forest Law Review* 49 (2014).

3. John C. P. Goldberg and Benjamin Zipursky, *Recognizing Wrongs* (Cambridge, MA: Harvard University Press, 2020).

4. Order, Jane Doe v. David K. Elam II, No. 14-9788 (C.D. Cal. April 4, 2018).

5. Rachel Bayefsky, "Remedies and Respect: Rethinking the Role of Federal Judicial Relief," *Georgetown Law Journal* 109 (2021).

6. Owen M. Fiss, *The Civil Rights Injunction* (Bloomington, Indiana: Indiana University Press, 1978), 6; see, e.g., the Civil Rights Act of 1964, 42 U.S.C. § 2000a-3(a); Carey v. O'Reilly Automobile Stores, 2019 WL 3412170 (S.D. Fla. May 31, 2019), report and recommendation adopted, 2019 WL 3408926 (S.D. Fla. June 17, 2019).

7. Kalani v. Starbucks Corp., 117 F. Supp. 3d 1078 (E.D. Cal. 2017), aff'd in relevant part, vacated in part, 698 Fed. Appx. 883 (9th Cir. 2017).

8. Hugo Martín, "Lawsuits Targeting Business Websites over ADA Violations Are on the Rise," *Los Angeles Times*, November 11, 2018, https://www.latimes.com/business/la-fi-hotels-ada-compliance-20181111-story.html.

9. Winter v. Nat. Res. Def. Council, 555 U.S. 7, 24 (2008). There is an extensive scholarly debate about whether courts should be required to issue injunctions to remedy statutory violations. Michael T. Morley, "Enforcing Equality: Statutory Injunctions, Equitable Balancing Under eBay, and the Civil Rights Act of 1964," *University of Chicago Legal Forum*, 2014 (2014).

10. Uniform Civil Remedies for Unauthorized Disclosure of Intimate Images Act (Uniform Law Commission, 2018, https://www.uniformlaws.org/viewdocument/final-act-3?CommunityKey=668f6afa-f7b5-444b-9f0a-6873fb617ebb&tab=librarydocuments. CCRI President Mary Anne Franks served as the reporter for the Uniform Law Commission's committee that drafted this proposal.

11. Ark. Code Ann. 16-129-101 et seq.; Iowa Code Ann. 659A.1 et seq.; S.D. Codified Laws 21-67-1 et seq.; Col. Rev. Stat. Ann. 13-21-1401 et seq.

12. New York Civil Rights Law § 51.

13. Ali v. Playgirl, 447 F. Supp. 723 (S.D.N.Y. 1978).

14. Hassell v. Yelp, No. S235968 (Sup. Ct. Cal. July 2, 2018).

15. Speech, Vice-President of the European Commission and EU Justice Commissioner Viviane Reding, European Commission, "The EU Data Protection Reform 2021: Making Europe the Standard Setter for Modern Data Protection Rules in the Digital Age," January 22, 2012, https://ec.europa.eu/commission/presscorner/detail/en/SPEECH_12_26.

16. Google v. Spain, Court of Justice of the European Union, C-131-12 (May 13, 2014).

17. Google v. CNIL, Court of Justice of the European Union, C-507/17 (September 24, 2017).

18. Leo Kelion, "Google Wins Landmark Right to Be Forgotten Case," *BBC News*, September 24, 2019.

19. Michelle Alexander, *The New Jim Crow: Mass Incarceration in the Age of Color Blindness* (New York: The New Press, 2010).

20. Citron and Franks, "Criminalizing Revenge Porn." For crucial recounting of the experience working on legislative reform on the nonconsensual disclosure of intimate images, see Mary Anne Franks, "'Revenge Porn' Reform: A View from the Front Lines," *Florida Law Review* 69 (2017).

21. Citron, *Hate Crimes in Cyberspace*, 126.

22. Citron, *Hate Crimes in Cyberspace*, 126.

23. Megan Specia, "Killings Spur Britons to Ask If Misogyny Is a Hate Crime," *New York Times*, October 11, 2020: A6.

24. Jennifer Fermino et al., "Anthony Weiner May Face Criminal Prosecution for Allegedly Sexting a 15-year-old Girl," *New York Daily News*, September 22, 2016, https://www.nydailynews.com/news/national/anthony-weiner-allegedly-sexted-15-year-old-girl-report-article-1.2800788.

25. Leslie Kendrick, "First Amendment Expansionism," *William and Mary Law Review* 56 (2015): 1212.

26. State v. VanBuren, 214 A.3d 791 (Sup. Ct. Vt. 2019).

27. State v. Katz, 2022 WL 152487 (Sup. Ct. Indiana January 18, 2022); State v. Michael Casillas, A19-0576 (Sup. Ct. Minn. December 30, 2020); People v. Austin, 155 N.E.3d 439 (Sup. Ct. Ill. 2020), cert. denied, 141 S. Ct. 233 (2020).

28. Michaels v. Internet Entertainment Group, 5 F. Supp.2d 823 (C.D. Cal. 1998).

29. Katie Hill v. The Daily Mail, Order Granting Special Motion to Strike Lawsuit, April 7, 2021.

30. Helen Norton, "(At Least) Thirteen Ways of Looking at Election Lies," *Oklahoma Law Review* 71 (2018): 131.

31. Bartnicki v. Vopper, 532 U.S. 514 (2001).

CHAPTER 8: THE DUTIES OF DATA GUARDIANS

1. Tim Cook, Remarks before the International Conference of Data Protection and Privacy Commissioners, October 24, 2018.

2. Marta Teperek, Maria J. Cruz, Elen Verbakel, Jasmin Bohmer, and Alastair Dunning, "Data Stewardship: Addressing Disciplinary Data Management Needs," *International Journal of Data Curation*, December 2018, http://www.ijdc.net/article/view/604/520.

3. 20 U.S.C. § 1681(a) (2000).

4. Danielle Keats Citron and Mary Anne Franks, "Cyber Civil Rights in the Time of COVID-19," *Harvard Law Review Blog*, May 14, 2020, https://blog.harvardlawreview.org/cyber-civil-rights-in-the-time-of-covid-19/.

5. Interview, "Talking about Section 230 with Mary Anne Franks," *Galley by Columbia Journalism Review* (n.d.), https://galley.cjr.org/public/conversations/-MfdcaH8450RYp43dV3y.

6. Danielle Keats Citron, "Cyber Civil Rights," *Boston University Law Review* 89 (2009); Danielle Citron and Benjamin Wittes, "The Internet Will Not Break: Denying Bad Samaritans Section 230 Immunity," *Fordham Law Review* 86 (2017); Danielle Citron and Mary Anne Franks, "The Internet as Speech Machine and Other Myths Confounding Section 230 Reform," *University of Chicago Legal Forum* (2020).

7. User Clip, "Danielle Citron Explains Content Moderation," House Intelligence Committee Hearing on "Deep Fake Videos," *C-Span*, June 14, 2019, https://www.c-span.org/video/?c4802966/user-clip-danielle-citron-explains-content-moderation.

8. Danielle Keats Citron, "Reservoirs of Danger: The Evolution of Public and Private Law at the Dawn of the Information Age," *Southern California Law Review* 80 (2007);

Benjamin C. Zipursky, "Reasonableness in and out of Negligence Law," *University of Pennsylvania Law Review* 163 (2015) ("the range of uses of 'reasonableness' in the law is so great that a list is not an efficient way to describe and demarcate it").

9. I have written about those best practices, served on working groups to devise best practices, and offered testimony on the topic. Danielle Keats Citron and Helen Norton, "Intermediaries and Hate Speech: Fostering Digital Citizenship for our Information Age," *Boston University Law Review* 91 (2011); Danielle Keats Citron, *Hate Crimes in Cyberspace* (Cambridge, MA: Harvard University Press, 2014); Danielle Keats Citron and Quinta Jurecic, "Platform Justice: Content Moderation at an Inflection Point," *Hoover Institute Aegis Series* (2018); "Misogynistic Cyber Hate Speech," Hearing before the Inter-Parliamentary Committee on Anti-Semitism for the Task Force on Online Hate, House of Commons, UK, October 27, 2011.

10. Gilad Edelman, "Everything You've Heard about Section 230 Is Wrong," *Wired*, May 6, 2021.

11. Edina Harbina, "Online Safety Bill: Not So Safe At All," *Lawfare*, July 8, 2020, https://www.lawfareblog.com/uks-online-safety-bill-not-safe-after-all; Thomas Reilly, Sam Jungyun Choi, Lisa Peets, and Marty Hansen, "UK Government Plans for an Online Safety Bill," *Inside Privacy* (December 18, 2020), https://www.insideprivacy.com/international/united-kingdom/uk-government-plans-for-an-online-safety-bill/.

12. European Commission, "The Digital Services Act: Ensuring a Safe and Accountable Online Environment," December 15, 2020, https://ec.europa.eu/info/strategy/priorities-2019-2024/europe-fit-digital-age/digital-services-act-ensuring-safe-and-accountable-online-environment_en

13. @cagoldberglaw, https://twitter.com/cagoldberglaw/status/1391133297967783946.

14. Andrew Smith, "New and Improved FTC Data Security Orders: Better Guidance for Companies, Better Protection for Consumers," FTC Business Blog, January 6, 2020, https://www.ftc.gov/news-events/blogs/business-blog/2020/01/new-improved-ftc-data-security-orders-better-guidance.

15. NAACP v. Alabama, 357 U.S. 449 (1958).

16. 5 U.S.C. § 552(a).

17. Hawkins v. Jamaica Hospital Medical Center Diagnostic and Treatment Center, No. 16-CV-4265, 2018 WL 1521774 (E.D.N.Y. March 28, 2018).

18. Anita L. Allen, *Unpopular Privacy* (New York: Oxford University Press, 2011).

19. 47 U.S.C. § 552(e)(1).

20. Khiara M. Bridges, *The Poverty of Privacy Rights* (Palo Alto, CA: Stanford University Press, 2017); Whalen v. Roe, 429 U.S. 589 (1977).

21. Thorne v. El Segundo, 726 F.2d 459 (9th Cir. 1983): 469–70.

22. The Illinois Biometric Identification Privacy Act conditions the collection of biometric information on consent given after firms inform consumers about the reason for the collection and how biometric data will be used and stored. 740 Ill. Comp. Stat. 14/20(2).

23. Paul Ohm and Scott Peppet, "What If Everything Reveals Everything?," in *Big Data*

Is Not a Monolith, ed. Cassidy R. Sugimoto, Hamid R. Ekbia, and Michael Mattioli (Boston, MA: MIT Press, 2016), 45.

24. Data Protection Act of 2021, https://www.gillibrand.senate.gov/imo/media/doc/DPA%20Bill%20Text.pdf.

25. Neil M. Richards and Woodrow Hartzog, "A Duty of Loyalty for Privacy Law," *Washington University Law Review,* forthcoming.

26. Richards and Hartzog, "A Duty of Loyalty for Privacy Law."

27. We can look to HIPAA by way of analogy. As Anita Allen explains in her important book *Unpopular Privacy,* HIPAA (passed in 1996) and the Privacy Rule (adopted in 2000) are not paternalistic because they "do not require patients to protect their own privacy." Instead, they set limits on the ways that covered health care entities can collect, use, and share personally identifiable health information. Anita Allen, *Unpopular Privacy* (New York: Oxford University Press, 2011), 114.

28. My colleague Woodrow Hartzog gave me the idea to call it the "data death penalty."

29. "Requests Stronger Measures against the Dating App Grindr," *Forbrukerrådt,* March 2021, https://www.forbrukerradet.no/news-in-english/requests-stronger-measures-against-the-dating-app-grindr/.

30. Press release, Hamburg Commissioner for Data Protection and Freedom of Information, "Speech Assistance Systems Put to the Test—Data Protection Authority Opens Administrative Proceedings against Google" (August 1, 2019), https://datenschutz-hamburg.de/assets/pdf/2019-08-26_press-release_Google-speech-assistant-systems.pdf.

31. California Consumer Privacy Act of 2018; California Privacy Rights and Enforcement Act of 2020; Virginia Consumer Data Protection Act of 2021.

32. Neil M. Richards and Woodrow Hartzog, "A Duty of Loyalty for Privacy Law," *Washington University Law Review* (2022); Woodrow Hartzog and Neil M. Richards, "Privacy's Constitutional Moment and the Limits of Data Protection," *Boston College Law Review* 61 (2020).

33. Ryan M. Calo, "Privacy and Markets: A Love Story," *Notre Dame Law Review* 91 (2016).

34. Snyder v. Phelps, 131 S. Ct. 1207 (2011).

35. Neil M. Richards, "Reconciling Data Privacy and the First Amendment," *UCLA Law Review* 52 (2005).

36. Bartnicki, 532 U.S. at 527.

37. Sorrell v. IMS Health, Inc., 131 S. Ct. 2653 (2011).

38. Neil M. Richards, *Intellectual Privacy* (Oxford: Oxford University Press, 2015), 1523.

CHAPTER 9: THE NEW COMPACT FOR SOCIAL NORMS

1. "Black to the Future," *United Shades of America, CNN,* episode 2, season 6 (May 9, 2021).

2. Gene Teare, "Introducing the Diversity Rider Program," *Crunchbase News,* August 26, 2020.

3. Venture Forward, https://ventureforward.org/human-capital/; "Guidance and Best Practice Examples for VCs, Private Equity, and Institutional Investors with regard to Diversity and Female Entrepreneurship," February 2021, https://ventureforward .org/wp-content/uploads/2021/02/Unconscious-Bias-Guidance-and-Best-Practice -Examples6.pdf.

4. Siri Chilazi, Anisha Asundi, and Iris Bohnet, "Venture Capitalists Are Using the Wrong Tools to Improve Gender Diversity," *Behavioral Scientist*, March 12, 2019.

5. Richard Robinson, "Venture Capitalists Must Do More Than Stand in Solidarity with Black Lives Matter," *Financial Times*, July 22, 2020, https://www.ft.com/ content/55a4d2e1-4d2b-4f19-a9b8-11534df4c688; Chilazi, Asundi, and Bohnet, "Venture Capitalists Are Using the Wrong Tools to Improve Gender Diversity."

6. Amy Lewin, "New Diversity 'Standard' for VC Firms Launches," *Sifted*, September 2020, https://sifted.eu/articles/diversity-vc-standard-launch.

7. Megan Rose Dickey, "Facebook Hires a VP of Civil Rights," *TechCrunch*, January 11, 2021, https://techcrunch.com/2021/01/11/facebook-hires-a-vp-of-civil-rights/.

8. Selena Hill, "Facebook Civil Rights V.P. Roy L. Austin Speaks Out about Audit and Progress on the Platform," *Black Enterprise*, July 15, 2021, https://www.blackenterprise .com/facebook-civil-rights-v-p-roy-l-austin-speaks-out-about-audit-and-progress-on -the-platform/?test=prebid.

9. Fatima Al Mahmoud, "Gang Rape on Facebook Live: Why Did Facebook Not Interrupt the Broadcast?," *Medium*, December 13, 2017, https://medium.com/@ fatimaalmahmoud/gang-rape-on-facebook-live-why-did-facebook-not-interrupt-the -broadcast-9cc72275c3aa.

10. "Facebook Live 'Broadcasts Gang Rape' of Woman in Sweden," *BBC*, January 23, 2017, https://www.bbc.com/news/world-europe-38717186.

11. David Schaper, "Should Viewers of Facebook Live Gang Rape Face Charges?," *National Public Radio*, April 4, 2017, https://www.npr.org/2017/04/04/522574666/ should-viewers-of-facebook-live-gang-rape-face-charges.

12. Episode 2, "The Garbage Can Model of Decision Making," *Sudhir Breaks the Internet* podcast, April 19, 2021; Mike Murphy, "Facebook Is Hiring 3,000 More People to Monitor Facebook Live for Murders, Suicides, and Other Horrific Video," *Quartz*, May 3, 2017, https://qz.com/974720/facebook-fb-ceo-mark-zuckerberg-is-hiring-3000-more -people-to-monitor-facebook-live-for-murders-suicides-and-other-horrific-video/.

13. Zoom interview with Julie Inman Grant, Australia's e-safety commissioner, November 18, 2020.

14. Jamie Condiffe, "Facebook and Google May Be Fighting Terrorist Videos with Algorithms," *MIT Technology Review*, June 27, 2017, https://www.technologyreview .com/2016/06/27/159096/facebook-and-google-may-be-fighting-terrorist-videos-with -algorithms/.

15. Interview with Mary Anne Franks, Robert M. Klein Distinguished Professor of Law, University of Miami School of Law, September 1, 2018. Franks urged tech companies to adopt hash strategies to filter and block nonconsensual porn starting in 2014.

16. Facebook Safety, "People Shouldn't Be Able to Share Intimate Images to Hurt Others," Facebook (May 22, 2018).

17. Steven Bellovin, "Facebook's Initiative Against 'Revenge Porn,'" SMBlog, September 16, 2017, https://www.cs.columbia.edu/~smb/blog/2017-11/2017-11-16.html.

18. Fight for the Future (@fightfortheftr), Twitter, May 24, 2018, 11:34 a.m.

19. David Bloom, "Facebook Wants Your Nude Photos: What Could Possibly Go Wrong?," Forbes, May 24, 2018, https://www.forbes.com/sites/dbloom/2018/05/24/facebook-wants-your-nude-photos-what-could-possibly-go-wrong/?sh=1d0127864587.

20. NCII Pilot, Facebook's Safety Center, https://www.facebook.com/safety/notwithoutmyconsent/pilot/partners.

21. Grant interview.

22. "What Is Private Detector and How Does It Work?," Bumble, https://bumble.com/en/help/what-is-private-detector.

23. Emma Batha, "After #MeToo, Phone App Allows You to Legally Consent to Sex," Reuters, Jan. 18, 2018, https://www.reuters.com/article/us-netherlands-tech-sex-apps/after-metoo-phone-appallows-you-to-legally-consent-to-sex-idUSKBN1F72F0.

24. Helena Horton, "Rise of 'Consent Apps' as Millennials Sign Contracts Before Sex," Telegraph (UK), May 2, 2018, https://www.telegraph.co.uk/news/2018/05/02/tap-yes-can-tapmillennials-sign-consent-apps/.

25. Gil Smart, "Martin County Native Develops 'Consent' App for Safer Sex," TC Palm (May 10, 2018), https://www.tcpalm.com/story/opinion/columnists/gil-smart/2018/05/10/consent-app-martincounty-lessen-sex-assaults/594093002/.

26. Jason Tashea, "Legal Technology: Tech Companies Are Creating Apps to Combat Sexual Assault," A.B.A. Journal 104 (2018): 33–34.

27. Today's Single Guy Needs Proof, Consent Amour, https://perma.cc/2U87-WGUC.

28. Got Consent?, ConsentAmour, https://consentamour.info/.

29. Alexandra Petri, "This Should Not Happen More Than Once," Washington Post, April 6, 2021, https://www.washingtonpost.com/opinions/2021/04/05/matt-gaetz-photos-should-not-happen-more-than-once/.

30. Martha Nussbaum, "Objectification and Internet Misogyny," in The Offensive Internet: Speech, Privacy, and Reputation, ed. Martha Nussbaum and Saul Levmore (Cambridge, MA: Harvard University Press, 2010), 87.

31. Nussbaum, "Objectification and Internet Misogyny."

32. Sophia Ankel, "Many Revenge Porn Victims Consider Suicide—Why Aren't Schools Doing More to Stop It?," The Guardian, May 7, 2018, https://www.theguardian.com/lifeandstyle/2018/may/07/many-revenge-porn-victims-consider-suicide-why-arent-schools-doing-more-to-stop-it.

33. Janene Pieters, Enschede Teen Commits Suicide Over Online Nude Photo, NL Times (February 21, 2017), https://nltimes.nl/2017/02/21/enschede-teen-commits-suicide-online-nude-photo.

34. Episode 2, "The Garbage Can Model of Decision Making," *Sudhir Breaks the Internet* podcast, April 19, 2021.

35. IWF, "Image Hash List," IWF Services, https://www.iwf.org.uk/our-services/hash-list.

36. Stephanie Mlot, 'Hash List' to Help Google, Facebook, More Remove Child Porn," *PC Magazine*, August 11, 2015; International Reporting Protocols, Annual Report, *The Internet Watch Foundation* (2020).

37. UK-Hosted Child Sexual Abuse, *The Internet Watch Foundation*, https://annualreport2020.iwf.org.uk/trends/uk/hosted.

38. "Latest Internet Watch Foundation report shows Europe now hosts 60% of child sexual abuse webpages," April 3, 2017, https://www.iwf.org.uk/news/latest-internet-watch-foundation-report-shows-europe-now-hosts-60-of-child-sexual-abuse.

39. IWF, "Classifiers," Annual Report 2020, https://annualreport2020.iwf.org.uk/tech/new/classifiers.

40. IWF, "IWF Taskforce," Annual Report 2020, https://annualreport2020.iwf.org.uk/tech/new/taskforce.

41. "Video Unavailable: Social Media Platforms Remove Evidence of War Crimes," *Human Rights Watch*, September 10, 2020.

CHAPTER 10: HOPE AND CHANGE

1. "FPF Finds Nearly Three-Quarters of Most Downloaded Mobile Apps Lack a Privacy Policy," *Future of Privacy Forum*, May 12, 2011.

2. John Kennedy and Annie Bai, "Apps Gone Wild? The FTC and California AG Seek to Rein in Mobile App Privacy Practices," *IAPP*, March 1, 2013.

3. Sam Kashner, "Both Huntress and Prey," *Vanity Fair*, October 20, 2014, https://www.vanityfair.com/hollywood/2014/10/jennifer-lawrence-photo-hacking-privacy.

4. Nancy Scola, "Kamala Harris's Crusade Against 'Revenge Porn,'" *Politico*, February 1, 2019, https://www.politico.com/magazine/story/2019/02/01/kamala-harris-porn-california-attorney-general-facebook-twitter-silicon-valley-224534/.

5. "Industry Best Practices Regarding the Non-Consensual Distribution of Sexually Intimate Images," https://oag.ca.gov/cyberexploitation/practices.

6. Jessica Guynn, "Google to Remove 'Revenge Porn' from Search Results," *USA Today*, June 19, 2015, https://www.usatoday.com/story/tech/2015/06/19/google-revenge-porn-search-results/28983363/.

7. Google Spain v. Agencia Española de Protección de Datos, Court of Justice of the European Union, May 13, 2014, https://curia.europa.eu/jcms/upload/docs/application/pdf/2014-05/cp140070en.pdf.

8. "Industry Appendix of Resources on Non-Consensual Distribution of Sexually Intimate Images," https://oag.ca.gov/cyberexploitation/appendix.

9. H.R. 5896, Intimate Privacy Protection Act of 2016, https://www.congress.gov/bill/114th-congress/house-bill/5896.

10. S. 2111, SHIELD Act of 2019, https://www.congress.gov/bill/116th-congress/senate-bill/2111.

11. Gina Martin, *Be the Change: A Toolkit for the Activist in You* (London: Little Brown, 2019), 5–7.

12. Martin, *Be the Change*, 6–7.

13. Zoom interview with Gina Martin, July 6, 2020.

14. Martin, *Be the Change*, 12.

15. Martin interview.

16. @thegobbledegook, June 16, 2018; https://www.globalcitizen.org/en/content/up-skirting-illegal-england-wales-gina-martin/.

17. "Up-skirting Now a Crime after Woman's Campaign," *BBC News*, April 12, 2019, https://www.bbc.com/news/uk-47902522.

18. Alicia Garza, *The Purpose of Power: How We Come Together When We Fall Apart* (New York: One World, Penguin Random House, 2020).

19. Law Commission, "Intimate Image Abuse."

20. Jungmin Seo and Seoyoung Choi, "Why Korean Feminism?," *Journal of Asian Sociology* 49 (December 2020): 384. WOMAD was an online community and website founded in 2016, which supposedly mirrored content from male-dominated websites, including explicit content assaulting male objects. The woman who was convicted of posting the man's image was a WOMAD user.

21. "South Korean Women Protest in Seoul over Hidden Sex Cameras," *BBC*, July 7, 2018, https://www.bbc.com/news/world-asia-44751327.

22. Nicola Smith, "South Korean Women Demand Equal Justice for Internet Sex Crimes," *Telegraph (UK)*, May 21, 2018, https://www.telegraph.co.uk/news/2018/05/21/south-korean-women-demand-equal-justice-internet-sex-crimes/.

23. Smith, "South Korean Women Demand Equal Justice"; Emily Pacenti, "My Life Is Not Your Porn: The Korean Social Movement You Haven't Heard Of," *Spire Magazine*, March 12, 2019, https://spiremagazine.com/2019/03/12/my-life-is-not-your-porn-the-korean-social-movement-you-havent-heard-of/.

24. Yenn Lee, "Online Consequences of Being Offline: A Gendered Tale from South Korea," *Medium*, January 21, 2019, https://medium.com/rawblog/online-consequences-of-being-offline-a-gendered-tale-from-south-korea-94f71f6c59e0.

25. Yenn Lee, "Online Consequences of Being Offline."

26. Jungmin Seo and Seoyoung Choi, "Why Korean Feminism?," *Journal of Asian Sociology* 49 (December 2020): 386.

27. Adam Taylor and Min Joo Kim, "'My Life Is Not Your Porn': South Korea's War against Spy Cameras and Sexual Harassment,'" *Independent (UK)*, July 31, 2018, https://www.independent.co.uk/news/world/asia/south-korea-spy-cams-metoo-sexual-harassment-ahn-hee-jung-a8470771.html.

28. Seo and Choi, "Why Korean Feminism?," 384.

29. Kelly Nguyen, "The Students and Stans Saving K-pop Idols from Deepfake Porn," *Vice i-D*, June 2, 2021.

30. Zoom interview with Won-mo Lee, Director General of Digital Sex Crimes Information Bureau Review Board, November 23, 2020.

31. "14 Pct of Women in Seoul Suffer from Digital Sexual Violence," *Yonhap News Agency*, December 2, 2019.

32. Introduction of the Digital Sex Victim Support Center by the Ministry of Gender Equality and Family, Ministry of Gender Equality and Family in Korea (September 5, 2018).

33. Digital Sex Crime Information Review Status Report (January 2021) (on file with author).

34. Digital Sex Crime Information Review Status Report (January 2021).

35. Lee interview.

36. Lee interview.

37. Lee interview.

38. Tiffany May and Su Hyun Lee, "Is There a Spy Camera in That Bathroom? In Seoul, 8,000 Workers Will Check," *New York Times*, Sept. 3, 2018.

39. Choe Sang-Hun, "South Korean Is Sentenced to 34 Years for Running Exploitative Chat Rooms," *New York Times*, April 9, 2021.

40. Jenna Gibson, "Will South Korea Finally Have Its Reckoning on Sex Crimes?," *The Diplomat*, August 14, 2020.

41. Grace Moon, "'Mitigating Factors': What's Behind South Korea's History of Giving Light Sentences For Sex Crimes?," *Vice World News*, July 20, 2020; Olivia Schieber, "South Korea Needs to Contend with Sexual Violence," *Foreign Policy*, August 10, 2020.

Recommended Reading

Sara Ahmed, *Queer Phenomenology: Orientations, Objects, Others* (Durham, NC: Duke University Press, 2006).

Sara Ahmed, *Living a Feminist Life* (Durham, NC: Duke University Press, 2017).

Anita Allen, *Uneasy Access: Privacy for Women in a Free Society* (Lanham, MD: Rowman & Littlefield, 1988).

Anita Allen, *Unpopular Privacy: What Must We Hide?* (Oxford: Oxford University Press, 2011).

Carol Anderson, *Eyes Off the Prize: The United Nations and the African American Struggle for Human Rights, 1944–1955* (Cambridge: Cambridge University Press, 2003).

Julia Angwin, *Dragnet Nation: A Quest for Privacy, Security, and Freedom in a World of Relentless Surveillance* (New York: Henry Holt and Company, 2014).

Rana Ayyub, *Gujarat Files: Anatomy of a Cover Up* (Delhi: self-published, 2016).

Samantha Barbas, *Laws of Image: Privacy and Publicity in America* (Stanford, CA: Stanford University Press, 2015).

Simone de Beauvoir, *The Second Sex* (1949), translated by Constance Borde and Sheila Malovany-Chevallier (New York: Vintage Books, 2011).

David Bell and Jon Binnie, *The Sexual Citizen: Queer Politics and Beyond* (Cambridge: Polity Press, 2000).

Ruha Benjamin, *Race after Technology: Abolitionist Tools for the New Jim Code* (Cambridge: Polity Press, 2019).

Kate Bornstein, *Gender Outlaw: On Men, Women, and the Rest of Us* (New York: Vintage Books, 2016).

Edward Bloustein, *Individual and Group Privacy* (New Brunswick, NJ: Transaction Publisher, 2003).

Patricia Boling, *Privacy and the Politics of Intimate Life* (Ithaca, NY: Cornell University Press, 1996).

Jennifer Finney Boylan, *She's Not There: A Life in Two Genders* (New York: Broadway Books, 2013).

Sarah Brayne, *Predict and Surveil: Data, Discretion, and the Future of Policing* (New York: Oxford University Press, 2021).

Khiara Bridges, *Reproducing Races: An Ethnography of Pregnancy as a Site of Racialization* (Berkeley: University of California Press, 2011).

Khiara Bridges, *The Poverty of Privacy Rights* (Stanford, CA: Stanford University Press, 2017).

David Brin, *The Transparent Society: Will Technology Force Us to Choose Between Privacy and Freedom?* (New York: Perseus Books Group, 1998).

Susan J. Brison and Katharine Gelber, eds., *Free Speech in the Digital Age* (New York: Oxford University Press, 2019).

Simone Browne, *Dark Matters: On the Surveillance of Blackness* (Durham, NC: Duke University Press, 2015).

Martin Buber, *Between Man and Man,* translated by Ronald Gregor Smith (Boston: Beacon Press, 1955).

Martin Buber, *I and Thou*, translated by Walter Kaufmann (New York: Touchstone, 1996).

Clay Calvert, *Voyeur Nation: Media, Privacy, and Peering in Modern Culture* (Boulder, CO: Westview Press, 2004).

P. Carl, *Becoming a Man: The Story of a Transition* (New York: Simon & Schuster, 2020).

Emily Chang, *Brotopia: Breaking Up the Boys' Club of Silicon Valley* (New York: Portfolio/Penguin, 2019).

Danielle Keats Citron, *Hate Crimes in Cyberspace* (Cambridge, MA: Harvard University Press, 2014).

Julie E. Cohen, *Configuring the Networked Self: Law, Code, and the Play of Everyday Practice* (New Haven, CT: Yale University Press, 2012).

Julie E. Cohen, *Between Truth and Power: The Legal Construction of Informational Capitalism* (New York: Oxford University Press, 2019).

Sasha Costanza-Chock, *Design Justice: Community-Led Practices to Build the Worlds We Need* (Cambridge, MA: MIT Press, 2020).

Kate Crawford, *Atlas of AI: Power, Politics, and the Planetary Costs of Artificial Intelligence* (New Haven, CT: Yale University Press, 2021).

Caroline Criado Perez, *Invisible Women: Data Bias in a World Designed for Men* (New York: Abrams Press, 2019).

Julia Dahl, *The Missing Hours* (New York: Minotaur Books, 2021).

Lennard J. Davis, *Enabling Acts: The Hidden Story of How the Americans with Disabilities Act Gave the Largest U.S. Minority Its Rights* (Boston: Beacon Press, 2015).

Hany Farid, *Fake Photos* (Cambridge, MA: MIT Press, 2019).

Lin Farley, *Sexual Shakedown: The Sexual Harassment of Women on the Job* (New York: Warner Books, 1978).

Michel Foucault, *The History of Sexuality,* vols. 1 and 2, translated by Robert Hurley (New York: Vintage Books, 1978).

Mary Anne Franks, *The Cult of the Constitution* (Stanford, CA: Stanford University Press, 2019).

Charles Fried, *An Anatomy of Values: Problems of Personal and Social Choice* (Cambridge, MA: Harvard University Press, 1970).

Barry Friedman, *Unwarranted: Policing without Permission* (New York: Farrar, Straus and Giroux, 2017).

Brett Frischmann and Evan Selinger, *Re-Engineering Humanity* (Cambridge: Cambridge University Press, 2018).

Erich Fromm, *The Art of Loving* (New York: Harper & Brothers Publishers, 1956).

Alicia Garza, *The Purpose of Power: How We Come Together When We Fall Apart* (New York: One World, 2020).

Erving Goffman, *The Presentation of Self in Everyday Life* (New York: Anchor Books, 1959).

Erving Goffman, *Stigma: Notes on the Management of Spoiled Identity* (New York: Simon & Schuster, 1963).

Carrie Goldberg, *Nobody's Victim: Fighting Psychos, Stalkers, Pervs and Trolls* (New York: Plume, 2019).

John Goldberg and Benjamin C. Zipursky, *Recognizing Wrongs* (Cambridge, MA: Belknap Press, 2020).

Jamal Greene, *How Rights Went Wrong: Why Our Obsession with Rights Is Tearing America Apart* (New York: Houghton Mifflin Harcourt, 2021).

James Griffin, *On Human Rights* (Oxford: Oxford University Press, 2008).

Elizabeth Grosz, *Volatile Bodies: Toward a Corporeal Feminism* (Bloomington: Indiana University Press, 1994).

Andrew Guthrie Ferguson, *The Rise of Big Data Policing: Surveillance, Race, and the Future of Law Enforcement* (New York: New York University Press, 2017).

Sue Halpern, *Migrations to Solitude* (New York: Pantheon Books, 1992).

Woodrow Hartzog, *Privacy's Blueprint: The Battle to Control the Design of New Technologies* (Cambridge, MA: Harvard University Press, 2018).

Deborah Hellman, *When Is Discrimination Wrong?* (Cambridge, MA: Harvard University Press, 2008).

Mar Hicks, *Programmed Inequality: How Britain Discarded Women Technologists and Lost Its Edge in Computing* (Cambridge, MA: MIT Press, 2018).

Katie Hill, *She Will Rise: Becoming a Warrior in the Battle for True Equality* (New York: Grand Central Publishing, 2020).

Jennifer Hirsch and Shamus Khan, *Sexual Citizens: A Landmark Study of Sex, Power, and Assault on Campus* (New York: W.W. Norton & Company, 2020).

Chris Jay Hoofnagle, *Federal Trade Commission: Privacy Law and Policy* (New York: Cambridge University Press, 2016).

Sarah Igo, *The Knowing Citizen: A History of Privacy in Modern America* (Cambridge, MA: Harvard University Press, 2018).

Julie Inness, *Privacy, Intimacy, and Isolation* (New York: Oxford University Press, 1992).

Sidney Jourard, *The Transparent Self* (New York: Litton Educational Publishing, Inc., 1964).

Kristin A. Kelly, *Domestic Violence and the Politics of Privacy* (Ithaca, NY: Cornell University Press, 2003).

Nancy Kim, *Consentability: Consent and Its Limits* (Cambridge: Cambridge University Press, 2019).

Jeff Kosseff, *The Twenty-Six Words that Created the Internet* (Ithaca, NY: Cornell University Press, 2019).

Jessica Lake, *The Face That Launched a Thousand Lawsuits: The American Women Who Forged a Right to Privacy* (New Haven, CT: Yale University Press, 2016).

Yasha Levine, *Surveillance Valley: The Secret Military History of the Internet* (New York: PublicAffairs, 2018).

Saul Levmore and Martha C. Nussbaum, eds., *The Offensive Internet: Speech, Privacy, and Reputation* (Cambridge, MA: Harvard University Press, 2010).

Deborah Lupton, *The Quantified Self* (Cambridge: Polity Press, 2016).

Deborah Lupton, *Data Selves* (Cambridge: Polity Press, 2020).

Catherine MacKinnon, *Sexual Harassment of Working Women* (New Haven, CT: Yale University Press, 1979).

Catherine MacKinnon, *Toward a Feminist Theory of the State* (Cambridge, MA: Harvard University Press, 1989).

Gina Martin, *Be the Change: A Toolkit for the Activist in You* (London: Sphere, 2019).

Rollo May, *Love and Will* (New York: W.W. Norton & Company, 1969).

Roger McNamee, *Zucked: Waking Up to the Facebook Catastrophe* (London: Penguin Books, 2019).

Paul Mendes-Flohr, ed., *Martin Buber: A Contemporary Perspective* (Syracuse, NY: Syracuse University Press, 2002).

Maurice Merleau-Ponty, *Phenomenology of Perception* (New York: Routledge, 2012).

Arthur Miller, *The Assault on Privacy: Computers, Data Banks, and Dossiers* (Ann Arbor: University of Michigan Press, 1971).

Janet Mock, *Redefining Realness: My Path to Womanhood, Identity, Love and So Much More* (New York: Atria Paperback, 2014).

Samuel Moyn, *The Last Utopia: Human Rights in History* (Cambridge, MA: Belknap Press, 2010).

Samuel Moyn, *Not Enough: Human Rights in an Unequal World* (Cambridge, MA: Belknap Press, 2018).

Thomas S. Mullaney, Benjamin Peters, Mar Hicks, and Kavita Philip, eds., *Your Computer Is on Fire* (Cambridge, MA: MIT Press, 2020, 2021).

Cecilia Muñoz, *More Than Ready: Be Strong and Be You . . . And Other Lessons for Women of Color on the Rise* (New York: Seal Press, 2020).

Helen Norton, *The Government's Speech and the Constitution* (Cambridge: Cambridge University Press, 2019).

Martha C. Nussbaum, *Women and Human Development: The Capabilities Approach* (Cambridge: Cambridge University Press, 2000).

Martha C. Nussbaum, *Hiding from Humanity: Disgust, Shame, and the Law* (Princeton, NJ: Princeton University Press, 2004).

Martha C. Nussbaum, *From Disgust to Humanity: Sexual Orientation and Constitutional Law* (New York: Oxford University Press, 2010).

Martha C. Nussbaum, *Creating Capabilities: The Human Development Approach* (Cambridge, MA: Belknap Press, 2011).

Martha C. Nussbaum and Jonathan Glover, eds., *Women, Culture, and Development: A Study of Human Capabilities* (Oxford: Oxford University Press, 1995).

Margaret O'Mara, *The Code: Silicon Valley and the Remaking of America* (Cambridge: Penguin Books, 2019).

Frank Pasquale, *The Black Box Society: The Secret Algorithms That Control Money and Information* (Cambridge, MA: Harvard University Press, 2015).

J. Roland Pennock and John W. Chapman, eds., *Privacy* (New York: Atherton Press, 1971).

Erica Posner, *Law and Social Norms* (Cambridge, MA: Harvard University Press, 2002).

Neil Richards, *Intellectual Privacy: Rethinking Civil Liberties in the Digital Age* (Oxford: Oxford University Press, 2015).

Neil Richards, *Why Privacy Matters* (Oxford: Oxford University Press, 2021).

Megan Richardson, *The Right to Privacy: Origins and Influence of a Nineteenth-Century Idea* (Cambridge: Cambridge University Press, 2017, 2020).

Dorothy Roberts, *Killing the Black Body: Race, Reproduction, and the Meaning of Liberty* (New York: Vintage Books, 2017).

Marc Rotenberg, Julia Horwitz, and Jeramie Scotts, eds., *Privacy in the Modern Age: The Search for Solutions* (New York: The New Press, 2015).

Jennifer Rothman, *The Right of the Publicity: Privacy Reimagined for a Public World* (Cambridge, MA: Harvard University Press, 2018).

George Rutherglen, *Civils Rights in the Shadow of Slavery: The Constitution, Common Law, and the Civil Rights Act of 1866* (New York: Oxford University Press, 2013).

Jean-Paul Sartre, *Being and Nothingness: A Phenomenological Essay on Ontology* (1943), translated by Hazel E. Barnes (New York: Washington Square Press, 1984).

Bruce Schneier, *Data and Goliath: The Hidden Battles to Collect Your Data and Control Your World* (New York: W.W. Norton & Company, 2015).

Scott Skinner-Thomson, *Privacy at the Margins* (Cambridge: Cambridge University Press, 2021).

Daniel J. Solove, *The Digital Person: Technology and Privacy in the Information Age* (New York: New York University Press, 2004).

Daniel J. Solove, *The Future of Reputation: Gossip, Rumor, and Privacy on the Internet* (New Haven, CT: Yale University Press, 2007).

Daniel J. Solove, *Understanding Privacy* (Cambridge, MA: Harvard University Press, 2008).

Susan Sontag, *On Photography* (New York: Picador, 1977).

Susan Sontag, *Regarding the Pain of Others* (New York: Picador, 2003).

Tristan Taormino, Celine Parreñas Shimizu, Constance Penley, and Mireille Miller-Young, eds., *The Feminist Porn Book: The Politics of Producing Pleasure* (New York: The Feminist Press at the City University of New York, 2013).

Astra Taylor, *The People's Platform: Taking Back Power and Culture in the Digital Age* (New York: Picador, 2014).

Shatema Threadcraft, *The Black Female Body and the Body Politic* (Oxford: Oxford University Press, 2016).

Fred Turner, *From Counterculture to Cyberculture: Stewart Brand, the Whole Earth Network, and the Rise of Digital Utopianism* (Chicago: University of Chicago Press, 2006).

Melvin I. Urofsky and David W. Levy, eds., *Letters of Louis D. Brandeis* (Albany: State University of New York Press, 1971).

Sara Wachter-Boettcher, *Technically Wrong: Sexist Apps, Biased Algorithms, and Other Threats of Toxic Tech* (New York: W.W. Norton & Company, 2017).

Judith Wagner DeCew, *In Pursuit of Privacy: Law, Ethics, and the Rise of Technology* (Ithaca, NY: Cornell University Press, 1997).

Ari Ezra Waldman, *Privacy as Trust: Information Privacy for an Information Age* (Cambridge: Cambridge University Press, 2018).

Ari Ezra Waldman, *Industry Unbound* (Cambridge: Cambridge University Press, 2021).

Robin West, *Caring for Justice* (New York: New York University Press, 1997).

Robin West, *Civil Rights: Rethinking Their Natural Foundation* (Cambridge: Cambridge University Press, 2019).

Alan Westin, *Privacy and Freedom* (New York: Atheneum, 1968).

George Edward White, *Tort Law in America: An Intellectual History* (New York: Oxford University Press, 1980).

Patricia Williams, *The Alchemy of Race and Rights: Diary of a Law Professor* (Cambridge, MA: Harvard University Press, 1991).

Mary Wollstonecraft, *A Vindication of the Rights of Women* (1792) (London: Penguin Books, 2004).

Christopher Wylie, *MindF*ck: Cambridge Analytica and the Plot to Break America* (New York: Random House, 2019).

Kenji Yoshino, *Covering: The Hidden Assault on Our Civil Rights* (New York: Random House, 2006).

Iris Marion Young, *Intersecting Voices: Dilemmas of Gender, Political Philosophy, and Policy* (Princeton, NJ: Princeton University Press, 1997).

Shoshana Zuboff, *The Age of Surveillance Capitalism: The Fight for a Human Future at the New Frontier of Power* (New York: Public Affairs, 2019).

Index

abortion, 62–63
accountability, 152
accountants, fiduciary obligations of, 2
Activision Blizzard, 22
activism, 196–205, 229–30
Acxiom, 13–14
ad-tech
    ad-blocking, 220
    ad-tech industrial complex, 8–10
    ad-tech market, 16–17, 99
    ad-tech surveillance, 9–10
    ad-tech trackers, 9–10
adult site tracking, 8–9
advertising, xiv, 8, 162. *See also* ad-tech
    personal data and, 8–11
    targeted, 22
advocacy efforts, how to get involved with,
    229–30
Airbnb, 4
AirDrop, 30, 82
Alexa, 5, 6, 7
Alexander, Michelle, 141
algorithmic assessments, 12, 103. *See also*
    algorithmic bias
algorithmic bias, 20–22, 68–71
Ali, Muhammad, 137
Allen, Anita, 119, 158

Amazon, 210
    Alexa, 5, 6, 7
    Alexa for Residential, 7
    algorithmic hiring at, 21
    bugging devices on, 26
    Echo Flex, 7
    Halo, 1–2, 20–21
    hiring at, 107
    smart assistants and, 5–7
American Bar association, 134
American Civil Liberties Union (ACLU),
    Maryland chapter, 94
American Media Inc., 33
Americans with Disabilities Act, 136, 150
Amnesty International, 46
analytics, 8
Anderson, Carol, 109
Andreessen, Marc, 65
Angwin, Julia, 10–11, 65
AnonIB, 74
anonymization of data, 16
Anti Cyberhate Coalition, 194
Anti-Defamation League, 192, 194
antidiscrimination principles, 107
Apple
    app privacy policies and, 191
    privacy policy of, 6

"appropriation" tort, 102

apps, 1–3, 5, 10, 191, 222. *See also specific apps and kinds of apps*

Arendt, Hannah, 113–14

Arkansas, 136

artificial intelligence (AI), 37–38, 47–48, 129, 160, 177–78

Ashley Madison, 23, 100

The Atlantic, 72

attitudes, changing, 180–86

Austin, Roy, 171

Australia, xiv

    e-Safety Commissioner, xvi, 39–40, 75, 176

    Facebook's hash technology pilot program in, 176–77

    intimate privacy violations in, 28–29, 80, 188

authoritarian regimes, 55

autonomy, securing, 113–16

Ayyub, Rana, 56, 78, 107–8, 114

Azerbaijan, 127–28

Backpage, 87

Bad Samaritans, 87, 90

bar associations, 134

Barlow, John Perry, 65

Bartiromo, Maria, 53

Bartnicki v. Vopper, 147

Bateman, David, 90, 93

battered women's movement, 118

Bayard, Mabel, 111

Bayer, 17

Becerra, Xavier, 129

Bedoya, Alvaro, 107

behavior, prediction of, xiv (*see also* algorithmic assessments)

Belfort, Jordan, 85

Bell, Derrick, 191

Bergeron, Robert, 97, 98, 101, 102, 103

Berners-Lee, Tim, 65

Bezos, Jeff, 33

bias, 20–22, 68–71, 69–71, 142–43

Bing, 91, 195

bin Laden, Osama, 51

Black Enterprise, 171

Black Lives Matter movement, 170, 200

blackmail, 31–33, 35–36

Blumenthal, Richard, 128–29

Bollaert, Kevin, 192

Brandeis, Louis, xii, xiii, 101, 111–13, 123, 139

Brazil, 35, 177

Bridges, Khiara, 61–62

Brin, Sergey, 66

Browne, Simone, 107

Buber, Martin, 116–17

bugging devices, 25–26, 33–34, 50, 100–101

Bumble, 177–78, 204

Buolamwini, Joy, 69

bureaucratic surveillance, 58–60

burner email, 221

Burrill, Jeffrey, 11, 13

California, 98, 127, 129, 138, 142, 146, 164, 190–91, 192

Calo, Ryan, 160

Cambodia, 55

Cambridge Analytica, 13, 176

Canada, 9, 89, 177, 186

Candid Board, 72

Candid Forum, 72

#CANHELP, 229

Cardin, Jon, 94

Castaño, Paula, 22

Catholic Church, 125, 127

cell phones. *See* mobile devices

Chang, Emily, 68

change, 180–86, 189. *See also* reform efforts;
    technology
Chauvin, Derek, 170
children
    books and movies for, 224–25
    educating, 224–25
    rates of victimization and, 40
    sextortion of, 95–96
Children's Online Privacy Protection Act
    (COPPA), 158
child sexual abuse material (CSAM), 37,
    174–75, 186–88, 193
China, 29–30, 57
choice, 4
Chope, Christopher, 199–200
Chopra, Rohit, 103
Choun-Sook, Jung, 204
Citron, Danielle Keats, 71, 190–96
civil lawsuits, 91–92, 101–2, 132
civil liberties, 107
civil rights, 209
    civil rights approach vs. human rights
        approach, 126–27
    human rights and, 108–9, 126–27
    injunctive relief and, 120–21
    as intimate privacy, 106–10
    personal data and, 157
    in United States, xviii–xix, 106, 108, 149
        (*see also specific legislation*)
    West's conception of, 108
Civil Rights Act of 1866, 108–9
Civil Rights Act of 1964, Title VII, 154–55
Clementi, Tyler, 183
Clinton, Bill, 26, 54
    administration of, 65
Clinton, Hillary, 51–52, 53
Clipper chip, 65–66
Cohen, Julie, xiv, 101
Coinbase, 4

Coleman, Daisy, 42
Collab Capital, 170
Collins, Patricia Hill, 68
Colorado, 98, 136
Color for Change, 169–70
Committee on Foreign Investment in the
    United States (CFIUS), 57
communications, securing privacy of, 220
Communications Decency Act (CDA),
    Section 230, 84–90
companies. *See also* tech companies; *specific*
    companies
    accountability of, 152
    bureaucratic surveillance and, 58–59
    as caretakers of privacy rights, xviii, 148,
        155, 210
    privacy policies and, 1–2, 4–5, 6, 191
    Section 230 and, 149–52
comprehensive federal privacy law, proposed
    Rule #1, 156–59
    Rule #2, 159–60
    Rule #3, 160–62
    Rule #4, 162–65
Computer Professionals for Social
    Responsibility, 65
consent, 116, 137, 145–46, 159, 161, 178–79
ConsentAmour, 178, 179
consent apps, 178–79
Consumer Financial Protection Bureau, 103
consumer privacy, 66–67, 129
consumer protection, xvii, 97–100
Consumer Reports, 15
consumer scoring marketplace, 4
consumption, ethical, 221
content moderation, 150, 151–53
Convirs-Fowler, Kelly, 82–83
Cook, Tim, 148–49, 165
copyright infringement, 90–93
Costeja González, Mario, 138, 139

Coulter, Ann, 52
Council of Europe, 125
Court of Justice of the European Union
    (CJEU), 138–39, 195
COVID pandemic, xvi, 18, 40, 128–29,
    181–82
Cox, Chris, 85–87, 150
Cranor, Lorrie, 5
Criado Perez, Caroline, 46–47
crime, data collection to fight, 58–60
criminal justice, rethinking, 140
Crossix, 12
Cruz, Ted, 149, 154
cultural practices, xvii
Cyber Civil Rights Initiative (CCRI), xvi,
    41–42, 145, 172, 177, 180, 190, 193,
    196, 202, 229, 230
Cyber Civil Rights Legal Project (CCRLP),
    90, 91, 134
Cyber Exploitation Task force, 190
cyber flashers, 30–31, 39, 82, 94
cyber mobs, 54
cyberstalking apps, 34–35. See also
    stalkerware
cycle tracking, 14–16

Dahl, Julia, 225
The Daily Caller, 45
Daily Mail, 146
D'Amico, Elisa, 90, 93, 132–33, 134, 192
data. See also data collection; intimate data;
    personal data
    anonymization of, 16
    digital reservoirs of, 17–19
    re-identification of, 16
data brokers, xiv, 11–14, 58–59, 162, 167
data collection, xiv
    bulk interception of, 58
    to fight crime and terrorism, 58–60

lifesaving, 18
    risks vs. rewards, 17–23
    smart devices and, 7–8
"data death penalty," 164
data guardians, duties of, 148–68
data markets, xiv–xv. See also data brokers
data mining, 11–12, 20–21, 103, 166–68
Data Protection and Privacy Commissioners
    (DPAs), 148, 164
data protection regulations, xvii. See also
    privacy laws
data selves, 3–8, 23
dating apps, 3–4, 6, 9–13, 18, 22, 88, 105–6,
    116, 155, 162, 177–79. See also specific
    apps
Davis, Antigone, 176–77
deepfake porn, 37–38, 78, 94, 108, 136, 203
    criminalization of, 142
    First Amendment implications for
        regulation of, 146–47
Deep Fakes, 37–38
deepfake technology, 37. See also deepfake
    porn
"deep learning" artificial intelligence, 37–38
Defamation Regulations of 2013, 90
delivery orders, 4
democracy, 121
Democratic National Committee, 13
Deneumostier, Bryan, 40
DeNicola, Nathaniel, 15
Deras, Miguel, 80
design, seductive, 6
destructive attitudes, internalization of,
    80–81
"dick pics," 30–31
digital citizenship, 183, 185–86
digital engagement, ethics of, 221
Digital Millennium Copyright Act, 153
digital services, 1–3

risks vs. rewards of, 17–23

digital sex crime information (DSCI), 202–3

Digital Sex Crime Out, 201–4

digital sexual identity fraud, 37–39

"Digital Stakeout," 59

digital surveillance, xiv

Digital Sex Crime Information Bureau (DSCIB), 202–3

digital voyeurs, 28–33

The Dirty, 87

disability status, rates of victimization and, xvi

discrimination, 21, 142–43

disgust, sexuality and, 115

District of Columbia, 142, 196

diversity initiatives, 169–70

Diversity VC, 171

doctors, health privacy laws and, 2

doctors' offices, intimate privacy violations in, 29

Doerr, John, 67

domestic abuse, 34–36, 118

Do Not Call registries, 165

dopamine hits, 6

Dowd, Maureen, 45

Dumont, Ed, 190–91

Duportail, Judith, 3–4

"duty of care," 155, 203

Echo Flex, 7

Edelman, Gilad, 152

education, 180–86, 210

educational tools, security of, 224

Electronic Communications Privacy Act, 86

Electronic Frontier Foundation (EFF), 65

emergency health data, 128–29

encryption, 219, 220

England, 143, 198. See also United Kingdom

Enright, Amy, 183

Equal Credit Opportunity Act, 129

equality, privacy and, 105, 107, 118–19, 141, 169–71, 199

equal opportunity, 171

Equifax, 14

ethical consumption, 221

ethnic background, rates of victimization and, xvi

European Commission, Digital Services Act, 155

European Convention on Human Rights, 125

European Court of Human Rights (ECHR), 125, 126, 128

European Economic Area (Norway, Ireland, Liechtenstein), 99

European Union, xvii. See also specific countries

Court of Justice of the European Union (CJEU), 138–39, 195

General Data Protection Regulation (GDPR) and, 3–4, 5, 8, 14, 99, 138, 164

liability for third-party content in, 89–90

personal data in, 99

right to privacy in, 138–39, 195, 205

everyday interactions, tips for, 219–21

Experian, 3, 14

extortion, 31–33, 35–36. See also sextortion

Facebook, xiv, 8–9, 89, 185, 186, 192, 210

advertising services on, 17, 21

ban on nonconsensual intimate images, 175–77

civil rights experts at, 171

Facebook Live, 172–73

harassment policy of, 197

internal reforms and, 171, 175–77, 204

Nonconsensual Intimate Imagery Task Force, 176–77

terms-of-service (TS) agreement, 175

facial recognitions systems, limits on, 210
Fair Credit Reporting Act (FCRA), 129,
    166
fair information practices, 97–98, 99
"false light" tort, 102
Falwell, Jerry Jr., 33
"Fappening," 192
Faraday, Michael, 10n
Faraday bags, 10–11, 10n
Farid, Hany, 38, 174
FBI (Federal Bureau of Investigation), xvi, 50,
    51–54, 65–66, 78, 207, 208
Federal Communications Commission
    (FCC), 164–65
Federal Trade Commission (FTC), 10,
    97–101, 103–4, 119, 129–30, 156, 163,
    164–65
FEMM, 161–62
femtech apps, 14–17, 19, 21–23. See also
    specific apps and kinds of apps
fertility apps, 19, 21–23, 100, 116, 129,
    161–62
financial data, 3
Finland, 46
Finlay, Chase, 75
First Amendment, 82–83, 87–88, 126–27,
    144–47, 154, 157, 166–68. See also free
    speech rights
"First Amendment expansionism," 144
flashing, 30–31, 82
Flo, 14, 16, 17, 100
Floyd, George, 170
Foley Hoag, 134
Ford, Michael, 95
Forsgrén, Bella, 46
Fourth Amendment, 150–51
France, 9, 186
Franks, Mary Anne, xvi, 43, 87, 131, 145, 165,
    175, 190, 192, 193, 194–95, 196

freedoms, enabled by intimate privacy, xvii–
    xviii
free market, xvii
free speech rights, xvii, 82–83, 87–88, 122–
    23, 125–27, 144–47, 166–68
FSB, 57
fusion centers, 58–59, 63

Gadot, Gal, 38
Gaetz, Matt, 180
gamelike behavior, nonconsensual porn and,
    74
Garza, Alicia, 200
Gasser, Urs, 224
Gatto, Mike, 193
Gebru, Timit, 69
Geller, Weny Mandell, 178
gender, 43, 114. See also LGBTQ
    community; girls; men; women
    discrimination and, 21
    gender-based objectification, 180
    gendered harms, 141
    gender equality, 107
    gender norms, 204
    gender stereotypes, 21
    heteronormativity and, 115
    intersectionality and, 141
    rates of victimization and, xvi
General Data Protection Regulation
    (GDPR), 3–4, 5, 14, 99, 138, 164
Genetic Information Non-Discrimination
    Act (GINA), 108, 157
genetic testing, consumer, 12
geo-blocking technology, 139
Georgetown University Law Center, "The
    Color of Surveillance," 106–7
Georgia, 95, 112
Germany, 90
    Network Enforcement Act of 2018, 90

Gillibrand, Kirsten, 161
girls
    hyper-surveillance of, 14–17
    intimate privacy violations as structural
        problem for, 119–20
global cooperation, xix
Glove Eve, 19
Glow, 15, 70, 71, 129
Glow Nurture, 19
GNS Healthcare, 12
Goffman, Erving, 117
Goldberg, Carrie, 88, 134, 192, 196
Goluboff, Risa, 109
Good Samaritan blocking, 86–88, 104, 150
Google, xiv, 66, 89, 138–39, 164, 170, 186,
        192, 193
    advertising system of, 70
    algorithmic bias and, 69–71
    change in search results policy, 194–95,
        205
    discrimination and stereotypes in search
        results, 21
    Google ad trackers, 8
    internal reforms and, 194–95, 205
    Keyword Planner, 69–70
    Maps, xiv
    nonconsensual porn and, 91
    racial bias and, 69–70
    smart assistants and, 5–7
gossip rags, xii
governments, xviii, 207–8. *See also*
        government surveillance; *specific*
        countries
government surveillance, 50–63, 225
    freedom from, 65–66
    of minority communities, 106–7
Granda, Giancarlo, 33
Grand Chamber of the European Court of
    Human Rights, 58

Grant, Julie, 173, 176
Gregoire, Claudia, 192
Grindr, 9, 11, 22, 57, 73, 88, 97, 98–99, 101,
        102, 103, 155, 162, 164
Griveaux, Benjamin, 47
Guam, 142, 196
guardians, guidance for, 224–25
Guynn, Jessica, 194–95

Halo, 20–21
Hamburg Commissioner for Data Protection
        and Freedom of Information, 164
Harris, Kamala, 190, 191, 192, 193–94, 196,
        199
Hartzog, Woodrow, 5, 161
Harvey, Del, 170, 192
hash technology, 174–77, 186–88, 203
hate crimes, 142–43
Hawaii, 142
Hawley, Josh, 149, 154
health apps, 5, 12, 14–17, 19, 21–22
Health Breach Notification Rule, 100
health data, 12
health data miners, 166–68
health devices, 18
Health Information Portability and
        Accountability Act (HIPAA), 15, 97,
        163, 168
health privacy laws
    doctors and, 2
    Health Information Portability and
        Accountability Act (HIPAA), 15, 97,
        163, 168
health-related purchases, 12
Herrick, Matthew, 88, 155
Hess, Amanda, 75
heteronormativity, 115
hidden cameras, 200–205. *See also* bugging
    devices

Hill, Kashmir, 4
Hill, Katie, 45–47, 127, 146, 187
hiring tools
    AI and, 107
    discrimination and, 21, 107
HIV status, 22, 97, 162
Hobhouse, Wera, 199
Hoffmann, Anna Lauren, 114
Holmes, Oliver Wendell Sr., 28
home devices, 5, 6–7, 18–19
    data collection and, 7–8
    for hotel rooms, 7
    for landlords, 7
    tips for, 223
home routers, updating, 223
homosexuality, xii
Hoover, J. Edgar, 50, 51, 55
Horowitz, Andreessen, 170
hotels, intimate privacy violations in, 31–32
Hoyle, Sarah, 170
human rights, xviii, 108–9, 124, 126–27
human rights approach, civil rights approach
    and, 126–27
Hyeong-wook, Moon, 204
hyper-surveillance, of women and girls,
    14–17

IBM, 69
Iceland, 78
identity, securing, 113–16
identity formation, 114
Illinois, Supreme Court of, 145
immigrants, subject to pregnancy surveillance,
    62–63
Imse, Elliott, 47
independent counsel, 54
India, 56
    nonconsensual porn in, 78
    stalkerware users in, 35

Indiana, Supreme Court of, 145
inequality, intimate privacy violations and,
    43–48
information, freedom of, 65–66
"informational capitalism," xiv–xv
information asymmetries, 103
information overload, 5
injunctive relief, 120–21, 135–36, 137, 138,
    164
Instagram, 47, 176, 183
insurance companies, 13
insurance industry, 20–21
interest-convergence theory, 199
International Conference of Data Protection
    and Privacy Commissioners (DPAs), 148
international cooperation, 186–88
internet
    pornography and, xvi (see also
        nonconsensual intimate images)
    securing privacy on, 220
Internet Association, 89
internet service providers (ISPs), 186
Internet Watch Foundation (IWF), 186–88
Interpol, 40
intersectionality, 141
intimacy, enabling, 116–19
intimate data
    advertising and, 8–11
    databases of, 17–23
    governments weaponizing, 50–63
    manipulation based on, 22
    selling of, 116
    sharing of, 122
intimate partners, tips for, 226
intimate privacy, 209
    attitudes toward, xvii, 76–81, 141–42,
        180–86, 204
    as a civil right, 106–10, 115–16, 119–24,
        128–30, 134, 136–37, 138, 149, 209

comprehensive approach to violations, 131–47

education and, 180–86, 210

freedoms enabled by, xvii–xviii

as a human right, 124, 125–28

laws to support, 209

as a moral and legal right, 106

protections of, 209–11

right to, 105–30, 134, 136–38, 149

social norms and, xii

strengthening, 209

violations of (*see* intimate privacy violations)

intimate privacy protections. *See* legislation; privacy laws

intimate privacy violations, xi–xii, 24–49, 97–102, 131–47, 196–205

bias and, 142–43

civil claims, 101–2

discrimination and, 142–43

economic consequences of, 44, 140

education about, 180–86

emotional harm of, 41–43

entrenched inequality and, 43–48

by the government, 50–57

harms caused by, 41–43, 139–40

LGBTQ community and, 105–6

patterns of victimization, 39–40

penalties for bias-motivated, 142–43

political consequences of, 45–48

as a single problem, 142

stereotypes reinforced by, 43–44

intimate surveillance, abuse and, 33–37

"intrusion on seclusion" tort, 102

Iowa, 136

IP addresses, blocking of, 88

iPhone, xiv, 30, 82. *See also* mobile devices

iPhone AirDrop, 30, 82

Ismayilova, Khadija, 127–28, 56

Israel, 28

Italy, 89, 177

Jack'd, 105–6, 107

Jacobs, Holly, 190, 193, 195, 196

James, Letitia, 105, 107, 129

Japan, 9, 30

Jefts, Kara, 42, 77

job market, 140. *See also* hiring tools

Johansson, Scarlett, 38

Johnson, Erica, 195

Johnson, Erious Jr., 59

Johnson, Venus, 193

Johnstone, Erica, 193

Jong-woo, Son, 204

Joo-bin, Cho, 204

journalism, xii

journalists, 56, 59, 69. *See also specific journalists*

judicial system, 156, 163–64

four types of wrongful privacy-invasive activities recognized by, 101

recognition of victims within, 132–33

removing barriers to justice, 133–35

rethinking criminal justice, 140–44

victim blaming and, 95–96

Jureic, Quinta, 45

justice

removing barriers to, 133–35

rethinking criminal justice, 140

K&L Gates, 90, 134

Kaspersky, 35

Kaye, David, 126

Kelly, R., 33

Kendrick, Leslie, 144

Kennedy, Anthony, 168

Khan, Lina, 101

Khan, Sadaf, 19
King, Martin Luther Jr., 50
Kleiner Perkins, 67
kompromat, 55
KPMG, 130
Kunlun Tech, 57

Lake, Jessica, 112
landlords, 7
Lauer, Matt, 118
law enforcement, 193
    abuses by, 50–51
    attitudes of, 76–80, 141–42, 204
    failure to help victims of nonconsensual
        porn, 91
    lack of responsiveness by, 76–81
    need to educate, 141–42
    negligence of, xvii
    victim blaming by, 77–80
Lawrence, Jennifer, 191–92
Leathers, Sydney, 45
Lee, Pamela Anderson, 77, 145–46
Lee, Won-mo, 202
Legal-Fling app, 178
legal tools, inadequacy of, 94–96
legislation, 120–21. *See also* privacy laws;
        specific laws
    failed, 82–84, 94–95
    practical hurdles, 90–93
Levchin, Max, 70
Lewinsky, Monica, 26, 54
LGBTQ community, 105
    disproportionately burdened by privacy
        invasions, 107–8, 140, 141
    victim blaming and, 80–81, 96
    victimization and, xvi, 47, 39–40, 80–81,
        96, 105–8
    vulnerability of, 105

liability, 84–90
life insurance companies, 13, 20–21
The Lives of Others, 225
Lloyd, Scott, 62
loyalty, 160–61

MacKinnon, Catharine, 118–19
Maddow, Rachel, 53
March Against Revenge Port, 229
Marcotte, Amanda, 75
marginalized groups, disproportionate
        burdens of, 59, 76–80 (*see also specific
        groups*)
Maris, Elena, 9
market interventions, need for, xix
Markle, Meghan, 39
The Markup, 10–11, 69, 70
Martin, Gina, 196–200
Martin, Noelle, 38–39
Martynenko, Anton, 95
Maryland, House of Delegates, 94
Massachusetts Group Insurance Commission,
        16
McCabe, Andy, 208
McCluskey, Lauren, 80
McDonald, Aleecia, 5
McNamee, Roger, 68
Medicaid, 61, 167
Medicare, 167
meditation apps, 98
Meineck, Sebastian, 9
men, rates of victimization and, xvi
mental health apps, 10
Meta, 210. *See also* Facebook
#MeToo movement, 199
Mexico, 89
Michaels, Bret, 145–46
Microsoft, 69, 186, 192, 194, 195, 210

mikvahs, intimate privacy violations in, 29

Minnesota, Supreme Court of, 145

minority communities. *See also specific groups*
  disproportionately burdened by privacy invasions, 107–8, 140, 141
  government surveillance of, 106–7
  negative impact of algorithmic decision-making on, 21–22
  rates of victimization and, xvi, xvii, 39–40, 45–47
  victim blaming and, 80–81, 96

Min-seo, 96

misogyny, 46–47, 204

Missouri, 62

mobile devices
  bombarded with sexually explicit material, 30
  data collection and, 7–8
  privacy settings, 221
  up-skirt photos and, 29

Modi, Narendra, 56

molka, 28, 201–2

monetary relief, 139

multifactor authentication (MFA), 220–21

mutual revelation, 117

MySpace, 205

Nain, Karuna, 176–77

National Association for the Advancement of Colored People (NAACP), 109, 157

National Center of Missing and Exploited Children (NCMEC), 174–75, 188, 203

National Enquirer, 33

National Network to End Domestic Violence (NNEDV), 176, 177

National Public Radio (NPR), 86

National Security Agency, 51

National Venture Capital Association, 171

Nature Cycles app, 15–16

Nebraska, 136

Netherlands, 186, 188

New York, 142
  Civil Rights Law, 136–37
  Department of Education, 107, 140
  Department of Financial Services, 13

New York City Ballet (NYCB), 75, 95

New York Post, 44

New York Times, 45, 111

New Zealand, 29, 36–37

Nkonde, Mutale, 169–70

Noble, Safiya, 21, 70–71

nonconsensual intimate images, xi–xii, xv, 35–37, 71–76, 84–90, 87, 127–28, 130–32, 145–46, 152, 188, 191–92, 200–205
  banned on Facebook, 175–77
  civil lawsuits and, 91–92
  copyright infringement and, 90–93
  during COVID pandemic, xvi
  criminalization of, 142, 196, 209
  disproportionately female and minority victims, 39–40
  economic consequences of, 44
  female victims of, 39–40
  gamelike behavior and, 74
  as "incurable disease," 42
  jurisdiction issues and, 91
  political consequences of, 45–47
  protesters and, 74–75
  removal of, 135–36
  shame caused by, 115
  victim-blaming and, 44–45, 47
  vulnerability and, 115

nondiscrimination, 160–61

norms, 151

Northeastern University, 6

Norton, Helen, 146
Norway, 99
notice, 4
notice-and-takedown regime, 153
Novak, Kathryn, 43–44
"Nth Room," 202–4
Nunes, Devin, 150
Nussbaum, Martha, 115, 180

Obama, Barack, 64, 65
Ocasio-Cortez, Alexandria, 45
Office of Refugee Resettlement (ORR), 62
Ohm, Paul, 16
OkCupid, 9–10
O'Mara, Margaret, 68
Oracle, 8, 12
Oregon, 59
Ovia Health, 21–22

Page, Larry, 66
Page, Lisa, 51–54, 63, 207–8
Paine, Thomas, 108
Pakistan, 177
Palantir, 58
Palfrey, John, 224
Panty Buster toy, 7
parents, guidance for, 224–25
Park, Soo-Yeu, 201–4
Parker, Kate, 181
Parliament (UK), 199–200
Pasquale, Frank, 12
password managers, 219
Patient Privacy Rights, 16–17
Paul, Rand, 52
Peel, Deborah, 16–17
peeping toms, 25
Penney, Jonathon, 154
penny press, 110–11

period-tracking apps, 14–15, 19, 21–22,
    161–62, 163
permission to consume and sell, 97–104
personal data, 97–100. See also intimate data
    advertising and, 8–11 (see also ad-tech;
        advertising)
    breaches of, 2–3
    civil rights and, 157
    collection of, xiv–xv, 1–6, 14, 156–59
    fair information practices and, 97–98
    firms hoarding, xiv, 1–3, 5
    overcollection of, xiv, 1–6
    penalties for collecting without permission,
        xvii
    permission to collect, xvii
    selling of, 5, 8, 97–102 (see also data
        brokers)
    used to humiliate and shame pregnant
        women seeking Medicaid, 61–62
    value of, xvii, 1–2, 10
Petri, Alexandra, 180
PGP encryption, 220
pharmaceutical companies, 166–68
PhotoDNY hash technology, 174
The Pillar, 11
Pinterest, 192, 194
Planned Parenthood, 62
Plaza, Aubrey, 38
policymakers, in United States, xvii
political campaigns, 13
polycystic ovary syndrome (PCOS), 16
pop culture, privacy invasion in, 25
porn-filtering software, racial discrimination
    and, 68–69
Pornhub, 9, 37, 40, 188
pornography, 8–9, 51, 71–76, 162. See also
    nonconsensual intimate images; specific
    sites

Post, Robert, 114
Pott, Audrie, 183
pregnancy apps, 19
pregnancy surveillance, 60–63
press, xii
privacy
    adding extra layer of privacy control,
        220–21
    definitions of, 94–95
    equality and, 105, 107, 118–19, 141,
        169–71, 199
    expectation of, xvii
    hope for, xvii
    as human rights with basic entitlements,
        148
    invasion of, xiv–xvi, 24–49
    male invocation of in service of female
        subordination, 118–19
    practical and moral significance of, xvii
    right to, 105–30
    violations of, xi–xii
Privacy Act of 1974, 52, 157, 158, 208
privacy harms
    disproportionate burden on women,
        minorities, and LGBTQ community,
        107–8
    intangibility of, 101–3
privacy laws, xvii, 209–11. *See also specific laws*
    comprehensive federal, 156–65
    founding article of, 112
    free speech and, 166–68
    gaps in, 83
    health privacy laws, 2, 10, 15, 97, 163,
        168
    inadequacy of current, xix, 2–3, 82–104
    proposed federal, 156–65
    telephone privacy laws, 164
privacy policies, 1–2, 4–5, 6, 191

privacy rights
    companies as caretakers of, xviii, 148, 155,
        210
    First Amendment and, 157
    free speech rights and, 122–23, 125–26,
        144–47
privacy settings, mobile devices, 221
privacy tort law, 101–102, 112–13, 139–40
private power, xviii
private sphere, 118
pro bono representation, 90, 91, 93, 132, 133,
    134–35, 198, 230
Prodigy, 85
product development, 171–73
Prosser, William, 101
protesters, 200–205
    government surveillance of, 59–60
    nonconsensual porn and, 74–75
pseudonymous lawsuits, 133–34
public power, xviii
public sphere, 118
public transportation
    cyber flashers and, 30
    intimate privacy violations in, 29
public Wi-Fi, avoiding, 221
"purely private matters," 165
"pure shame," 114
Putin, Vladimir, 55

Rabkin, Jeffrey, 190
race
    intersectionality and, 141
    racial discrimination, 68–70
    racial equality, 107 (*see also* equality)
    rates of victimization and, xvi
Rad, Sean, 6
Radha, Matt, 185
Raji, Deborah, 68, 69, 70

rape videos, 36–37

ratters, 40

reasonableness standard, content moderation
      and, 150–53

reasonable steps approach, 150–56

Rebeca, Júlia, 42

Reddit, 37–38

Reding, Viviane, 138

reform efforts, 121, 189–90. *See also*
      legislation
   failed, 82–84, 94–95
   getting involved with, 230
   practical hurdles, 90–93
   public sentiment and, 199

Remote Access Trojan (RAT) malware, 40

reporters, xii

reproductive data, 14–15, 16–17

reproductive freedom, data collection to
      impede, 62

respect, securing, 113–16

Retina-X, 100–101

"revenge porn," xi–xii, xvi, 35–36, 131–32,
      192, 202. *See also* nonconsensual
      intimate images

Revenge Porn Helpline, 229–30

Richards, Neil, 7, 112, 161, 168

Ridley, Daisy, 38

rights. *See specific kinds of rights*

"right to be forgotten," 138, 195, 205

"right to be left alone" article, 110–13

right to privacy, 123, 126, 138–40, 205

Rivers School, 183

Roosevelt, Eleanor, 109

Rosenblum, Ellen, 59

Russia
   intimate privacy violations in, 48
   IWF and, 186
   kompromat in, 55, 56–57

stalkerware users in, 35
   targeting of journalists in, 56

Rutherglen, George, 108–9

"safety pants," 29–30

Saint-Exupéry, Antoine de, 189

Sales, Nancy Jo, 6

Sartre, Jean-Paul, 114

Schatz, Brian, 149

School of American Ballet, 75

schools, 183–84

Schools Consent Project, 181

"scored society," 12

searches, online, 12

Secret, 192

Section 230, 137–38, 149–50
   legal shield of, 84–90, 172
   need to reform, 137–38, 149–54, 188
   US Congress and, 149–52, 154

"seductive surveillance," 5

Seifullah, Annie, 44–45, 107, 140

self-development, xviii, 113, 122

self-regulation, tech companies and, 66–67

Sensity, 48

September 11, 2001, terrorist attacks of, 51

services, personalization of, xiv

sex robots, 48

sextortion, xvi, 31–33, 35–36, 40, 94, 95–96,
      127–28, 202, 203–4

sex toy apps, 7–8

sex trafficking, 86

sexual assault, 36–37, 118, 141. *See also* rape
      videos

sexual autonomy, 41, 113, 132. *See also*
      autonomy

sexual equality, 107. *See also* equality

sexual expression, 147

sexual harassment, 118

sexuality, disgust and, 115
sexually transmitted infections (STIs), 9. *See also* HIV status
sexual orientation, xvi. *See also* LGBTQ community
sex videos, 145–46
Sift, 4
Simpson, Brandon, 43–44
Singapore, intimate privacy violations in, 28, 29
Siri, 5, 6
site operators, as caretakers of privacy rights, xviii
Slaughter, Rebecca Kelly, 129–30
smart phones. *See* mobile devices
"social approval," 6
social media, 162, 165, 169, 183, 192, 197–98, 203–4. *See also* tech companies; *specific platforms*
    education and, 185
    Section 230 and, 149
    social and cultural normalization of surveillance in, 64–71
social norms, 64–71. *See also* attitudes
    intimate privacy and, xii
    new compact for, 169–88
software updates, 223
Solove, Daniel J., 225
Soltani, Ashkan, 9–10
Sontag, Susan, 28
Sorrell v. Ims Health, 166–68
South Africa, xvi
South Dakota, 136
South Korea, xiv
    intimate privacy protections in, 209
    intimate privacy violations in, 28–29, 32, 36, 39–40, 77, 89, 96, 188, 200–205, 209

mass protests and activism in, 200–205
    National Police, 39
Sovath, Luon, 55
Spain, 138
Speier, Jackie, 196
Spielman, Amanda, 30–31
Spinner, 22
Spotify, 170
SpyFone, 101
spying, 1–23, 100–101
stalkerware, 34–35, 100–101
stalking, 24–26, 34–35
Starr, Kenneth, 54, 55
Starr Report, 54
startups, 153
state attorneys general, 163. *See also specific states*
stereotypes, 21, 43–44
stigma, 45–46, 140
#StopSkirtingtheIssue, 199
"Straightboyz" website, 40
Streisand, Barbra, 92
"Streisand Effect," 92
"strict scrutiny review," 145
Strzok, Peter, 51–54, 63, 207–8
Sudjic, Olivia, 15–16
Sullivan, Joseph, 192
Suomela, Iiris, 46
Supreme Court of California, 138
Supreme Court of Georgia, 112
Surovell, Scott, 82–83
surveillance, 100–101, 225
    ad-tech surveillance, 9–10
    bureaucratic surveillance, 58–60
    government surveillance, 14–17, 50–63, 65–66, 106–7, 225
    intimate surveillance and, 33–37
    pregnancy surveillance, 60–63

surveillance (*continued*)
    "seductive surveillance," 5
    social and cultural normalization of, 64–81
surveillance tools, 25–27, 33–34
Suvor, Daniel, 191
Swann, Cody, 178
Sweeney, Latanya, 10, 16
Swift, Taylor, 38

Take Back the Tech! 229
Taobao, 30
targeted advertising, 22
tech companies, xvii, 192, 193, 195, 196. *See also specific companies*
    blind spots of, 67–71
    consumer privacy and, 66–67
    dominated by men, 64–71
    duties of care and, 203
    exportation of biases around the world, 71
    government oversight of, 66
    hiring of women and minorities by, 67–68
    hiring practices of, 67–68, 169–71
    hyper-surveillance of, 14–17
    internal reforms, 194–95
    market interventions and, xix
    privacy and safety practices and, xiv
    product development and design at, 171–73
    racial and gender diversity in, 169–71
    Section 230 and, 84–90, 154
    self-regulation and, 66–67
    social and cultural normalization of surveillance in, 64–71
    US Congress and, 66
technology
    cautious optimism about, 173–80
    erosion of privacy and, xii
    privacy-enhancing, 173–80
tech startups, 170–71

teenagers, 224–25
telephone privacy laws, 164
terrorism, 51, 58–60
Texxxan, 87
Thiel, Peter, 68
3D avatars, 48
Tinder, 3–4, 6, 57
TITAN Fusion Center, 59–60
tort law, 150
toxic masculinity, 43
tracking. *See also* surveillance
    ad-tech trackers, 8–9
    pornography and, 8–9
TrafficJunky, 9
transgender people, 114
transparency, 152, 203
TransUnion, 14
Tripp, Linda, 26
Troullinou, Pinelopi, 5
Truman, Harry S., 109
Trump, Donald, 13, 51–54, 207–8
    administration of, 18, 62
    "pee tape" and, 55
Trust and Safety Professional Association, 151
Tumblr, 192, 194, 195
Twitter, 9, 46, 170, 172, 186, 192, 194, 195, 198, 201

uConsent, 178
UGotPosted, 192
"Uncomfortable Courage" protests, 201
"unfair and deceptive commercial acts and practices" (UDAP) laws, 98, 156
Uniform Civil Remedies for Unauthorized Disclosure of Intimate Images Act (UDII Act), 136
Uniform Law Commission, 136

United Kingdom, xiv, 28–29, 186, 196–200,
209
after Brexit, 3–4
bulk interception in, 58
bureaucratic surveillance in, 58
criminal justice system in, 143
cyber flashers in, 30–31, 39
Facebook's hash technology pilot program
in, 177
General Data Protection Regulation
(GDPR) and, 3–4, 5, 14, 99
Home Office's Child Abuse Image
Database, 186
Information Commissioner's Office
(ICO), 14
intimate privacy violations in, 78, 81, 200
Law Commission, 143
Law Commission Report on Intimate
Image Abuse, 81, 94
liability for third-party content in, 90
Ministry of Justice, 200
Office for Standards in Education
(Ofsted), 30–31
Office of Communications (Ofcom), 155
Online Safety Bill, 155
Pornhub traffic in, 9
reform efforts, 155
Revenge Porn Helpline in, 229–30
sexist online abuse during election in, 46
up-skirt photos in, 196–200
United States, xiv. See also specific states
bureaucratic surveillance in, 58–60
civil rights in, xviii–xix, 106, 108, 149
consumer protection in, 97–100
criminalization of nonconsensual porn
in, 209
cyber flashers in, 82
data collection in, 14

Facebook's hash technology pilot program
in, 177
health privacy laws in, 10
inadequacy of laws in, 2–3
increase in nonconsensual porn during
pandemic, xv–xvi
intimate privacy protections in, 209–11
intimate privacy violations in, 28, 29,
31–32, 48, 84–90, 91, 97–102, 138,
152, 188, 207–9
IWF and, 186
permission to consume and sell in, 97–104
personal data in, 97–100
policymakers in, xvii
Pornhub traffic in, 9
privacy policies and, 4–5
reform efforts, 149–52
stalkerware users in, 35
United States-Mexico-Canada Trade
Agreement, 89
Universal Declaration of Human Rights, 126
up-skirt photos, 29–30, 72, 94, 95, 196–99
USA Today, 194
US Centers for Disease Control and
Prevention (CDC), 57
US Conference of Catholic Bishops
(UCCB), 11
US Congress, 50–51, 62, 161, 163–64,
180, 196. See also legislation; specific
legislation
fusion centers and, 60
need for change and, 189
reasonable steps approach and, 155–56
Section 230 and, 87, 137–38, 149–52,
154–56
tech companies and, 66
US Copyright Office, 92–93
US Date, 12

US Department of Health and Human
Services (HHS), 163
US Department of Homeland Security, 58
US Department of Justice (DOJ), 51–54,
109, 142–43, 207–8
US Department of the Treasury, 57
usernames, 223
US Supreme Court, 87, 88, 147, 157,
166–68

Vanity Fair, 192
Venkatesh, Sudhir, 185
venture capital (VC) firms, 169–71, 173
Vermont, 100, 167–68
Vibratissimo, 7
VICE, 9, 62
victim activists, 196
victim blaming, 95–96, 192
judicial system and, 95–96
by law enforcement, 77–80
nonconsensual porn and, 44–45
victims, 230. See also injunctive relief; victim
blaming
getting them what they want, 135–40,
194–95
pro bono representation for, 90, 91, 93,
132, 133, 198, 230 (see also Cyber
Civil Rights Initiative (CCRI))
resources for, 195–96
suicide and, 183
victims' groups, 193
video voyeurism, 94, 95
"viewpoint-based discrimination," 166–67
Vimeo, 33, 34
Violence Against Women Reauthorization
Act of 2021, 196
Virginia, 98, 142, 164
House of Delegates, 82–83

Vogel, Colette, 195
VOIC.org.uk, 230
Vox, 22
voyeurism, 39
digital voyeurism, 28–33
video voyeurism, 94, 95
vulnerability, xiv–xvi, xvii
nonconsensual porn and, 115
reciprocal, 117

"wake words," 223
Waldman, Ari, 91
Wales, 143, 198
Wall Street Journal, 17, 103
Warner, Mark, 128–29, 149
Warren, Ned, 111
Warren, Samuel, xii, xiii, 101, 111–13, 123,
139
Washington Post, 13, 18, 23, 72–73, 180
Waterbury, Alexandra, 75, 95
wearable tech, health devices, 1–2
We-Consent, 178
Weiner, Anthony, 45, 143
Weinstein, Harvey, 118
Weld, William, 16
wellness apps, 19
West, Robin, 108
We-Vibe, 7
Whelan, Ryan, 198–200
whistleblowers, 6, 59
White, Edward, 108–9
Williams, Maisie, 38
Williams, Randall, 62
Wired, 1–2, 65, 66, 152
Wiretap Act of 1968, 50–51
Without My Consent, 195–96
Wittes, Benjamin, 150
Wollstonecraft, Mary, 108

women. *See also* girls
    disproportionately burdened by privacy
        invasions, 76–80, 107–8, 140, 141
    intimate privacy violations as structural
        problem for, 119–20
    negative impact of algorithmic decision-
        making on, 21–22
    poor, 60
    rates of victimization and, xvi, 39–40, 45–47
    victim blaming and, 80–81, 96
women's rights movement, 131
Wyden, Ron, 11, 85–87, 150

Xbox Live, 195

Yahoo, 186, 192, 194, 195
Yeltsin, Boris, 55
Yes to Sex, 178
Young, Iris Marion, 113
YouTube, 33, 34, 70, 192, 202

Zen, 98
Zideyah, Ayah, 47
Zoom, 181–82
Zuckerberg, Mark, 65, 172–73